The Pollan Family Table

The Pollan Family Table

THE BEST RECIPES *and* KITCHEN WISDOM *for* DELICIOUS, HEALTHY FAMILY MEALS

CORKY, LORI, DANA, *and* TRACY POLLAN

Foreword by MICHAEL POLLAN

PHOTOGRAPHS BY JOHN KERNICK

Scribner

NEW YORK LONDON TORONTO SYDNEY NEW DELHI

SCRIBNER
A Division of Simon & Schuster, Inc.
1230 Avenue of the Americas
New York, NY 10020

First Scribner hardcover edition October 2014

SCRIBNER and design are registered trademarks
of The Gale Group, Inc., used under license by
Simon & Schuster, Inc., the publisher of this work.

For information about special discounts
for bulk purchases, please contact Simon &
Schuster Special Sales at 1-866-506-1949 or
business@simonandschuster.com.

The Simon & Schuster Speakers Bureau can bring
authors to your live event. For more information
or to book an event, contact the Simon & Schuster
Speakers Bureau at 1-866-248-3049 or visit our
website at www.simonspeakers.com.

Interior design by Jan Derevjanik
Jacket design by Gabriele Wilson
Jacket photographs by John Kernick
Photographs copyright © John Kernick
Photograph on page 28 copyright © Quentin Bacon
Food styling by Susie Theodorou
Prop styling by Amy Wilson

Manufactured in the United States of America

10 9 8 7 6 5 4 3 2 1

Library of Congress Cataloging-in-Publication
Data is available.

ISBN 978-1-4767-4637-1
ISBN 978-1-4767-4639-5 (ebook)

for Grandma Mary, where it all began

contents

foreword by michael pollan

LOOKING BACK, THERE WERE DEFINITELY HINTS THAT THE FAMILY TABLE OF MY childhood was something special, but at the time I figured everyone must have dinners pretty much like ours: all of us sitting down together for a home-cooked meal at 6:00 p.m. sharp, everybody serving themselves from the same pot or platter, taking turns telling about the day at school, joking around, and, sure, occasionally tormenting a younger sibling for sport. I don't want to sound sentimental about it—sweetness and light were not always the rule. The four of us bickered a lot. My father, who endured a two-hour daily commute on the Long Island Expressway, sometimes didn't get home until the dishes were done, so the Pollan family table was often a matriarchy. And with three sisters, the table talk tended to bog down on the relative charms of the various Monkees and their haircuts rather more than I, the only boy, would have liked. But as most kids probably feel about the household they grew up in, whatever it is must be what's normal. Right?

Well, yes and no. It is true that back in the sixties and seventies, the institution of the family dinner in America was considerably more robust than it is now—when it has become the exception in many households rather than the rule. Fast-food franchises had begun to colonize suburban roadsides, but visits to these places, which we cherished, were emphatically special occasions. (Compare that to today, when one of every three American children will visit a fast-food restaurant on any given day.) In our house, the idea of a frozen dinner, or take-out, or eating in front of the TV (another rare treat) was entertained only on weekend nights when my parents went out. In the sixties, the average American was still spending more than an hour a day preparing food, a figure that has since fallen by more than half—to 27 minutes a day.

So it was a much different world, but already in those days, signs of the changes to come were in the air. Most nights there were at least one or two young guests at

our table, usually friends of ours whose mothers worked and seldom cooked. (My mother went back to work when I was in high school, but even then preparing a family dinner remained a priority.) These guests were always grateful for my mom's cooking, and when we stopped to think about it, this made us appreciate just how good we had it. But there were also kids who came to dinner at our house as often as they could just because my mom's cooking was so incredible. Our friends would come over after school (the horrible word "playdate" had not yet been coined, since no one ever thought to plan these things, they just happened) and linger long enough into the afternoon to be invited to stay for dinner. They invariably ate like refugees.

My best friend, Dan, was a pale, skinny latchkey kid whose own mother never, ever cooked and seemed to regard the family meal as an anthropological

curiosity. There was a period when Dan ate dinner at our house more nights than not, much to the consternation of my sisters, who felt he consumed not only too much food, but too much attention as well. One of my sisters eventually declared Dan was "ruining our family" and that if he didn't stop coming to dinner every night, she would. So Dan lay low for a while, and the boycott was averted, but eventually he drifted back to our table, doing his best to keep quiet and attract less notice. But he never failed to extravagantly thank my mother, whom he called (and still calls) "Mrs. Pollan," for the delicious dinner. No one appreciated her cooking more than Dan.

Since those days, the Pollan family table has branched into five family tables, as each of us kids has carried the traditions forward into our own homes. The four of us routinely consult one another—and Corky, our mother—about meals, exchange recipes, and compare notes on culinary hits and misses. And when the whole 21-person, three-generation family gathers on certain weekends and the big holidays, we invariably cook together. In the week before such a gathering, the email traffic is heavy as we decide what to make and who will do what. Corky is nominally in charge, but she's raised an opinionated bunch of chefs who all weigh in with ideas and seasoning suggestions. And our kids, "the cousins," are always very much in the mix, mashing potatoes, slicing apples for a pie, mixing up big bowls of whipped cream. This is how the everyday habits of home cooking get passed down, one generation to another.

IF ANY OF US TOOK MY MOTHER'S TABLE FOR GRANTED WHEN WE WERE growing up, none of us does now. The world has changed in ways that make family dinner something that is no longer a given but that must be achieved, often against great odds. The American household is a very different place today. In 60 percent of American families, both parents work at jobs; in many other families, there is only one parent. Our kids' after-school schedules have never been busier, and their homework load has never been heavier.

Something had to give, and in many homes what gave was sitting down to a home-cooked family meal. The food industry has been only too happy to accommodate our busyness with a cornucopia of what it aptly calls "home-meal replacements"—frozen microwaveable entrées simulating every cuisine known to civilization, and appealing to every demographic in the household. At the same time, the supermarket has gone from just selling food to cooking it for us too, offering a panoply of take-out options from rotisserie chicken to sandwiches. (A sandwich is the most popular meal in America today, both at lunch and dinner.) And then there are always the restaurants—fast food, fast casual, and fine dining. Never in history has it been easier, or more tempting, not to cook.

But even those of us who have trouble finding the time to put a real dinner on the table have come to realize what is lost when we don't do it. It is no coincidence that the rise in obesity in America closely tracks the decline in home cooking. Why? Because corporations don't cook as well as humans do (something implicitly acknowledged when we refer to what they do as "food processing" rather than "cooking"). They use the cheapest possible raw ingredients, which they render appealing by adding far more salt, fat, and sugar than a human ever would. Then, to disguise the fact their dishes have been prepared so far away and long ago, they add lots of novel chemicals no human keeps in his or her pantry: stabilizers, preservatives, texturizers, emulsifiers, artificial flavors, and colors. Industrial corporations are also adept at making certain labor-intensive special-occasion foods—such as french fries or dessert—so inexpensive and ubiquitous that we eat these foods far more often than we would if someone had to actually cook or bake them. My mom occasionally made homemade french fries, and they were fabulous, but they were such a pain to make (and such a mess to clean up!) that she didn't do it every day—more like once a month. The practical realities of daily home cooking and cleaning encourage us to use the best ingredients we can afford and then prepare them as simply as possible—right there, a pretty good recipe for healthy eating.

So it's almost impossible to eat a healthy meal when industry is doing the cooking. But there are other, subtler problems with industrial eating. Those home-meal replacements? They're not designed to feed a family, just an individual, with the result that each member of the family winds up eating something different, turning the home into a kind of restaurant. I have no research to back this claim, but I'm convinced that when people eat from the same pot or platter, they share something more than the food. Eating the same meal helps put everyone on the same emotional page. Also, the single-serving portions undermine the ability of a family to sit down at the same time, since each of them needs to be microwaved separately, one after another. "Family dinner" in these homes begins to fragment, and before long each member of the family is eating different things at different times. Solitary eating in front of the television or computer soon follows.

The loss of that common experience of eating a meal together is far reaching. This is going to sound like a big claim to make for something as simple as family dinner, but I believe that institution is essential not only to a family's health and well-being but also to our society as a whole. Because at the dinner table we literally civilize our children, teaching them how to take turns, to share, to listen to other people's point of view, and to argue without insulting. The family meal is the nursery of democracy.

NOW, IT'S ONE THING TO RECOGNIZE THE IMPORTANCE OF THIS DAILY PRACTICE, and quite another to actually do it—to get a home-cooked meal on the table more nights than not. That's where I think you're going to find *The Pollan Family Table* immediately helpful and, in time, essential. My mother and sisters are not only superb cooks but also eminently practical women who face the same challenges most people do—busy schedules, kids with too much

MICHAEL F.

homework, picky eaters, etc.—and have figured out how to put beautiful meals on the table most nights of the week. I know this firsthand, because I've enjoyed their cooking for years, and have cooked many of these recipes myself.

In some cases, these are the dishes we loved as kids—don't miss the Speedy Skillet Beef with Peppers and Pineapple (page 63) or the Mashed Potato Casserole with Spinach, Carrots, and Gruyère (page 234)—midweek standbys that have never lost their appeal, especially to kids. But my sisters and mother all live in Manhattan, and have soaked up the city's vibrant food and farmers' market scene, which has broadened and enlivened their repertoire. I'm thinking especially of the Jalapeño, Pork, and Hominy Chili (page 182), the Halibut Puttanesca en Papillote (page 100), and the Citrus-Roasted Chicken with Grand Marnier (page 29). Here you'll find modern American cuisine at its very best, and exactly the dish to try when your family's bored with dinner and you've run out of ideas.

My mother and sisters are not professional cooks, and this, oddly enough (or maybe not so oddly), probably explains why this eminently practical cookbook really *works*. Because most of us aren't professional cooks either. They never lose sight of the few core principles that set this cookbook apart: All the dishes can be made with ingredients available at any American supermarket; most can be put on the table in less than an hour (some in half that time); the recipes take nothing for granted and never assume lots of prior experience in the kitchen; and they all appeal equally to kids and adults.

This last principle strikes me as particularly important today. The rise of a distinct "kids' cuisine"—chicken nuggets and their ilk—is a particularly insidious development, one that food marketers have worked hard to promote. (No wonder: They sell us more food when each member of the family is eating something different.) But it's a trap for parents, complicating the cooking of family meals and undermining the virtues of sharing while stunting the development of kids' taste for real, grown-up food. To my mind, one of the best things about this book is that it marks out a broad and delicious common ground, offering a great many dishes you will discover that both adults and children will be able to enjoy

MICAELA

equally—and together. Feeding our children well is one of the pillars of good parenting, and that pillar today is tottering. Many of us have come to feel powerless before the forces—of modern life, of food marketing—that are undermining our ability to put a home-cooked meal on the table. We're losing control of our family's eating, ceding it to companies that have insinuated themselves into what once was, and needs to again become, a family affair. More than anything else, I think you will find that *The Pollan Family Table* is an empowering book. Rather than argue for the importance of family meals—something you already know, or you probably wouldn't have picked it up—it will, one practical step at a time, help you to make them a nightly reality, straightforward to prepare, and delicious to enjoy together.

introduction

THE KITCHEN HAS ALWAYS BEEN THE CENTER OF GRAVITY IN OUR HOME. WHEN we were growing up our mother cooked as we sat at the kitchen table and did our homework. We ate our after-school snacks and recounted our days at school as Mom chopped, blended, and basted. Tracy and Dana would argue over whose job it was to set the silverware and later Michael and Lori (debating Rolling Stones versus Beatles) carried the serving platters brimming with one of our mother's classic meals: coq au vin, wild rice pilaf, and broccoli hollandaise. This was a typical dinner for us, unusual and sophisticated for the time. While we studied, Mom would pore over her cookbooks, making notes and revisions in the margins, rising to the challenge of a new or exotic dish.

These meals were the cornerstone of our family, and they continue to inspire all four of us. Although life would at times pull us away from our kitchen traditions, they never fully disappeared, and when we had our own kids, they returned.

The idea for this book came about when we three Pollan sisters—Dana, Tracy, and Lori—realized that we were continually calling each other to ask, "What are you making for dinner tonight?" We kept turning to each other for fresh ideas whenever we felt stuck or we would regularly call Mom and ask for one of her recipes. Although we each had a large repertoire of our families' favorite dishes, we would find ourselves, time and again, unable to remember the whole range of possibilities. After a while, our mental list of go-to recipes became smaller and smaller. Our kids would invariably text us on their way home from school asking, "What's for dinner?" For them the question was simple—they expected a delicious meal would be waiting for them at the end of a long day. But for so many, this is a question that triggers dread and anxiety: "What *should* I make for dinner tonight?" As cooks we were often in a rut, bored with preparing the same old recipes and tired of eating the same old meals. We decided at this point it was time to collect all our family dishes and write them down.

This book is the result. We've collected the very best Pollan family recipes, a number of them passed down through generations, yet simplified to accommodate today's busy lifestyles and modernized to reflect our healthier food choices. More essentially this book helps cultivate kitchen traditions where they may have lapsed under the pressure of modern life or were never established to begin with. We believe that these traditions are vitally important to everyone's health and happiness—and that it is never too late to find your way in the kitchen.

The Pollan Food Philosophy

IT WAS OUR GRANDPA MAX, CORKY'S DAD, WHO INSPIRED OUR CORE philosophy. He would walk in from his garden with a large watermelon in hand, slice it open, take a bite, and declare it "sweet as sugar." The peaches he'd pick from his trees were more luscious than any store-bought peaches. At an early age we were exposed to fresh and freshly picked fruits and vegetables and we tasted the difference. Back then we weren't concerned if fresh-picked was healthier—it just tasted more delicious. Today, when we choose organic and locally grown produce, we're not motivated by their current popularity. It stems from our early memories. It's our inheritance, our grandfather's legacy.

The key to how we cook and how we shop is common sense. Our dishes are rich in vegetables, whole grains, and beans, and lower in fat and processed ingredients. We don't deny ourselves the judicious use of carbs, cheese, or butter. If a sauce or dish cries out for a tablespoon or two of butter or a splash or two of cream, we go for it, but it has to be in moderation. Whenever possible we shop at farmers' markets or stores with local produce. Ingredients can influence the success of any dish. When vegetables are seasonal and fresh they simply taste so much better; they'll also have less pesticide residues. When it comes to chicken, eggs, milk, and fish we're pretty inflexible. We buy only organic or free-range, sustainably raised chickens and eggs, organic milk, and fish that's wild-caught or farmed sustainably—despite having to pay a bit more. Beef is an occasional treat, so we opt for grass-fed, knowing it's pricey,

MAX STALLER

PRODUCE WAREHOUSE

but knowing also that this beef is raised without growth hormones and antibiotics. Our essential philosophy is to try to pick the healthiest options our budget will allow.

Gathering around the dinner table has been and still is the highlight of our day. Our long-standing tradition of eating together is now extended to three generations—all 21 of us—and defines our cooking style. Over the past generation the country has moved away from dinners that appeal to all and toward a whole set of foods specifically designed and marketed to children, such as chicken tenders. We believe that eating together is more than just everyone sitting down at a table; it's about the communal meal, which at its best is the ritual of sharing food, of cooking together, eating together, and laughing together. Our recipes return families to the idea of a common pot. These are meals we cook for our own families—and they work.

MICHAEL P.

Bringing Our Families Back Together

THERE ARE SUCH POWERFUL EXTERNAL FORCES PULLING CHILDREN AND
parents in opposite directions, maneuvering kids toward unhealthy choices
when it comes to what they eat. *How do families come back together around
the dinner table?* Everyone is just too busy leading separate lives! It seems that
as soon as we acknowledge that it's impossible to "do it all," cooking for our
children and eating together fall by the wayside. This is the reality even though
research shows that children who have regular family dinners are more likely
to get better grades in school, are more emotionally stable, are happier, and have
overall healthier lifelong eating habits.

People today are stymied. Everyone knows the importance of healthy eating
and about the dangers of consuming too much processed food. And many have
come to realize that they should go back to eating "real food." But for so many
the time crunch is epidemic; finding time to cook healthy food has never been
more daunting.

The four of us lead busy lives and know this problem firsthand. We're not professional chefs—our knife skills may not be as sharp as those of culinary school graduates. We are home cooks like our mothers, grandmothers, and great-grandmothers before us, who taught us to be comfortable in the kitchen and not to fear cooking. We have developed real-life answers to the age-old question, "What should I make for dinner tonight?"

Let's Get Started

BEGINNING A NEW ROUTINE OF HOME-COOKED MEALS FIVE OR SIX NIGHTS a week is no more realistic than suddenly going from a sedentary lifestyle to an everyday workout regimen. Cooking can be time consuming, and often people get home too late to make preparing a complete meal practical. If you're just starting out, we suggest that you set a goal that can easily be attained—start with one night a week and build on that. Sometimes we have time to prepare a main course and that's all. There are simple ways to fill up your family's plates and satisfy their appetites with healthy sides. Our advice is to cut yourself some slack—you don't have to do this every night. The idea is to do the best you can, whatever your circumstances. The important takeaway is that it's not all-or-nothing and it's never too late to start!

In these pages we replace that perpetual quandary all of us face every day— "What's for dinner?"—with the question we love to hear from our families and friends as they walk in the door: "What smells so good?"

How to Use Our Book

THE POLLAN FAMILY TABLE HAS A NUMBER OF SPECIAL FEATURES THAT GUIDE you to cooking success. In these pages we've taken the guesswork out of meal planning.

Each recipe offers a "Market" list and "Pantry" list that make shopping for dinner stress free. Just snap a photo of the page with your cell phone and you don't have to worry about writing out a shopping list! In fact, ingredients in the market list are grouped as you will find them in your supermarket. Ingredients in the pantry list are listed in the order they appear in the recipe.

We simplify your cooking life by providing you with all the necessities for a well-stocked pantry and all the tools to have on hand for kitchen victory. In our chapter "Culinary ABCs" we translate esoteric cooking terms and techniques into straightforward language. In "Sage Advice" we share tips and methods that we've learned through the years that make cooking easier and quicker. Our most important kitchen tip is *mise en place*, which literally means "putting in place." Having all of your ingredients prepared, washed, cut, and measured, and all your utensils and pans at the ready, will guarantee you efficiency and success in the kitchen. "It's Easier Than You Think" explains how you can create your own recipe components such as breadcrumbs, salad dressing, and marinara sauce—items that you might have previously bought at the store. These homemade versions are less expensive, healthier, infinitely more delicious, and surprisingly, so easy to make! People are craving information about what to eat and how to maintain a healthy diet. You'll also find "Food for Thought" interspersed among the recipes, highlighting the particular health benefits of the ingredients we cook with. They educate and make you feel good about your healthy choices.

Reflections

WE GREW UP WITH A CELEBRATORY REVERENCE FOR SHARED MEALS, AND THIS has been formative for each of us. In time we moved out of the house and began families of our own. Life has taken each of us in different directions. While we have developed personal predilections and preferences in our cooking styles, our core philosophy remains the same, and we wrote this cookbook together in one united voice. Somehow, whatever our individual paths, we always follow the breadcrumbs (or croutons) back to the foundation upon which our bonds were built: the big, noisy, welcoming Pollan Family Table.

LORI

All of us are home cooks who've had the good fortune of having a great-grandmother, grandmother, and mother who happened to be exceptional and exceptionally resourceful cooks. Our mother's love of cooking was born in the kitchen of her mother, Mary. For Mary, feeding her children and grandchildren was how she expressed her love. She was a remarkable cook, but her real passion was for baking, especially the traditional Jewish sweets that she had learned from her mother, Tzena. When we visited my grandparents' house I would be drawn inside from playing with my cousins to watch as she made strudel. She would take a ball of dough, no bigger than a grapefruit, and painstakingly knead it, stretch it, and pull it until it covered the entire, floured kitchen table. I would look on in amazement, watching my grandmother perform this crazy magic trick, which ultimately yielded the most mouthwatering, flaky, hot apple strudel.

Mary baked by feel and by eye—the old-fashioned way—and never used written recipes. So when I asked her as a teenager to teach me some of my favorites, I had to observe carefully and translate her instructions into cooking terms I was familiar with—a handful of nuts (let's say a quarter cup), add flour "until it's workable—not too wet, not too dry" (my guesstimate was 3 cups), 30 drops of vanilla (I noted ½ teaspoon). My grandmother Mary taught me a powerful lesson: Cooking is not a science but an art, mistakes are okay, messes are fine— the pleasure is in the creating and the sharing of the result. I still have my little red hardcover notebook—spine now held in place by packing tape, pages dotted with cooking stains—filled with her loving instructions for mandelbrot, nut cake, and strudel. Two of these family recipes are in this book.

TRACY

Out of the four of us Pollan kids I was probably the most enthusiastic eater. A good meal could actually be an emotional experience. I remember sitting down to a birthday dinner my mother had prepared for me— duck à l'orange and French onion soup. I stared at the feast in front of me and big fat salty tears began streaming down my face. My mother asked me what was wrong. Wasn't this exactly what I had requested for my birthday meal? I struggled to reply. I was not crying out of sadness, but because it was so beautiful, so perfect.

It wasn't only my mother's cooking that I craved— I would beg her to try to replicate the delectable feasts they served at the Walt Whitman Elementary School cafeteria. I didn't understand the irony in simply asking my mother, a master chef (in my eyes) and devotee of Julia Child, to knock off dishes that had been served from a steam table by someone in a hairnet. My all-time favorite cafeteria classic was something they called "chicken steak." She attempted several variations; chicken cutlets fried like a steak, a steak breaded and served like fried chicken—but it was never quite right. She finally threw up her hands in frustration and cried, "Is it chicken or is it steak?" I have to admit that to this day I have no idea. But it really was delicious.

My gusto for eating soon led to an interest in cooking. I would follow my mother around the kitchen watching and trying to find any way to help. One of the first dishes my mother taught me to make was hollandaise sauce. Though she always served it with broccoli, I soon realized it was equally delicious with asparagus, artichokes, or any other vegetable. I don't know if it was the fact that I loved it so much or simply that I could create something so elegant myself. Whatever the reason, we had hollandaise sauce with almost every meal after that.

My culinary education wasn't all smooth sailing. I remember once thinking I could employ my mother's technique of frying steak on a bed of kosher salt to avoid using oil. The only problem was, I was frying eggs. This was disastrous to the eggs as well as the frying pan, which had to be soaked in the sink overnight and was never quite the same. And there was the time I spent an entire afternoon simmering a huge pot of vegetables to make my own broth. I proceeded to take the enormous vessel of richly aromatic stock over to the sink to strain but had forgotten to put a bowl under the colander. My husband, Michael, walked by and said, "Isn't there anything you can do with all of that liquid? It seems a shame to waste it." I realized what I had done. Three hours of hard work literally went down the drain.

DANA

When Macklin, my firstborn, was little he took food fussiness to the extreme: a bottle of milk for breakfast and a bagel with vegetable cream cheese for lunch and dinner was all he'd eat. Macklin was even particular about which part of the bagel he'd eat. He only ate the soft insides, so we had to "shuck" it for him. I rationalized that the bagel diet was okay since there were all those tiny specks of carrot and red pepper in the cream cheese. Still, I was frustrated because when it came to food options it seemed that I couldn't make an offer he wouldn't refuse. I became convinced that I was stunting his growth.

Influenced by his preschool peers, Macklin eventually tried a McDonald's chicken nugget. He loved it. I recall conflicting emotions—thrilled that he liked something new, but feeling somehow inadequate as a mother. It was obviously such an unhealthy choice. So I created my own chicken nuggets, omitting

processed ingredients, but he literally would not bite. And so McNuggets, bagels, and the occasional peanut butter and jelly sandwich (crusts cut off, of course) served as the staples of Macklin's diet for the first six or seven years of his life.

Finally, after many family meals with my siblings and their children at my parents' home, Macklin was gradually lured into the pleasures of real food. Nana's oven-baked fried chicken cut off the bone (with plenty of ketchup) was a huge hit. So were Thanksgiving turkey bathed in gravy and Nana's Passover brisket. Over the years Macklin's palate expanded to include just about everything and anything, though he is conscious about making healthy food choices. (By the way, he is now six feet four.)

CORKY

Meals have always been at the center of our family life, so we get together any chance we can, and not just for holidays and birthdays. But early on we faced an obstacle: our old refectory dining table could only seat ten, proving a challenge to our ever-growing family. My husband, Stephen, and I were determined the family tradition would continue, with everyone able to sit together, rather than relegating the youngest to "the kids' table." So ours became the ever-lengthening table. First we hired a woodworker to add an extension, then another, until we literally burst through the dining room wall to create a new wing that jutted out into the driveway before we finally had a room long enough to comfortably accommodate all 21 of us.

The kids and I text and phone each other all week in advance of our dinners, swapping recipes, talking about new cooking techniques, learning from one another. Gradually a menu emerges. It might be chicken Marsala along with a hearty vegetable bake to please the vegetarians, a spring lettuce salad, and a strawberry-rhubarb crumble. Or it could be orecchiette with broccoli, artichoke hearts, and sun-dried tomatoes; salmon for the fish lovers; a Caesar salad; lots of garlic bread; and chocolate cream pie.

Each of us contributes a dish or two and everyone gets involved in the preparation. It's no surprise that with so many cooks in the kitchen there are the occasional "animated discussions." Tracy, after taking a look at the small mound of potatoes, incredulous that someone thought that two pounds of potatoes would feed all 21 of us? (Resulting in a quick trip to the market.) Dana voicing surprise that we were not aware that tenting grilled steaks locks in their juices? (Now we always tent.) And Lori challenging the need for both *butter and oil in the broccoli sauté? (I prevailed; it was delicious.)*

Even the grandkids (all 11 cousins) happily help us in the kitchen, some competing for vegetable peelers, cheese graters, and potato brushes; others for dishes, flatware, and water and wineglasses for the table. Everyone is eager to be part of the bustling activity and the conversation: the younger ones—Mica, Savannah, Aquinnah, and Schuyler—secretly plotting the inevitable sleepover at Tracy and Mike's; the older ones—Sam, Hallie, Isaac, Macklin, and Jack— doubling over with laughter as they quote Ron Burgundy lines from Anchorman. *Then there are the youngest ones: Esmé rehearsing dialogue for her after-dinner play; and Cameron, playing with Coco, our cat. No matter our age, everyone in our household knows that cooking and eating together is where the fun is.*

the pollan pantry

key ingredients to have on hand in your pantry or cabinet

THERE'S NOTHING MORE FRUSTRATING THAN PLANNING TO COOK A GREAT meal, only to open your pantry and discover that you're missing a key ingredient. In fact, we've found that having a well-stocked pantry is one of the most critical components to successfully preparing home-cooked meals. It saves time and makes the cooking process easier.

Our list is extensive. It comprises what we believe are the most basic and essential ingredients. You don't need to buy everything at once. Pick out the ones you'll use most often and then add to them over time. All of these pantry list items can be found in the grocery store, and they have a long shelf life, so they can be used over and over again.

■ **OILS**

Canola (organic)

Extra virgin olive

Grapeseed

Organic olive oil cooking spray

Safflower

Sesame

■ **VINEGARS**

Aged balsamic

Balsamic Vinegar Glaze (page 269, or your favorite store-bought)

White balsamic

Apple cider

Champagne

Raspberry

Red wine

Sherry

White wine

■ **THE SPICE DRAWER**

Bay leaves

Black pepper (we like whole peppercorns and a grinder)

Cayenne pepper

Chili powder

Crushed red pepper flakes

Dried oregano

Garlic powder

Ground chipotle chile pepper

Ground cinnamon

Ground coriander

Ground cumin

Ground nutmeg

Herbes de Provence

Herb salt

Kosher salt

Paprika

Sea salt (good-quality)

Smoked paprika

■ **THE CUPBOARD**

Breadcrumbs, plain (page 264, or your favorite store-bought)

Croutons (page 264)

Grains (bulgur, pearl barley, and quinoa)

Honey, pure

Legumes, canned organic (black beans, cannellini beans, kidney beans, and chickpeas)

Legumes, dried (French and brown lentils)

Low-sodium organic beef broth

Low-sodium organic chicken broth

Low-sodium organic vegetable broth

Marinara sauce (your favorite store-bought, or homemade in your freezer, page 268)

Pastas (various shapes and types)

Polenta

Raw nuts (almonds, blanched hazelnuts, pecans, and walnuts)

Rice (basmati, brown, and long-grain white)

Tomatoes, canned (whole, crushed, and diced)

Tomato paste

■ THE FRIDGE

Capers

Dijon mustard

Ketchup

Maple syrup, pure

Mayonnaise

Organic low-sodium soy sauce

Raw seeds (shelled pumpkin, pine nuts, and sesame)

Sun-dried tomatoes in oil

■ SPIRITS

Dry sherry

Dry white wine

Mirin

Red wine

■ BAKER'S DOZEN

All-purpose flour

Baking powder

Baking soda

Brown sugar (light and dark)

Confectioners' sugar

Cornstarch

Granulated sugar

Old-fashioned rolled oats

Pure vanilla extract

Semisweet chocolate chips

Sweetened condensed milk

Sweetened shredded or flaked coconut

Yellow cornmeal

■ SPECIAL SHOUT-OUT!

Parchment paper—we use this all the time

essential utensils

indispensable cooking tools

HAVING THE RIGHT TOOL FOR THE JOB IS JUST AS IMPORTANT AS A WELL-STOCKED pantry. It can be overwhelming when you are faced with too many choices of fancy gadgets on the utensil wall of your local cookware store. Certain tools seem unnecessary but others are indispensable. So whether you are stocking your kitchen for the first time or you simply want to edit and add to what you already own, here are three separate lists to help you get organized: the tools we use on a regular basis, the ones that you may not have known would make your life easier, and the luxury items.

■ MUST-HAVES

Blender

Box grater

Cake pans
(round, rectangular, and square)

Casseroles
(small, medium, and large)

Colander

Cutting boards
(we like to have two,
one dedicated to meat)

Dish towels

Dry measuring cups

Electric hand mixer

Garlic press

Kitchen scissors or shears

Kitchen timer

Ladles

Liquid measuring cups (glass or
plastic with a spout)

Measuring spoons

Mesh strainer

Nested mixing bowls

Nonstick skillets
(small, medium, and large)

Paring, serrated, and chef's
knives (medium and large)

Potato masher

Pot holders and/or oven mitts

Rimmed baking sheets

Roasting pan
(standard is 9 by 13 inches)

Rolling pin

Saucepans (medium and large)

Slotted spoon

Spatulas
(silicone, rubber, and metal)

Spring-loaded tongs

Stainless-steel skillets
(medium and large)

Stockpot (large)

Vegetable peeler

Whisk

Wooden spoons

■ TOOLS YOU CAN'T BELIEVE YOU LIVED WITHOUT

Bench scraper

Bundt pan

Cheese plane

Cooling rack

Dutch oven

Immersion blender

Instant-read thermometer

Jars for salad dressing

Juicer

Mandoline

Metal turner

Muffin pans

Pastry brush (silicone)

Pepper mill

Pizza slicer

Potato brush

Salad bowl

Salad tongs

Salt cellar

Sifter

Spider (great for lifting food
from cooking liquid)

Vegetable steamer

Zester

■ INDULGENCES

Cast-iron skillet

Food mill

Food processor

Kitchen scale

Knife sharpener

Meat pounder

Microplane grater

Olive oil spigot

Pastry blender

Pizza stone

Rice cooker

Salad spinner

Silicone mat
(perfect for cookie baking)

Stand mixer

culinary ABCs

cooking terms explained in straightforward language

YOU'RE IN THE MIDDLE OF COOKING A NEW DISH AND SUDDENLY YOU REALIZE you're in trouble. You have no idea how to "sweat" the vegetables or "deglaze" the pan. At one time or another we've all found ourselves in this quandary since cookbooks often fail to define terms they use. Here, in simple language, are our translations of the most commonly used cooking terms. Many of them are used in this book, but we've included a few that aren't so you can turn to these ABCs whenever you need a straightforward answer to a vexing kitchen question.

BASTE: Spooning, brushing, or squirting a liquid such as melted butter, barbecue sauce, or broth on food as it's cooking to prevent it from drying out and to add to its flavor.

BLANCH: Immersing food (typically fruits and vegetables) in boiling water for a very short period of time, to set the color or partially cook it.

BOUQUET GARNI: A selection of aromatic herbs (most often parsley, thyme, and bay leaf) tied together or wrapped in cheesecloth to flavor soups, stews, and sauces.

BRAISE: Cooking foods slowly in a small amount of liquid at low heat in a Dutch oven or a covered skillet. The slow cooking tenderizes the food and enriches the flavor.

BRINE: Immersing meat, poultry, or fish in a solution of water, salt, and sugar for a few hours (or as long as two days) before cooking. This method enhances the food's tenderness and succulence.

BROWN: Cooking the surface of meat, poultry, or vegetables until they turn mahogany brown, thereby increasing flavor and releasing aroma.

CARAMELIZE: Primarily means cooking sugar until it liquefies, turns deep brown, and gives off a nutty aroma. Vegetables are said to caramelize when they have a browning reaction (see "Maillard reaction") when grilled or roasted.

CHIFFONADE: Cutting herbs or green vegetable leaves such as basil, spinach, kale, sage, etc., into long thin strips by stacking the leaves, rolling them tightly, then cutting across the roll with a sharp knife.

CHOP: Cutting foods into small pieces that can be uneven in size.

CREAM: Beating one or more ingredients together, usually sugar and butter, until they're light and airy.

DEGLAZE: Adding a liquid (water, wine, or broth) to a pan after browning or roasting meat, poultry, or vegetables in order to dissolve the browned bits left (see "Fond") in the bottom of the pan. The resulting flavorful liquid can form the base for a pan sauce.

DEMI-GLACE: A rich brown sauce made from reduced veal and beef stock, used to make classic sauces.

DICE: Cutting foods into small cubes of the same size.

DOCK: Pricking rolled-out dough to prevent air bubbles from forming when the dough is baked.

DREDGE: Coating food with a dry ingredient such as flour, cornmeal, breadcrumbs, or sugar before or after cooking.

DRIZZLE: Slowly pouring a thin stream of liquid in a random pattern over the surface of a food.

DUST: Lightly sprinkling food with a dry ingredient such as flour, confectioners' sugar, salt, or pepper before or after cooking.

EMULSION: A combination of two liquids that ordinarily don't dissolve into each other: oil and vinegar is an example of a temporary emulsion; mayonnaise is an example of a permanent emulsion.

FOND: The browned bits and caramelized drippings left in the bottom of a pan after the browning or roasting of meat, poultry, or vegetables. They form a flavorful base for quick pan sauces when deglazed with a liquid.

GRATIN: A dish with a lightly browned crust of breadcrumbs and melted cheese.

GREMOLATA: An Italian garnish of minced garlic, parsley, and lemon rind traditionally served with osso buco but also used as a topping for roasts and fish.

JULIENNE: Cutting foods into long thin matchsticks of the same size.

MAILLARD REACTION: The result of a chemical reaction between an amino acid, a reducing sugar, and heat. It's responsible for the browning of meats, seafood, breads, and other protein-heavy foods, which gives them their aromas and flavors.

MARINATE: Placing foods in a prepared liquid (classically a mixture of oil, spices, herbs, wine, or vinegar) to flavor them prior to cooking.

MEUNIÈRE: A simple sauce made of butter, lemon juice, and parsley most often used for fish that's been dredged (see "dredge") in flour and cooked in butter.

MINCE: Cutting food into very small pieces.

MIREPOIX: A mixture of diced onions, celery, and carrots cooked in butter or oil, and used as a flavor base for soups, stews, and sauces.

NAP: Completely covering food with a light coating of sauce so that it forms a thin even layer.

PISTOU: An uncooked sauce of garlic, olive oil, and basil. Classically known as the French version of Italy's pesto, minus pine nuts and cheese. Today, a pistou may include grated Parmesan or other cheeses.

POACH: Submerging and cooking delicate foods (such as eggs, fish, fruits, or chicken) in a barely simmering liquid.

PUREE: Mashing food to a thick, smooth consistency.

REDUCE: Boiling down a liquid or a sauce to concentrate it and increase the flavor.

ROUX: A mixture of equal parts flour and fat that's cooked slowly over low heat and added to soups and sauces to thicken them and enrich their flavor.

SAUTÉ: Cooking food rapidly in a small amount of fat over high heat, constantly stirring or shaking the pan so the food doesn't stick.

SEAR: Quickly browning the surface of food over high heat so that the surface develops a flavorful brown crust.

SEPARATE (EGGS): Removing the egg yolk from the egg white, allowing one part to be used without the other, or to use each part for different purposes.

SHOCK: Plunging just-blanched vegetables into an ice water bath to stop the cooking and lock in flavor, texture, and color.

SHRED: Pulling or tearing chicken and meats into strips, often using two forks. For shredding vegetables and cheeses, a grater is commonly used.

SIMMER: Cooking food in a liquid at a low temperature so the liquid only occasionally bubbles.

SOFFRITO: The Italian version of the French mirepoix is a mixture of chopped onions, garlic, and celery that's lightly cooked and serves as a foundation for soups, sauces, and stews.

STOCK OR BROTH: Though the name is often used interchangeably, there is a difference between the two. Both stocks and broths are made from slowly simmering scraps and bones of meat, chicken, or fish (or an assortment of vegetables for a vegetable stock or broth). No salt, pepper, herbs, or seasonings are added to a stock, while a broth is seasoned. Both are used for making soups, sauces, and braises.

SWEAT: Cooking small uniform pieces of food (most often vegetables) in butter or oil over low heat, without browning them, until they're softened and translucent.

TENT: Loosely covering meat or poultry just out of the oven with a large sheet of aluminum foil. This allows the air to circulate so the food finishes cooking and the juices are reabsorbed.

ZEST: The thin colored layer of peel that covers citrus fruits and contains aromatic oils. It's removed with a zester, a vegetable peeler, or a grater.

sage advice

valuable cooking techniques, tricks, and shortcuts

IN THE YEARS WE'VE SPENT AT THE STOVE, WE'VE LEARNED SHORTCUTS, TIPS, and tricks. Some are simple (why a pot lid should be left ajar when boiling) and some surprising (how to cook delicious steaks indoors in a skillet on an ordinary stove). These tips will help make cooking easier and speedier, and your meals even more scrumptious.

- Always take the time to read the recipe through to the end before you start to cook. We find that cooking goes much smoother and quicker when you know all the steps in advance. What's more, there might be a mention of a technique that you're not familiar with and you'll need time to check it out.

- The most important tip we have learned is to set your *mise en place* (literally, "putting in place") before beginning to cook. Carefully wash, prepare, cut, and measure all the ingredients as well as laying out utensils, pots, and pans that are needed for a dish before starting to cook it. This simple practice will assure success in the kitchen.

- Taste, Taste, Taste! There's no other way to ensure that what you're cooking has the flavor you're trying to achieve. Check the amount of salt, pepper, and other seasonings throughout the cooking process, but especially right before serving, since their strength can become diluted.

- When possible, remove poultry and meat from the refrigerator 1 hour before cooking to let it reach room temperature. This will guarantee even cooking.

- When roasting a whole chicken, position the legs to the back of the oven. Legs take longer than breasts to cook, and the back of the oven is the hottest spot.

- You can cook steaks to perfection *indoors* on any stove by heating a cast-iron skillet until it's very, very hot and searing the steaks on all sides, including the edges. After they're seared, flip them every 10 to 15 seconds until they're nicely browned. This method allows the steaks to cook faster and more evenly and results in unusually moist and tasty meat.

- Always leave the pot lid ajar when boiling food. This simple trick will eliminate nasty foam spillovers onto your burners.

- Always cut vegetables the same size when preparing them for a recipe, so they all finish cooking at the same time.

- Green vegetables, carrots, beets, and cauliflower should be added to water that's already boiling so that they cook more quickly and preserve both vitamins and color. Starchy vegetables, such as potatoes, corn, and butternut squash, should be started in cold water that's gradually brought to a boil—this helps prevent the vegetables from breaking apart while the pieces cook through.

- You can caramelize vegetables quickly in very little oil by putting the vegetables and as little as 1 teaspoon of oil in a cold skillet. Cover the pan and turn the heat to medium. When liquid accumulates in the pan, increase the heat to high, and when the oil starts to sizzle, turn the heat back down to medium. The vegetables will emerge perfectly cooked and evenly browned.

- To brighten and boost the flavor of soups, stews, and sauces, add an acid—such as lemon juice or a flavored vinegar—instead of salt.

- Steal a trick from chefs when cooking onions. Sauté onions slowly at a lower temperature and for much longer than the recipe calls for. They'll turn sweet, golden, and delicious and add a wonderful depth of flavor to any dish.

- Add a small piece of Parmesan cheese rind to stews and soups for added flavor. Our trick: Save the rind when you've used up the cheese and store it in the freezer.

- To obtain the maximum amount of juice from lemons and limes, roll them with the palm of your hand on a cutting board or counter before juicing.

- Cook pasta 1 minute less than suggested in the directions on the package. After draining the pasta add it to the pan with the sauce and cook a few minutes longer to combine the flavors.

- Tired of discarding barely used fresh ginger? Wrap it tightly in plastic and store it in the freezer. You can slice or grate it while still frozen, and it will keep in the freezer for months.

- To keep brown sugar from turning into a block as hard as cement, simply place the box of sugar in a resealable plastic bag and store it in the refrigerator. It will stay soft and malleable for months.

- If a recipe calls for a nonreactive pot or pan, use one of stainless steel, glass, ceramic, or enamel-coated metal. Nonreactive cookware is suggested when cooking very acidic or alkaline foods; using "reactive" cookware (aluminum and cast iron) might add a metallic flavor to a dish.

- If a soup or sauce you're cooking looks fatty or greasy, just add a few ice cubes to the pot. The fat will cling to the ice, making it easy to scoop out.

- To remove lumps from gravies or sauces, simply strain through a fine sieve and then reheat. They'll turn out smooth and lump free.

- When a recipe calls for honey, maple syrup, or molasses, lightly coat your measuring cup or spoon with cooking spray first and it will easily pour out.

- For juicier burgers, don't overhandle the meat or flatten the burgers with a spatula.

- Before cutting chicken breasts into cutlets, beef into strips, or shredding cheese, place them in the freezer for about 15 minutes until firm and they'll be easier to slice or shred.

- When mincing garlic, sprinkle it with a little salt and the garlic won't stick to the knife.

- Always measure skillets and baking pans across their tops, not across their bottoms.

- Measure ingredients carefully. Use metal or plastic nested cups for dry ingredients, glass or plastic measuring cups with a spout for liquids.

- To measure flour, always *spoon* (never *scoop*) the flour from the canister or bag into a measuring cup, mound it up, then level it off with the straight edge of a spatula or a knife.

- When a recipe calls for "1 cup sifted flour," sift the flour *before* measuring it. If a recipe calls for "1 cup flour, sifted," sift the flour *after* measuring it.

- Dip your hands in cold water instead of flour when working with sticky cookie, pie, or pizza dough.

- To remove silk from an ear of corn, wipe the ear with a dampened paper towel.

- Keep chocolate chips, nuts, or berries from sinking to the bottom by dusting them with flour before adding to a batter.

- No need to run to the store if you need buttermilk for pancakes or another recipe. Just add 1 tablespoon of lemon juice or white vinegar to 1 scant cup (7 ounces) whole or 2% milk and let it rest for 5 to 7 minutes.

- Roast, toast, or warm nuts before using them in a recipe for heightened flavor and aroma and an added crunch.

- *Always* let your roasted meats and poultry rest for 10 minutes before serving. This intensifies the flavor, returns moisture to the meat, and makes slicing easier.

poultry

PHYLLIS

I REMEMBER HOW SPECIAL A CHICKEN DINNER WAS WHEN I WAS GROWING UP. Chicken was more expensive than beef, so my mom would serve it only on birthdays or holidays. But it wasn't only chicken. Roast turkey for Thanksgiving, goose for Christmas, and duck for New Year's Eve were equally fabulous. Her way with poultry was inspiring.

Today, chicken is less expensive, so Americans consume more of it than any other meat. It's an ideal medium for absorbing a wonderful range of seasonings and flavors. The taste of chicken is so familiar and comforting that we persuade our kids to try exotic and unfamiliar foods by telling them, "You'll like it, it tastes just like chicken."

For my mom it was easy. She went to the butcher and bought a whole bird. These days we stand in the poultry section of the supermarket confronted by limitless choices. Do we want legs or breasts, thighs or cutlets? Do we buy bone-in and skin-on? And do we go for one of the big commercial brands or do we go local? Must the chicken be organic? What about cage-free? Do we want "air-chilled" (meaning chicken that's not soaked in ice water during the cooling process)? Answers to these last questions are no-brainers. We go with organic cage-free chickens or ones that are raised locally, and for air-chilled birds whenever we can. — CORKY

PRESALTING CHICKEN

We're big proponents of the presalting method of preparing chicken championed by the late chef Judy Rodgers of the Zuni Café and food science writer Harold McGee. This method produces chicken that is tender and succulent, yet never tastes salty.

- Purchase the chicken the day before, or that morning for an evening meal, since you must do the salting at least 6 hours before cooking.

- Remove the chicken from its store wrapping and dry it thoroughly.

- Measure out ¼ to ½ teaspoon of kosher salt per pound of chicken.

- Salt the chicken all over on all sides as well as inside.

- Cover it loosely with plastic wrap and refrigerate, or if you're planning to roast the bird, leave it unwrapped for crisper skin.

- One hour before cooking, remove the chicken from the refrigerator to let it reach room temperature.

perfect roast chicken dinner in one hour

4 servings

■ **FROM THE MARKET**

Whole chicken
(3½ to 4 pounds)

Carrots (4 small)

Yukon gold potatoes
(10 small)

Parsnips (4 small)

Unsalted butter (1 tablespoon)

■ **FROM THE PANTRY**

Kosher salt

Black pepper

Extra virgin olive oil
(2 tablespoons)

Low-sodium chicken broth
(1 cup)

Dry white wine (½ cup)

Cornstarch (1 tablespoon)

Balsamic vinegar
(1 tablespoon)

When I was growing up, roast chicken was my ultimate comfort food. My mother's chicken would come out of the oven golden brown, moist, and delicious, and she served it with roasted vegetables and chicken gravy. After cooking chicken for many years I've discovered that quick roasting at a high temperature delivers chicken like my mom used to make. —CORKY

1 whole chicken (3½ to 4 pounds), giblets removed

Kosher salt

Freshly ground black pepper

4 small carrots, peeled and cut on the diagonal into 1-inch pieces

10 small Yukon gold potatoes, scrubbed and quartered

4 small parsnips, peeled and cut on the diagonal into 1-inch pieces

2 tablespoons extra virgin olive oil

1 cup low-sodium chicken broth

½ cup dry white wine

1 tablespoon cornstarch mixed with 1 tablespoon water

1 tablespoon balsamic vinegar

1 tablespoon unsalted butter

Remove the chicken from the refrigerator 1 hour before cooking to allow it to reach room temperature. Dry the chicken with paper towels and liberally season it inside and out with salt and pepper.

Set racks in the upper and lower thirds of the oven and preheat the oven to 450°F. Place an ovenproof skillet on the lowest rack.

When the oven reaches 450°F, pull the lower rack out and carefully place the chicken in the hot skillet, breast side up and legs to the back of the oven (the hottest spot). Roast for 15 minutes.

Meanwhile, spread the carrots, potatoes, and parsnips on a rimmed baking sheet and drizzle with the olive oil, ½ teaspoon of salt, and ⅛ teaspoon of pepper; toss to thoroughly coat.

After the chicken has roasted for the 15 minutes, place the baking sheet with the root vegetables on the top rack of the oven. Reduce the temperature to 425°F and roast the chicken and vegetables for 35 minutes without opening the door.

Remove the chicken from the oven. Check the internal temperature with an instant-read thermometer inserted into the breast; the chicken is done when it registers 165°F.

Transfer the chicken to a platter. Tent and let it rest while you make the gravy. The chicken's temperature will climb to 170°F.

Turn off the oven. Remove the baking sheet, flip the vegetables over, and return them to the oven to keep warm.

Set the skillet with any remaining chicken juices on a burner over medium-high heat. Slowly add the chicken broth and wine, turn the heat to high, and bring to a boil, scraping up any brown bits in the bottom of the pan, about 2 minutes. Stir in the cornstarch mixture and boil, whisking, until slightly thickened, about 3 minutes. Add the vinegar and the butter, swirling the skillet until the butter melts. Pour the gravy into a gravy boat.

Transfer the chicken to a cutting board and carve as desired. Arrange the chicken on a clean platter, and surround with the vegetables. Serve, passing the gravy separately.

citrus-roasted chicken with grand marnier

4 servings

This dish is such a stunner and a crowd-pleaser. The depth of the Grand Marnier with the zestiness of the citrus creates the most amazing flavor.

¼ cup plus 2 tablespoons extra virgin olive oil

¼ cup plus 1 tablespoon fresh lemon juice

¼ cup fresh honey tangerine (Murcott orange) juice

½ cup dry white wine

1 tablespoon whole-grain mustard

3 tablespoons Grand Marnier (or other orange liqueur)

1 tablespoon light brown sugar

½ teaspoon paprika

¼ teaspoon crushed red pepper flakes

½ medium red onion, cut lengthwise, then cut into thin half-moon slices

7 or 8 sprigs fresh thyme

Kosher salt

Freshly ground black pepper

8 or 9 pieces chicken (breasts, thighs, and legs; about 4 pounds)

10 cloves garlic, peeled

1 lemon, washed, thinly sliced, and seeded

1 honey tangerine (Murcott orange), washed, thinly sliced, and seeded

For the marinade, in a small mixing bowl, combine ¼ cup of the oil, the lemon and tangerine juices, the wine, mustard, Grand Marnier, brown sugar, paprika, red pepper flakes, onion, 2 of the thyme sprigs, 1½ teaspoons of salt, and ½ teaspoon of pepper.

Place the chicken in a large plastic bag. Pour in the marinade, seal, and turn to coat completely. Marinate in the refrigerator for at least 1 hour or overnight.

Remove the chicken from the refrigerator, ideally 1 hour before cooking if you have marinated it overnight. Set racks in the middle and upper third of the oven. Preheat the oven to 450°F.

(recipe continues)

Place a colander over a large mixing bowl and drain the chicken, reserving the marinade along with the onion and thyme. Remove the chicken and dry thoroughly with paper towels. Pour the marinade, onion, and thyme into a rimmed baking sheet.

In a large skillet, heat 1 tablespoon of the remaining oil over medium-high heat until shimmering. Add half the chicken pieces skin side down (do not crowd them) and reduce the heat to medium. Cook for 4 to 5 minutes, undisturbed, until a dark golden crust forms. Remove the chicken from the skillet and place on the baking sheet, skin side up, on top of the marinade.

Wipe the skillet clean. Add the remaining tablespoon of oil and repeat with the remaining chicken. Transfer the chicken to the baking sheet, reserving the oil in the skillet. Turn off the heat and let the skillet cool for 1 minute.

Add the garlic to the oil in the skillet and turn the heat to medium. Cook the garlic for 3 minutes, flipping it halfway through until the garlic is lightly browned on both sides. Transfer the garlic to the baking sheet with the chicken.

Arrange the lemon and tangerine slices around and under the chicken. Lay 3 sprigs of thyme on top and season with salt and pepper. Bake on the middle rack for 25 to 30 minutes, until the internal temperature reaches 165°F on an instant-read thermometer and the juices run clear.

Remove the baking sheet from the oven and raise the temperature to broil. Transfer the chicken pieces to a serving platter, leaving the marinade, citrus, onion, and garlic on the sheet. Broil on the upper rack for 4 to 5 minutes, until the citrus slices caramelize. Remove the sheet from the oven and arrange the citrus, garlic, and onion under, on, and around the chicken. Garnish with a few sprigs of thyme.

Pour the liquid from the baking sheet into a small saucepan over medium-high heat and bring to a boil. Reduce the heat to low and simmer until the sauce reduces by a third, 8 to 10 minutes.

Serve the chicken warm with the sauce passed separately.

crunchy oven-fried chicken

4 servings

Fried chicken has always been a favorite, but our method of oven-frying chicken delivers that deep-fried crunch without the calories. Our secret? We bake the chicken on an elevated cooling rack so both top and bottom cook at the same time for added crispness.

3 cups buttermilk, well shaken

4 cloves garlic, peeled and lightly crushed

1 chicken (3½ to 4 pounds), giblets, wings, and backbone removed, cut into 8 pieces (2 legs, 2 thighs, breast split into 4 pieces)

Organic olive oil cooking spray

2 cups plain Breadcrumbs (page 264, or your favorite store-bought)

1 teaspoon paprika

Kosher salt

Freshly ground black pepper

■ **FROM THE MARKET**

Whole chicken (3½ to 4 pounds), giblets, wings, and backbone removed, chicken cut into 8 pieces (2 legs, 2 thighs, breast split in 4 pieces)

Buttermilk (3 cups)

Garlic (4 cloves)

■ **FROM THE PANTRY**

Organic olive oil cooking spray

Plain Breadcrumbs (2 cups; page 264, or your favorite store-bought)

Paprika (1 teaspoon)

Kosher salt

Black pepper

In a large bowl, combine the buttermilk and garlic. Add the chicken and turn to coat. Cover and refrigerate for at least 20 minutes or overnight.

Set a rack in the upper third of the oven and preheat the oven to 400°F. Line a rimmed baking sheet with foil and place a footed wire cooling rack on top. Spray the foil and cooling rack with oil.

In a large shallow dish, combine the breadcrumbs, paprika, 1½ teaspoons of salt, and ½ teaspoon of pepper. Working with one piece at a time and using tongs, remove the chicken pieces from the buttermilk, drain, and dredge in the breadcrumbs until coated. Place the chicken pieces, skin side up, on the cooling rack. Discard the buttermilk and garlic.

Spray each chicken piece lightly with oil. Bake the chicken for 20 minutes, then remove and lightly spray again with oil. Return to the oven and bake for an additional 20 minutes, until the crust is golden and the internal temperature reaches 165°F on an instant-read thermometer. Serve hot.

parmesan-crusted chicken fontina

4 to 6 servings

■ **FROM THE MARKET**

Chicken cutlets, thin
(8 cutlets, 1½ pounds total)

Large eggs (3)

Parmesan cheese (1 ounce)

Fontina cheese (4 ounces;
preferably Danish)

■ **FROM THE PANTRY**

Kosher salt

Black pepper

All-purpose flour (¾ cup)

Plain Breadcrumbs
(1 cup; page 264, or your
favorite store-bought)

Extra virgin olive oil
(about ½ cup)

My kids always loved when I made chicken cutlets for dinner until one day, as kids do, they decided they were tired of them. One of our favorite restaurants took the dish up a notch by adding nutty, creamy Fontina cheese melted on top. I tried this at home, and it was an instant hit.—DANA

8 thin chicken cutlets (about 1½ pounds total)

Kosher salt

Freshly ground black pepper

¾ cup all-purpose flour

3 large eggs

1 cup plain Breadcrumbs (page 264, or your favorite store-bought)

2½ tablespoons freshly grated Parmesan cheese

½ cup or less extra virgin olive oil, as needed

4 ounces Fontina cheese, thinly sliced with a cheese plane

Preheat the oven to 350°F. Line a large plate with paper towels.

Season the chicken liberally with salt and pepper. Place the flour in a wide, shallow dish. Place the eggs in a second wide, shallow dish and beat until blended. In a third dish combine the breadcrumbs, Parmesan cheese, and ¼ teaspoon of pepper.

Taking the chicken cutlets one at a time, dip them on both sides first in the flour, then the egg, and then the seasoned breadcrumbs, pressing the cutlets so they are completely coated. Set the cutlets aside on a baking sheet or platter.

Place a large nonstick skillet over medium heat and add enough oil (2 to 3 tablespoons) to coat the bottom of the pan. When the oil is shimmering, add 4 of the cutlets in a single layer and cook until golden brown, 3 to 4 minutes. Flip the cutlets and cook until golden brown on the other side, an additional 2 to

CAMERON

MITCHELL

3 minutes. Remove the pan from the heat and transfer the cutlets to the paper towel–lined plate. Add more oil to the pan (again, enough to coat the bottom) and repeat with the remaining cutlets.

Arrange the cutlets in a single layer on a clean rimmed baking sheet and top each with an equal portion of Fontina cheese. Bake until the cheese is melted, 3 to 5 minutes. Serve hot.

chicken marsala
with mushrooms and sage

4 servings

■ **FROM THE MARKET**

Chicken cutlets, thin
(8 cutlets, 1½ pounds total)

Cremini or baby
bella mushrooms
(about 12 ounces)

Unsalted butter
(4 tablespoons, or ½ stick)

Fresh sage (1 small bunch)

Dry Marsala wine (1 cup)

■ **FROM THE PANTRY**

Kosher salt

Black pepper

Extra virgin olive oil
(¼ cup)

All-purpose flour (½ cup)

Low-sodium chicken broth
(1 cup)

Our chicken Marsala is sure to please. It's rather different from a traditional one—the sage coupled with the mushrooms adds a wonderfully deep flavor. This dish is not just for family meals—it is elegant enough to serve when entertaining friends.

8 thin chicken cutlets (about
 1½ pounds total)

Kosher salt

Freshly ground black pepper

4 tablespoons extra virgin olive oil

3 cups stemmed and thinly sliced
 cremini or baby bella mushrooms,
 cut ¼ inch thick

½ cup all-purpose flour

4 tablespoons (½ stick) unsalted
 butter

1 tablespoon chopped fresh sage

1 cup dry Marsala wine

1 cup low-sodium chicken broth

Season the chicken with salt and pepper.

Heat 1 tablespoon of the oil in a large skillet over medium heat. When the oil is shimmering, add the mushrooms and season with salt and pepper. Sauté until the mushrooms have given off their liquid, and continue cooking until the moisture evaporates and the mushrooms are lightly browned, 5 to 7 minutes. Transfer to a small mixing bowl and set aside. Remove the skillet from the heat and wipe clean with paper towels.

Place the flour in a wide, shallow dish. One at a time, lightly coat both sides of the cutlets, shaking off any excess. Place the cutlets on a baking sheet or platter.

Return the skillet to medium heat. Add 2 tablespoons of the oil and 1 tablespoon of the butter. When the butter has melted, add the sage and sauté for 30 seconds. Place 4 of the cutlets in the pan in a single layer on top of the sage and cook until light golden brown, about 3 minutes. Flip the cutlets and brown the other sides, an additional 2 to 3 minutes. Transfer the cooked chicken to a large plate, tent with foil, and keep warm.

Return the skillet to the heat and repeat with the last tablespoon of oil, 1 tablespoon of the butter, and the remaining chicken. Transfer to the tented plate. Allow the skillet to cool slightly, reserving the butter and oil in the pan.

Add the Marsala wine and chicken broth to the pan and bring to a boil over medium-high heat. Using a wooden spoon or spatula, scrape up any brown bits from the bottom of the pan. Boil until the sauce is reduced by half, 8 to 10 minutes. Swirl in the remaining 2 tablespoons of butter. Once the butter is combined, reduce the heat to medium-low and add the mushrooms and any accumulated juices. Season with salt and pepper. Spoon the sauce and mushrooms over the chicken and serve hot.

Food for Thought

Eating mushrooms regularly has been linked to a lower risk of breast cancer in studies of Chinese and Korean women. And, in a study in *Nutrition Journal,* researchers concluded that consuming button mushrooms may help prevent heart disease. The good news is that no matter how you eat them—stir-fried, grilled, or roasted—they retain their nutrients.

lemony chicken francese

4 servings

■ **FROM THE MARKET**

Chicken cutlets, thin
(8 cutlets, 1½ pounds total)

Large eggs (2)

Whole or 2% milk
(2 tablespoons)

Unsalted butter
(2 tablespoons)

Italian (flat-leaf) parsley
(1 small bunch)

Garlic (1 clove)

Lemons (2)

■ **FROM THE PANTRY**

All-purpose flour (1 cup)

Kosher salt

Black pepper

Extra virgin olive oil
(about ½ cup)

Dry white wine (½ cup)

Low-sodium chicken broth
(1 cup)

Capers (1 tablespoon)

Chicken Francese has always been one of our favorite meals when going out to dinner. We always thought of it as an elaborate dish, so we never attempted to re-create it at home. After a little experimentation, we came up with an easy, foolproof recipe that's great for a family meal or company.

1 cup all-purpose flour

2 large eggs

2 tablespoons milk (whole or 2%)

8 thin chicken cutlets (about
    1½ pounds total)

Kosher salt

Freshly ground black pepper

½ cup or less extra virgin olive oil,
    as needed

½ cup dry white wine

1 clove garlic, minced

1 cup low-sodium chicken broth

1 tablespoon capers, drained

2 tablespoons fresh lemon juice

2 tablespoons unsalted butter

1 tablespoon finely chopped Italian
    (flat-leaf) parsley

4 lemon wedges for garnish

Put the flour in a wide, shallow dish. In another wide, shallow dish beat together the eggs and milk until blended.

Season the chicken cutlets with salt and pepper. Dredge one at a time in the flour, shaking off the excess, then dip in the eggs, coating both sides. Dredge once more in the flour and shake off the excess. Place the cutlets on a baking sheet or platter.

Place a large nonstick skillet over medium-high heat and add enough oil (2 to 3 tablespoons) to coat the bottom of the pan. When the oil is shimmering, add 4 of the cutlets in a single layer and cook until golden brown, 2 to 3 minutes. Flip the cutlets and cook the other sides for an additional 2 minutes. Remove the pan from the heat and transfer the cutlets to a large platter.

Blot any remaining oil in the skillet with paper towels. Add 2 to 3 tablespoons of oil and repeat with the remaining cutlets.

Blot the skillet with paper towels. Return it to medium heat. Add the wine, scraping the bottom with a wooden spoon for about 30 seconds to deglaze the pan. Add the garlic and chicken broth, increase the heat, and bring to a boil. Reduce the heat to medium, add the capers, and season with salt and pepper.

Return the cutlets to the skillet and, using tongs or a spatula, flip them once, fully immersing them in the sauce. Transfer the chicken to a serving platter. Add the lemon juice and butter to the sauce and stir until the butter is melted and the sauce is bubbling. Pour the sauce over the chicken and sprinkle with parsley. Garnish the platter with lemon wedges and serve hot.

easy chicken parmesan with fresh mozzarella

4 servings

■ **FROM THE MARKET**

Chicken cutlets (4 cutlets, 6 ounces each/1½ pounds total)

Italian (flat-leaf) parsley (1 small bunch)

Fresh basil (1 small bunch)

Large egg (1)

Parmesan cheese (1 ounce)

Fresh mozzarella cheese (3 to 4 ounces)

■ **FROM THE PANTRY**

Kosher salt

Black pepper

All-purpose flour (1 tablespoon)

Plain Breadcrumbs (1 cup; page 264, or your favorite store-bought)

Garlic powder (½ teaspoon)

Extra virgin olive oil (¼ cup)

Perfect Marinara Sauce (½ cup; page 268, or your favorite store-bought)

Chicken Parmesan is an age-old favorite that delights both children and adults. Pair it with crispy garlic bread and a fresh salad and you have the perfect meal for the whole family.

FOR THE BREADED CHICKEN CUTLETS

4 chicken cutlets (6 ounces each, 1½ pounds total), pounded to ½ inch thick

Kosher salt

Freshly ground black pepper

1 large egg

1 tablespoon all-purpose flour

1 cup plain Breadcrumbs (page 264, or your favorite store-bought)

2 tablespoons freshly grated Parmesan cheese

½ teaspoon garlic powder

1 teaspoon finely chopped Italian (flat-leaf) parsley

4 tablespoons extra virgin olive oil

FOR THE CHICKEN PARMESAN

½ cup Perfect Marinara Sauce (page 268, or your favorite store-bought)

¾ cup shredded fresh mozzarella cheese

5 or 6 basil leaves, torn into ½-inch pieces

Set a rack in the middle of the oven and preheat the oven to 400°F. Line a plate with paper towels.

FOR THE BREADED CHICKEN CUTLETS

Lightly season both sides of the cutlets with salt and pepper. Place on a baking sheet or platter and set aside.

In a wide, shallow dish, whisk the egg. Add the flour and continue whisking until fully incorporated. In another wide, shallow dish, combine the breadcrumbs,

Parmesan cheese, garlic powder, parsley, ½ teaspoon of salt, and ¼ teaspoon of pepper. Mix well.

Dredge a cutlet in the egg mixture, gently draining any excess, then dip in the seasoned breadcrumbs, pressing it until completely coated. Return the cutlet to the baking sheet. Repeat with the remaining cutlets.

Heat 2 tablespoons of the oil in a large nonstick skillet over medium heat. When the oil is shimmering, place 2 of the cutlets in the pan. Cook until golden brown, 2 to 3 minutes. Flip and cook until brown on the other side, an additional 2 to 3 minutes. Transfer the chicken to the paper towel–lined plate to drain any excess oil. Wipe the pan clean with paper towels and repeat with the remaining oil and chicken.

FOR THE CHICKEN PARMESAN
Place the cutlets on a rimmed baking sheet. Top each cutlet with 2 tablespoons of the marinara sauce and 2½ tablespoons of the fresh mozzarella cheese. Bake for 5 to 7 minutes, until the cheese is melted. Change the oven setting to broil and cook for a few minutes more until the cheese is bubbling and beginning to brown.

Garnish with the basil and serve hot.

grilled herbed chicken breast

4 to 6 servings

This savory chicken turns any salad into a light weeknight main course—simply slice the cutlets into strips and top your favorite salad.

4 chicken cutlets (4 ounces each, 1 pound total), pounded to ½ inch thick

Kosher salt

Freshly ground black pepper

2 tablespoons extra virgin olive oil

2 cloves garlic, minced

¼ cup dry white wine

3 sprigs fresh thyme

8 sprigs Italian (flat-leaf) parsley

■ FROM THE MARKET

Chicken cutlets (4 cutlets, 4 ounces each, 1 pound total)

Italian (flat-leaf) parsley (1 small bunch)

Fresh thyme (3 sprigs)

Garlic (2 cloves)

■ FROM THE PANTRY

Kosher salt

Black pepper

Extra virgin olive oil (2 tablespoons)

Dry white wine (¼ cup)

Liberally season the chicken with salt and pepper.

In a wide, shallow dish, mix 1 tablespoon of the oil with the garlic, wine, and thyme. Lay the cutlets in the marinade and turn to coat. Top each cutlet with 2 parsley sprigs, cover the dish with plastic wrap, and refrigerate for at least 20 minutes and up to 8 hours.

Heat the remaining 1 tablespoon of oil in a grill pan or skillet over medium-high heat. If using a grill pan, make sure to coat the ridges of the pan in oil with a pastry brush or paper towel. When the pan is hot and the oil is shimmering, add the chicken cutlets and cook undisturbed until browned on the bottom, about 3 minutes. Flip the chicken and cook on the other side for 2 to 3 minutes more. Remove from the heat and let rest for 5 minutes. Serve as is, or cut into slices and use to top your favorite salad.

hunter's chicken stew with tomatoes and mushrooms

4 servings

Our hunter's stew is an Italian take on the classic Polish dish, with chicken as a stand-in for pork. The tender morsels of chicken are smothered in a luscious gravy, making this a dish that the family loves.

1 whole chicken (3½ to 4 pounds), giblets and backbone removed, cut into 8 serving pieces

Kosher salt

Freshly ground black pepper

3 tablespoons extra virgin olive oil

1 large Spanish onion, thinly sliced

8 cremini or baby bella mushroom caps, thickly sliced

4 cloves garlic, finely chopped

2 tablespoons all-purpose flour

1 cup dry white wine

¾ cup low-sodium chicken broth

One 14.5-ounce can diced tomatoes with juice

1 teaspoon minced fresh thyme leaves

1 tablespoon finely chopped fresh sage leaves

1 bay leaf

■ **FROM THE MARKET**

Whole chicken (3½ to 4 pounds), giblets and backbone removed, chicken cut into 8 serving pieces

Spanish onion (1 large)

Cremini or baby bella mushrooms (8)

Fresh thyme (1 bunch)

Fresh sage (1 bunch)

Garlic (4 cloves)

■ **FROM THE PANTRY**

Kosher salt

Black pepper

Extra virgin olive oil (3 tablespoons)

All-purpose flour (2 tablespoons)

Dry white wine (1 cup)

Low-sodium chicken broth (¾ cup)

Canned diced tomatoes (one 14.5-ounce can)

Bay leaf (1)

Set a rack in the middle of the oven and preheat the oven to 375°F.

Season the chicken liberally with salt and pepper.

In a Dutch oven or a large ovenproof pot, heat 2 tablespoons of the oil over medium-high heat until shimmering. Add 4 of the chicken pieces, skin side down. Cook undisturbed until the skin is golden, about 7 minutes. Flip the chicken pieces and cook until brown, about 4 minutes more. Transfer to a platter and repeat with the remaining pieces of chicken. Set aside.

Wipe the Dutch oven clean with paper towels and add the remaining 1 tablespoon of oil. Heat over medium-high heat until shimmering. Add the onion, mushrooms, and garlic. Cook, stirring occasionally, until the vegetables are tender and fragrant, about 8 minutes.

(recipe continues)

Add the flour and cook, stirring constantly, until the flour is thoroughly mixed with the onion and mushrooms, about 2 minutes.

Raise the heat to high and stir in the wine, scraping up any brown bits at the bottom of the pan. Add the chicken broth, tomatoes and their juice, thyme, sage, the bay leaf, 1½ teaspoons of salt, and ⅛ teaspoon of pepper. Reduce the heat to medium-low and add the browned chicken and any accumulated juices, submerging the pieces into the liquid. Cover and place the pot in the oven.

Bake until the chicken is tender, about 30 minutes. Take off the lid and bake for an additional 10 minutes.

Remove the pot from the oven and, using tongs, transfer the chicken to a platter. Return the pot to the burner, turn the heat to high, and cook until the sauce is thickened, about 4 minutes. Remove the bay leaf. Spoon the mushrooms and sauce over the chicken and serve.

quick chicken thighs provençal

4 servings

■ FROM THE MARKET

Bone-in, skin-on chicken
thighs (8)

Fresh rosemary
(a few sprigs)

Fresh thyme (a few sprigs)

Garlic (3 large cloves)

Kalamata pitted olives
(⅓ cup)

■ FROM THE PANTRY

Kosher salt

Black pepper

Extra virgin olive oil
(2 tablespoons)

Dry white wine (1 cup)

Red wine vinegar (½ cup)

Canned diced tomatoes
(one 14.5-ounce can)

Capers (1 tablespoon)

Chicken thighs cook almost as quickly as chicken cutlets, and they remain lusciously moist and flavorful. In this ever-so-easy dish their flavor is enhanced by olives, capers, rosemary, and thyme.

8 bone-in, skin-on chicken thighs

Kosher salt

Freshly ground black pepper

2 tablespoons extra virgin olive oil

1 tablespoon minced garlic

1 cup dry white wine

½ cup red wine vinegar

One 14.5-ounce can diced tomatoes
with juice

1 tablespoon capers, drained

1 teaspoon minced fresh thyme

1 teaspoon minced fresh rosemary

¼ cup pitted and halved kalamata
olives

Preheat the oven to 250°F.

Dry the chicken thoroughly and season liberally on all sides with salt and pepper.

Place a large Dutch oven or a deep skillet with a lid over medium-high heat. Add the oil and, when shimmering, add 4 of the chicken thighs, skin side down, and cook undisturbed until the skin is golden brown, 5 to 7 minutes. Flip and cook the other side for an additional 4 minutes. Transfer the chicken to a platter and repeat with the remaining 4 thighs. Drain all except for 1 tablespoon of fat from the pan.

Reduce the heat to medium, add the garlic to the fat in the pan, and cook, stirring, for 1 minute. Raise the heat to high, pour in the wine and vinegar, and boil until reduced slightly, about 5 minutes. Add the tomatoes and their juice, the capers, thyme, rosemary, olives, ¾ teaspoon of salt, ⅛ teaspoon of pepper, and the chicken along with any accumulated juices. Reduce the heat to low, cover the pan, and cook for 15 minutes.

Uncover the pan and continue cooking until the chicken is no longer pink and the centers register 165°F on an instant-read thermometer, about 25 minutes. Transfer the chicken to an ovenproof casserole or serving dish and place in the oven to keep warm.

Return the Dutch oven to medium-high heat and boil the sauce until it is reduced and thickened, about 10 minutes. Pour the sauce over the chicken and serve.

perfect juicy turkey burgers

6 servings

■ **FROM THE MARKET**

Ground turkey (2 pounds, preferably dark meat)

Italian (flat-leaf) parsley (1 small bunch)

Red onion (1 small)

Garlic (1 clove)

Unsalted butter (2 tablespoons)

Parmesan cheese (1 ounce)

Swiss, cheddar, or jalapeño Jack cheese (6 slices; optional)

Hamburger buns (6, preferably whole-grain)

■ **FROM THE PANTRY**

Extra virgin olive oil (4 teaspoons plus extra for coating hands)

Dijon mustard (1½ teaspoons)

Ketchup (1 teaspoon)

Kosher salt

Black pepper

This turkey burger is always a hit and a great alternative for those who don't eat red meat. The savory mix of seasonings and the pat of butter in the center of these patties give them all the juice and flavor of a traditional beef burger.

2 pounds ground turkey (preferably dark meat)

4 teaspoons extra virgin olive oil plus extra for coating hands

1 tablespoon finely grated red onion

1½ teaspoons Dijon mustard

1 tablespoon finely chopped Italian (flat-leaf) parsley

1 clove garlic, minced

1 teaspoon ketchup

Kosher salt

Freshly ground black pepper

1 tablespoon freshly grated Parmesan cheese

2 tablespoons cold unsalted butter, cut into 6 pieces

6 slices Swiss, cheddar, or jalapeño Jack cheese (optional)

6 hamburger buns (preferably whole-grain)

Your favorite burger toppings for serving

Place the turkey in a large mixing bowl. Add 1 teaspoon of the oil, the onion, mustard, parsley, garlic, ketchup, ½ teaspoon of salt, and ½ teaspoon of pepper and mix well.

Put the Parmesan cheese in a small dish. One at a time, dip the butter pieces into the Parmesan, making sure to coat all sides.

Oil your hands and form the turkey into 6 patties. Make an indentation in the center of each patty and press a piece of butter into it. Mold the meat gently over the butter to completely enclose it in the turkey.

(recipe continues)

MACKLIN

JACK

Heat a large grill pan or skillet over medium-high heat. Add the remaining 1 tablespoon of oil to lightly coat the bottom of the pan. When the oil is hot, arrange the patties in the pan and cook until the meat is brown, about 5 minutes. Flip the burgers and place a slice of cheese on top, if desired. Cook for 4 to 5 minutes more, until cooked through. Place the burgers on the buns and serve with your favorite toppings.

AQUINNAH

bite-size turkey meatballs

makes 40 to 45 one-inch meatballs

■ **FROM THE MARKET**

Ground turkey (1 pound; preferably dark meat)

Spicy turkey sausage (1 large, about 3 ounces)

Sweet turkey sausage (1 large, about 3 ounces)

Italian (flat-leaf) parsley (1 small bunch)

Shallot (1)

Garlic (2 cloves)

Large egg (1)

White bread (1 slice)

Whole or low-fat milk (2 tablespoons)

■ **FROM THE PANTRY**

Perfect Marinara Sauce (6 to 8 cups: page 268, or two 32-ounce jars of your favorite store-bought)

Garlic powder (½ teaspoon)

Plain Breadcrumbs (¼ cup: page 264, or your favorite store-bought)

Kosher salt

Black pepper

Organic canola oil (1 tablespoon)

Extra virgin olive oil (3 tablespoons)

These mini meatballs are so versatile. They are delicious as a dinner sandwich on a crusty Italian hero with melted mozzarella cheese, or served with any pasta. We especially love them in baked ziti and lasagna. Combining the dark meat turkey with the sausages yields incredible flavor, and is a lighter alternative to traditional beef or veal meatballs.

6 to 8 cups Perfect Marinara Sauce (page 268, or your favorite store-bought)

1 slice bread, crust removed, torn into pieces

2 tablespoons whole or low-fat milk

1 pound ground turkey (preferably dark meat)

1 large spicy turkey sausage (about 3 ounces), casing removed

1 large sweet turkey sausage (about 3 ounces), casing removed

1 large egg, lightly beaten

1 tablespoon finely chopped shallot

2 cloves garlic, minced

½ teaspoon garlic powder

1 tablespoon finely chopped Italian (flat-leaf) parsley

¼ cup plain Breadcrumbs (page 264, or your favorite store-bought)

Kosher salt

Freshly ground black pepper

1 tablespoon canola oil (to coat hands)

3 tablespoons extra virgin olive oil

Heat the marinara sauce in a large saucepan over medium-high heat until bubbling. Reduce the heat to low and let it simmer while preparing the meatballs.

Put the bread in a small mixing bowl and pour the milk on top; stir with a fork until mashed.

In a large mixing bowl, combine the ground turkey, spicy and sweet sausages, egg, shallot, garlic, garlic powder, parsley, milky bread, breadcrumbs, ½ teaspoon of salt, and ¼ teaspoon of pepper. Mix the ingredients until fully blended; for this job, there's no better tool than your hands coated with canola oil.

Scoop heaping teaspoons of the turkey mixture and form into 1-inch balls. Place them on a large baking sheet.

Heat the olive oil in a large skillet over medium heat until shimmering. Add the meatballs and cook, turning until they are browned on all sides, about 5 minutes. Remove the meatballs with a slotted spoon and put them into the simmering marinara sauce. Cook for 20 minutes and serve as you like. If you are making a double batch, store in an airtight container and freeze.

meat

LIKE MANY AMERICAN FAMILIES, WE POLLANS GREW UP LOVING MEAT. SOME form of meat appeared on our table three or four nights a week: boeuf bourguignon, London broil, brisket for holidays, beef carbonnade, and our all-time favorite, roast beef with Yorkshire pudding. There were also lamb chops and leg of lamb, pork chops and pork roasts, and for breakfast, bacon and sausages.

Meat was widely considered to be highly nutritious, high in protein and rich in iron. And our dad—who was not overly fond of vegetables–would eagerly devour whatever meat dish was put before him.

Though we still enjoy eating meat, it no longer has a starring role in our diet. Many other families, too, now eat beef more sparingly. To reflect this change we've created recipes for scrumptious dishes in which a small amount of meat goes a long way. Pastas, beans, grains, and vegetables now take center stage, as we've discovered that plants and grains can supply much of the protein we need, as well as the iron.

In addition to changes in the way we cook meat, we've also made changes in the way we buy it. We look for grass-fed whenever possible. We love the texture and the taste, and since grass-fed meat tends to be lower in fat and calories, eating it is a guilt-free pleasure. Happily, grass-fed has become easier to find. It's now available in many local supermarkets. We know it costs more, but to us it's worth it; with grass-fed we get less–hormones, pesticides, additives, and antibiotics.

patricia's "marry me" roast beef tenderloin

6 servings

■ **FROM THE MARKET**

Beef tenderloin (2½ pounds)

Garlic (2 cloves)

Extra large beef bouillon cubes (2)

Worcestershire sauce (2 teaspoons)

Unsalted butter (1 tablespoon)

■ **FROM THE PANTRY**

Dijon mustard (1½ teaspoons)

Tomato paste (1 tablespoon)

Black pepper

Red wine (¾ cup)

Dry sherry (1 tablespoon)

Low-sodium beef or low-sodium chicken broth (1 cup)

Cornstarch (1 tablespoon)

This recipe was given to me by my son, Sam's, beloved nanny, Patricia. I prepared it for dinner one night for my best childhood friend, the actress Jennifer Grey. She quickly added the recipe to her repertoire. Single at the time, Jennifer would make this dish to impress the men she was dating. In time she realized she had to be careful whom she cooked it for because they would invariably ask her to marry them after the meal—it is that delicious. I serve it for special occasions and dinner parties.—TRACY

2½ pounds beef tenderloin

2 extra large beef bouillon cubes

2 cloves garlic, minced

1½ teaspoons Dijon mustard

1 tablespoon tomato paste

Freshly ground black pepper

2 teaspoons Worcestershire sauce

1 tablespoon unsalted butter

¾ cup red wine

1 tablespoon dry sherry

1 cup low-sodium beef or low-sodium chicken broth

1 tablespoon cornstarch mixed with 2 tablespoons cold water

Poke the meat with a knife or thick skewer to make small holes all over. Set aside.

In a small mixing bowl, combine the bouillon cubes, the garlic, mustard, tomato paste, ⅛ teaspoon of pepper, and the Worcestershire. Pour in ¼ cup of boiling water to dissolve the bouillon. Using the back of a wooden spoon, crush the bouillon cubes. Keep crushing and stirring until you've made a nice thick paste.

Rub the paste all over the meat, rotating it to coat all sides well. Transfer the meat to a roasting pan, cover loosely with foil, and marinate for a minimum of 30 minutes or up to 1 hour.

(recipe continues)

While the meat is marinating, set a rack in the middle of the oven and preheat the oven to 425°F.

Pour enough water into the roasting pan to come to a depth of ¼ to ½ inch. Place the pan in the oven and roast, covered, for 15 minutes.

Remove the foil and rotate the pan. Continue cooking and check after 10 minutes that there is still liquid in the pan; add ¼ cup of hot water if needed. Roast for an additional 5 minutes for rare, an additional 15 minutes for medium-rare, and an additional 20 minutes for medium, or until the center of the roast registers the desired temperature on an instant-read thermometer.

RARE: 125°F (approximate total cooking time 30 minutes)
MEDIUM-RARE: 130°F (approximate total cooking time 40 minutes)
MEDIUM: 140°F (approximate total cooking time 45 minutes)

Transfer the roast to a platter or cutting board, cover with foil to keep warm, and allow it to rest while you prepare the gravy.

Place the roasting pan with all of the drippings on a burner over medium heat. Scrape up the brown bits with a wooden spoon. Add the butter and stir. Whisk in the wine, sherry, and chicken broth. Add the cornstarch-water mixture, whisking until thickened, another 2 to 3 minutes.

Slice the roast and arrange on a platter. Serve the gravy separately.

speedy skillet beef with peppers and pineapple

4 servings

Beef with peppers and pineapple was a dish we fondly remember from when we were young. It was rather sweet and a tad chewy, but we loved the way it tasted and our mom loved how quick and easy it was to prepare. We've now updated this retro dish and added red peppers to the green, used fresh pineapple instead of canned, and skirt steak instead of flank. The result is a tangy, fork-tender version of the original.

3 tablespoons plus 1 teaspoon extra virgin olive oil

2 tablespoons low-sodium soy sauce

1 tablespoon mirin

¼ cup red wine

1 pound skirt steak, trimmed and cut against the grain into ½-inch strips

½ cup ketchup

¼ teaspoon finely grated fresh ginger

¼ teaspoon powdered mustard

One 6-ounce can pineapple juice

1 small yellow onion, cut in half lengthwise and thinly sliced crosswise

2 large cloves garlic, minced

1 large red bell pepper, sliced into ¼-inch strips

1 large green bell pepper, sliced into ¼-inch strips

Kosher salt

Freshly ground black pepper

1½ cups fresh pineapple, cut into ½-inch cubes)

■ **FROM THE MARKET**

Skirt steak
(1 pound, trimmed)

Red bell pepper (1 large)

Green bell pepper (1 large)

Yellow onion (1 small)

Garlic (2 large cloves)

Fresh ginger (1 knob)

Fresh pineapple
(1 small, or 1½ cups cut
into ½-inch cubes)

Pineapple juice
(one 6-ounce can)

Powdered mustard
(¼ teaspoon)

■ **FROM THE PANTRY**

Extra virgin olive oil
(3 tablespoons plus
1 teaspoon)

Low-sodium soy sauce
(2 tablespoons)

Mirin (1 tablespoon)

Red wine (¼ cup)

Ketchup (½ cup)

Kosher salt

Black pepper

In a medium mixing bowl, mix together 1 teaspoon of the oil, the soy sauce, mirin, and wine. Add the steak, stir to coat, and set aside to marinate for 15 to 30 minutes.

Meanwhile, in a small mixing bowl, combine the ketchup, ginger, mustard, and pineapple juice for the sauce. Whisk together and set aside.

Lift the meat from the marinade using tongs and drain it in a colander. Discard the marinade.

(recipe continues)

In a large skillet over medium-high heat, heat 1 tablespoon of the oil until shimmering. Add half the steak in one layer without crowding. Quickly sear it on one side, about 1 minute, flip with tongs, and sear the other side, about 1 minute more, being careful not to overcook. Using the tongs, transfer the meat to a plate. Let the skillet cool slightly and discard any leftover juices. Wipe the skillet clean with paper towels. Add 1 more tablespoon of the oil to the pan and repeat with the remaining steak.

Wipe the skillet clean once again and add the remaining 1 tablespoon of oil. When the oil is shimmering, add the onion and cook, stirring, until it starts to turn brown, about 5 minutes. Add the garlic and the peppers and sauté until the peppers are lightly cooked but still crisp, about 4 minutes. Pour in the sauce. Add the steak and any juices that have accumulated on the plate, 1 teaspoon of salt, and ¼ teaspoon of pepper. Cook, stirring, to coat the meat with the sauce, about 1 minute. Add the pineapple and cook until heated and slightly softened, about 3 minutes. Serve hot.

spicy beef chilaquiles

4 to 6 servings

■ **FROM THE MARKET**

Ground beef chuck
(80% lean; 1 pound)

White onion (1 small)

Garlic (5 cloves)

Chipotle peppers in adobo
sauce (1 small can)

Canned tomato sauce
(one 8-ounce can)

Organic refried beans
(one 16-ounce can)

Monterey Jack cheese
(6 ounces)

Plain corn tortilla chips
(1 small bag)

■ **FROM THE PANTRY**

Chili powder
(2 tablespoons)

Dried oregano (1 teaspoon)

Crushed red pepper flakes
(½ teaspoon)

Paprika (1½ teaspoons)

Cayenne pepper
(⅛ teaspoon)

Ground coriander
(1 teaspoon)

Ground cumin (1 teaspoon)

Kosher salt

Black pepper

(continued on next page)

Dinners in our house were very special when "make your own tacos" were on the menu. Any taco leftovers would often resurface the next night as chilaquiles, a dish with as many versions as there are Mexican cooks. It is such a breeze to make, and our seasoning mix eliminates the need for any preservative-laden flavoring packets or commercially processed sauces.

FOR THE SEASONING MIX

2 tablespoons chili powder

1 teaspoon dried oregano

½ teaspoon crushed red pepper
flakes, or to taste

1½ teaspoons paprika

⅛ teaspoon cayenne pepper

1 teaspoon ground coriander

1 teaspoon ground cumin

Kosher salt

Freshly ground black pepper

FOR THE CHILAQUILES

1 tablespoon extra virgin olive oil plus
extra for coating the dish

1 small white onion, chopped

5 cloves garlic, minced

1 tablespoon drained, finely chopped
chipotle pepper in adobo sauce

1 pound ground beef chuck
(80% lean)

½ cup tomato sauce

½ cup low-sodium chicken broth

2 teaspoons apple cider vinegar

1 teaspoon dark brown sugar

20 to 25 corn tortilla chips,
or as needed

One 16-ounce can organic refried
beans

1½ cups shredded Monterey Jack
cheese

FOR THE SEASONING MIX

Combine the chili powder, oregano, red pepper flakes, paprika, cayenne pepper, coriander, cumin, 1½ teaspoons of salt, and ⅛ teaspoon of black pepper in a small mixing bowl or jar with a cover and stir or shake to mix. Set aside.

FOR THE CHILAQUILES

Preheat the oven to 375° F. Lightly oil a shallow 2½-quart casserole.

Heat 1 tablespoon of oil in a large skillet over medium-high heat until shimmering. Add the onion, garlic, chipotle, and the seasoning mix. Cook, stirring frequently, until the onion is softened and fragrant, about 2 minutes. Slowly add the ground beef, breaking the meat up with a fork until it's no longer pink. Stir to thoroughly blend with the seasonings, about 5 minutes.

Add the tomato sauce, chicken broth, vinegar, and brown sugar. Simmer, stirring frequently, until the liquid has reduced and the mixture has thickened, about 15 minutes.

Line the bottom of the prepared casserole with a single layer of tortilla chips.

Layer on half the beef, half the refried beans, and half the cheese. Repeat with a second layer of tortilla chips, beef, and beans, but no cheese on this layer. End with a layer of tortilla chips. Cover the casserole with foil and bake for 20 minutes.

Remove the foil and sprinkle on the remaining cheese. Bake for an additional 5 minutes, until the cheese is bubbly. Let stand for 5 minutes before serving.

TIP: Since so little of the canned chipotles in adobe sauce is used in this recipe, transfer what is left in the can to a glass jar and store in the refrigerator, where it will keep for weeks. These peppers and the adobo sauce are terrific additions to any dish in need of a bit of depth and heat.

(From the Pantry continued)

Extra virgin olive oil
(1 tablespoon plus extra for coating)

Low-sodium chicken broth
(½ cup)

Apple cider vinegar
(2 teaspoons)

Dark brown sugar
(1 teaspoon)

bistro burger
with caramelized onions

6 servings

Sometimes there is nothing better than a big, messy burger. The caramelized onions offer a deep, rich, sweet flavor, which contrasts beautifully with the earthiness of the beef, making this perfection on a bun.

1 large Vidalia onion, cut in half lengthwise and thinly sliced crosswise

1 tablespoon extra virgin olive oil

Kosher salt

2 pounds ground beef chuck (80% lean)

1 teaspoon finely grated red onion

1 teaspoon steak sauce

Freshly ground black pepper

2 tablespoons cold unsalted butter, cut into 6 pieces

6 slices of Swiss, cheddar, or jalapeño Jack cheese (optional)

6 hamburger buns (preferably whole-grain)

Your favorite burger toppings for serving

■ **FROM THE MARKET**

Ground beef chuck (80% lean; 2 pounds)

Vidalia onion (1 large)

Red onion (1 small)

Steak sauce (1 teaspoon)

Unsalted butter (2 tablespoons)

Swiss, cheddar, or jalapeño Jack cheese (6 slices; optional)

Hamburger buns (6, preferably whole-grain)

■ **FROM THE PANTRY**

Extra virgin olive oil (1 tablespoon)

Kosher salt

Black pepper

Place a large dry nonstick skillet over medium-high heat. When the pan is hot, add the sliced onion and stir continually until it is a rich, dark golden brown, about 10 minutes. Add the oil and ½ teaspoon of salt and cook, stirring, for an additional 3 minutes. Set aside.

Place the ground chuck in a large mixing bowl. Add the grated onion, steak sauce, ½ teaspoon of salt, and ¼ teaspoon of pepper and mix well.

Using your hands, form the meat into six patties. Make an indentation in the center of each patty and press a piece of butter into it. Mold the meat gently over the butter to completely enclose it in the beef.

Heat a large grill pan or skillet over medium-high heat. When the pan is hot, add the patties and cook until the meat begins to brown, 2 to 3 minutes; for the juiciest burgers, leave them untouched until you are ready to flip them. Flip the

SAVANNAH

burgers and, if desired, top with a slice of cheese. Cook for an additional 3 minutes for rare, 4 minutes for medium-rare, and 5 minutes for medium.

Arrange the burgers on the buns, and top each with a few spoonfuls of the caramelized onions. Serve hot with your favorite toppings.

SAM

TIP: Caramelized onions usually take a good 30 to 40 minutes to get nice and brown, but this method we discovered in *The New York Times* starts with a dry pan and dramatically cuts the cooking time.

herb and garlic-crusted rack of lamb with mint pesto

4 servings

■ **FROM THE MARKET**

Rack of lamb (8 ribs, about 2 pounds, well trimmed of fat)

Italian (flat-leaf) parsley (1 bunch)

Fresh mint (2 bunches)

Fresh thyme (1 bunch)

Fresh rosemary (5 sprigs)

Garlic (7 large cloves)

Lemon (1)

■ **FROM THE PANTRY**

Extra virgin olive oil (½ cup plus 2 tablespoons)

Kosher salt

Black pepper

Dijon mustard (1 teaspoon)

Sherry vinegar or red wine vinegar (2 tablespoons)

Granulated sugar (2 tablespoons)

We often had lamb chops when we were growing up, but a rack of lamb was a special treat. Though the lamb/mint combination shouts spring, this succulent dish is a winner year-round. The garlicky crust adds zest to the lamb and that classic accompaniment—mint jelly—gets upgraded to mint pesto.

FOR THE LAMB

6 large cloves garlic

¼ cup Italian (flat-leaf) parsley

1 tablespoon fresh thyme leaves

2 teaspoons fresh rosemary leaves

2 tablespoons extra virgin olive oil

8-rib rack of lamb, well trimmed of fat (about 2 pounds)

Kosher salt

Freshly ground black pepper

FOR THE MINT PESTO

1½ cups tightly packed fresh mint leaves

½ cup tightly packed Italian (flat-leaf) parsley leaves

1 large clove garlic

½ cup extra virgin olive oil

1 teaspoon Dijon mustard

2 tablespoons sherry vinegar or red wine vinegar

2 tablespoons fresh lemon juice

2 tablespoons granulated sugar

Kosher salt

Freshly ground black pepper

Set a rack in the upper third of the oven and preheat the oven to 450°F.

FOR THE LAMB

In a food processor, combine the 6 cloves garlic, ¼ cup parsley, thyme, and rosemary and pulse for 1 minute. Add 2 tablespoons of the oil and process until the garlic is finely chopped.

Season the lamb liberally with salt and pepper, and spread the garlic and herb puree all over with a spatula. Place the lamb on a rimmed baking sheet and set aside while you make the mint pesto.

FOR THE MINT PESTO

Wash and dry the food processor and add the mint, ½ cup parsley, 1 clove garlic, ½ cup oil, mustard, vinegar, lemon juice, sugar, 1 teaspoon of salt, and ⅛ teaspoon of pepper. Process until smooth. Transfer to a serving bowl and set aside.

Roast the lamb for 15 to 20 minutes, until nicely browned. Rotate the baking sheet and continue to roast until an instant-read thermometer, inserted in the center of the lamb, registers the desired temperature.

RARE: 125–130°F
MEDIUM-RARE: 130–135°F
MEDIUM: 140–145°F

Remove the lamb from the oven, tent with aluminum foil, and let rest for 8 minutes.

Transfer the lamb to a cutting board and carve into double chops. Serve with the mint pesto passed separately.

Food for Thought

Garlic is good for what ails you! Not only does it help ward off the common cold, but it's great for your heart. Studies have shown that eating a clove of garlic a day can lower cholesterol by up to 20 percent and can lend a hand in reducing blood pressure. It is filled with vitamins and minerals, and research suggests that consumption of garlic is effective in reducing the risk of certain cancers.

roasted fruit-stuffed pork loin

6 servings

■ **FROM THE MARKET**

Boneless pork loin
(2½ to 3 pounds, rolled
and tied by the butcher)

Dried apricots (4 ounces)

Dried pitted prunes
(4 ounces)

Port wine (⅓ cup)

■ **FROM THE PANTRY**

All-purpose flour
(⅓ cup)

Kosher salt

Black pepper

Extra virgin olive oil
(2 tablespoons)

Low-sodium beef broth
(1 cup)

Red wine (1 cup)

Balsamic vinegar
(1 tablespoon)

Handsome and impressive, this pork roast is ideal for entertaining. Yet it also gets high marks from my grandchildren. The blend of fork-tender meat and tangy fruit delivers a crowd-pleasing fusion of flavors.—CORKY

¾ cup quartered dried apricots

¾ cup quartered dried pitted prunes

⅓ cup port wine

1 boneless pork loin (2½ to 3 pounds), rolled and tied by the butcher

⅓ cup all-purpose flour

Kosher salt

Freshly ground black pepper

2 tablespoons extra virgin olive oil

1 cup low-sodium beef broth

1 cup red wine

1 tablespoon balsamic vinegar

In a small mixing bowl, combine the apricots, prunes, and port wine. Cover and set aside to marinate for at least 15 minutes, or overnight if desired.

Preheat the oven to 450°F.

Twist a long, narrow, sharp knife into the pork loin, first from one end and then from the other. Using the handle of a long wooden spoon, force a hole through the full length of the loin. Reinsert the knife and twist it around to make the hole an inch or so wide.

Drain the fruit, reserving the liquid, and with your fingers or a long-handled spoon, stuff the fruit into the loin. Stand the roast up on one end to stuff it, then turn it over and stuff the other end so there is fruit all the way to the center.

In a large dish or platter, mix the flour, 1 teaspoon of salt, and ½ teaspoon of pepper. Dredge the loin in the seasoned flour, including both ends to seal in the fruit. Shake off any excess.

Heat a Dutch oven over high heat. Add the oil and when it shimmers, add the loin. Using tongs, brown the loin on all sides, including both ends, until crusty brown bits appear on the loin, 8 to 10 minutes.

Transfer the loin to a plate and pour off the fat from the pot. Return the loin to the Dutch oven, add the beef broth, red wine, marinade, and any leftover fruit. Roast uncovered for 15 minutes.

Lower the heat to 375°F and continue roasting for an additional 30 minutes. Check the thickest part of the loin (avoiding the fruit) with an instant-read thermometer. When it registers 145°F, remove from the oven, transfer to a cutting board, and tent with foil to finish cooking, about 10 minutes.

While the loin rests, place the Dutch oven over high heat and add the vinegar. Boil, scraping the brown bits from the bottom of the pan with a wooden spoon, until the sauce is reduced and slightly thickened, about 8 minutes.

Slice the pork loin and arrange on a platter. Spoon some of the sauce over it and serve, passing the remaining sauce separately.

sweet and hot sausage hero melt

4 servings

■ **FROM THE MARKET**

Italian sausage
(1 pound, a mix of
sweet and hot)

Spanish onion (1 large)

Green bell pepper (1 large)

Red bell pepper (1 large)

Yellow or orange bell
pepper (1 large)

Garlic (4 large cloves)

Canned tomato sauce
(one 8-ounce can)

Italian hero or sub
sandwich rolls
(4 rolls, 7 to 8 inches long,
preferably whole-grain)

Provolone cheese
(8 to 10 thin slices, about
4 ounces)

■ **FROM THE PANTRY**

Extra virgin olive oil
(2 tablespoons)

Dried oregano (½ teaspoon)

Crushed red pepper flakes
(⅛ teaspoon)

Kosher salt

Sausage melts are a fabulous fallback dish when working late, or when kids' sports or ballet classes cut down on cooking time. They're easy to get on the table in record time, to the delight of hungry kids.

2 tablespoons extra virgin olive oil

1 pound Italian sausage (a mix of sweet and hot)

1 large Spanish onion, halved lengthwise and thinly sliced crosswise

4 large cloves garlic, sliced into slivers

1 large green bell pepper, cut into ¼-inch strips

1 large red bell pepper, cut into ¼-inch strips

1 large yellow or orange bell pepper, cut into ¼-inch strips

½ teaspoon dried oregano

⅛ teaspoon crushed red pepper flakes, or to taste

Kosher salt

One 8-ounce can tomato sauce

4 Italian hero or sub sandwich rolls (7 to 8 inches long, preferably whole-grain)

8 to 10 thin slices provolone cheese

Line a plate with paper towels.

In a large heavy skillet, heat 1 tablespoon of the oil over medium-high heat until it shimmers. Add the sausages and cook, turning with tongs, until they are browned on all sides and no longer pink in the middle, 12 to 15 minutes. Transfer to the paper towel–lined plate to drain. When cool, remove the sausages to a cutting board and slice in half lengthwise, then crosswise in thirds.

Wipe the pan clean with paper towels. Heat the remaining 1 tablespoon of oil over medium-high heat until shimmering. Add the onion and cook until soft and golden, stirring occasionally, about 5 minutes. Add the garlic and cook for 3 minutes. Stir in the bell peppers, dried oregano, red pepper flakes, and ½ teaspoon of salt and mix well. Continue to sauté until the peppers are lightly charred and tender, about 8 minutes.

Return the sausages to the pan and add the tomato sauce. Reduce the heat to medium and cook until heated through, about 8 minutes.

Meanwhile, preheat the broiler.

Split the rolls in half lengthwise and hollow out some of the bread on each of the bottom halves, forming a cavity. Put the rolls cut side up on a rimmed baking sheet and place an equal portion of the sausages and peppers on each roll bottom. Top these with provolone cheese. Broil until the bread crisps and the cheese melts, 2 to 4 minutes. Close the heroes and serve hot.

Food for Thought

You'll want to use all three colors of bell peppers, since each color offers its own health benefits. Green is high in vitamin A, red is supercharged with vitamin C, and yellow and orange are rich in carotenoids and antioxidants. And 1 cup of chopped peppers of any color provides 100 percent of the recommended daily intake of vitamin C.

fish and seafood

WE SPENT EVERY SUMMER OF OUR CHILDHOOD ON THE ISLAND OF MARTHA'S Vineyard, Massachusetts. School would let out and the very next day we loaded up the big family station wagon and squeezed into it (the six of us, two dogs, a cat, and usually one or two friends). You may be wondering how we would all fit, but this was before the age of using seat belts, and all of our luggage was affixed precariously to the roof with rope.

Our passion for seafood is tied to those halcyon summer days on the Vineyard. Every meal we ate told a story of how that food came to our plates and to our table. It was an adventure story composed of clamming at Quitsa Pond, trips to the dock to see the fishermen unload that day's catch, and perhaps our favorite activity of all, the visit to our local fish market to select our lobsters. Each of us picked out our own "pet" lobster, named it, cared for it, and played with it, rubber bands around the claws, until dinner. This fun with shellfish would culminate with the big lobster races, an approximate three-yard dash along our front porch. Crowding around the twine finish line we'd each scream our lobster's name in anticipation of the big win. As for what happened afterward, well, let's just say there were no winners except us. We would don our plastic bibs and feast on sweet buttery lobster, local corn, and warm pie teeming with blueberries we had picked ourselves.

What we took away from our time on the Vineyard, specifically from the meals we enjoyed, was an appreciation for food sourced locally, although we would never have put it that way then. We just knew that we were surrounded by water and from that water came an amazing bounty.

 Today when preparing fish and seafood we try to continue to source as locally as possible. It's so tricky knowing which fish are safe and which should be avoided. But Monterey Bay Aquarium has a website called Seafood Watch (www.montereybayaquarium.com) that posts up-to-date lists of fish on a "green" list. The seafood on this list is deemed "abundant, well managed, and caught or farmed in environmentally friendly ways." Use this list to determine

SCHUYLER

which fish to buy at your local market. If the fish we use in the recipe is not available, you can substitute another similar in taste and texture. Ask your fishmonger for suggestions if you need them.

The beauty of cooking fresh fish is that the subtle flavors need very little help, and we love to throw fish on the grill for an easy summer meal. When cooking indoors in the winter, panfrying, roasting, or cooking in parchment ("en papillote") is a good alternative.

beer-battered fish tacos with mango salsa

4 to 6 servings

■ **FROM THE MARKET**

Skinless white fish fillets
(1½ pounds; cod, halibut, or
tilapia will all work fine)

Iceberg or romaine lettuce
(1 head)

Red bell pepper (1)

Red onion (1 small)

Jalapeño chile (1 small)

Fresh cilantro (1 small bunch)

Mangos (2)

Limes (2)

Corn or flour tortillas
(12 to 18)

Canned chipotle peppers
in adobo sauce
(1 small can)

Beer (one 12-ounce bottle;
preferably Mexican)

■ **FROM THE PANTRY**

Kosher salt

Black pepper

Mayonnaise (1 cup)

All-purpose flour (1 cup)

Ground cumin (¼ teaspoon)

Cayenne pepper (¼ teaspoon)

Organic canola oil (1 quart)

Sea salt

We started making these yummy fish tacos on Martha's Vineyard many summers ago. We would all pile into the car and head to our local fish market, Larsen's, to choose the freshest catch of the day. We like to make an assembly line of savory south-of-the-border toppings and let everyone create their own masterpiece.

FOR THE SALSA

2 cups finely diced mango

½ cup finely diced red bell pepper

¼ cup finely diced red onion

½ teaspoon finely chopped
jalapeño chile

2 tablespoons chopped fresh cilantro

2 tablespoons fresh lime juice

Kosher salt

Freshly ground black pepper

FOR THE CHIPOTLE MAYONNAISE

1 tablespoon minced canned chipotle
pepper, with 2 teaspoons of the
adobo sauce

1 cup mayonnaise

Kosher salt

FOR THE FISH TACOS

1½ pounds skinless white fish fillets
(cod, halibut, or tilapia), cut into
1 by 3-inch strips

Kosher salt

Freshly ground black pepper

1 cup all-purpose flour

¼ teaspoon ground cumin

¼ teaspoon cayenne pepper

1 cup beer

12 to 18 corn or flour tortillas

1 quart canola oil

Sea salt

2 cups shredded iceberg or
romaine lettuce

1 lime, cut into wedges

FOR THE SALSA

In a small mixing bowl, combine the mango, red pepper, onion, jalapeño, cilantro, lime juice, ½ teaspoon of kosher salt, and ⅛ teaspoon of pepper. Mix well and set aside.

FOR THE CHIPOTLE MAYONNAISE

Combine the chipotle, adobo sauce, mayonnaise, and ¼ teaspoon of kosher salt in a small mixing bowl. Mix until smooth and refrigerate until you're ready to use.

FOR THE FISH TACOS

Preheat the oven to 300°F. Line a baking sheet with paper towels or brown paper.

Season the fish with ½ teaspoon of kosher salt and ⅛ teaspoon of pepper; cover and refrigerate.

In a mixing bowl, combine the flour, cumin, cayenne, ½ teaspoon of kosher salt, and ⅛ teaspoon of pepper. Add the beer and whisk until completely smooth.

Wrap the tortillas in foil and place in the warm oven.

In a large, deep skillet over medium-high heat, heat the oil to 375°F. If you don't have a thermometer, insert the handle of a wooden spoon into the oil. If bubbles form around the wood and begin to float, your oil is hot enough.

Put one third of the fish in the batter and mix gently until well coated. One at a time, lift the pieces with metal tongs, allowing excess batter to drip off, and place in the hot oil. Fry the strips for 2 to 3 minutes, until nicely browned, then flip to the other side, loosening with the tongs if they stick to the bottom of the pan. Cook on the second side for an additional 1 to 2 minutes, until golden brown. Remove the fish from the oil with the tongs and transfer to the paper towel–lined baking sheet to drain. Repeat with the remaining fish and batter. Sprinkle the fish with sea salt to taste.

Arrange the fish on a platter and serve with the salsa, chipotle mayonnaise, shredded lettuce, lime wedges, and warm tortillas.

pan-seared salmon with salsa verde

4 servings

FROM THE MARKET

Salmon (4 skinless
6-ounce fillets)

Italian (flat-leaf) parsley
(1 bunch)

Fresh cilantro (1 bunch)

Fresh mint (1 bunch)

Fresh chives (1 bunch)

Shallot (1 large)

Garlic (1 clove)

Lemons (2)

FROM THE PANTRY

Capers (1 tablespoon)

Dijon mustard (1 teaspoon)

Extra virgin olive oil
(⅓ cup plus 2 tablespoons)

Red wine vinegar
(1½ teaspoons)

Sea salt

Black pepper

When we are really pressed for time, this is our go-to salmon dish. The salsa verde gives it a light fresh flavor and an elegant look. Those who do not like cilantro can use basil instead.

FOR THE SALSA VERDE

1 clove garlic, halved

1 tablespoon capers, drained

1 tablespoon roughly chopped shallot

1 teaspoon Dijon mustard

½ cup packed Italian (flat-leaf)
    parsley leaves

½ cup packed fresh cilantro leaves

½ cup packed fresh mint leaves

¼ cup finely sliced fresh chives

⅓ cup extra virgin olive oil

1½ teaspoons red wine vinegar

1 tablespoon fresh lemon juice

Sea salt

Freshly ground black pepper

FOR THE SALMON

Four 6-ounce skinless salmon fillets

2 tablespoons extra virgin olive oil

Sea salt

Freshly ground black pepper

4 lemon wedges

Preheat the oven to 450°F.

FOR THE SALSA VERDE

In a food processor or blender, combine the garlic, capers, shallot, mustard, parsley, cilantro, mint, and chives. Blend until coarsely chopped. Slowly add ⅓ cup of oil, the vinegar, lemon juice, and 2 tablespoons of water, and blend until smooth, stopping to scrape down the sides with a rubber spatula as needed. Transfer to a small bowl and season with salt and pepper.

(recipe continues)

FOR THE SALMON

Coat each fillet with 1½ teaspoons of oil and generously season with salt and pepper.

Place a large dry ovenproof skillet over medium-high heat. When the pan is very hot, lay the salmon fillets rounded side down and cook until a nice brown crust forms, about 3 minutes. Carefully flip the fillets to the other side and place the skillet in the oven. Cook for 3 to 5 minutes for a rare center, or 6 to 7 minutes for more well-done.

Place the salmon fillets on individual plates and spoon salsa verde down the center of each fillet. Garnish each plate with a lemon wedge, and pass the remaining sauce separately.

Food for Thought

The fresh herbs in the salsa verde not only add flavor and color to this dish, they also offer important health benefits. Each contains powerful antioxidants and is rich in vitamins and minerals. Parsley, for instance, exceeds almost every other vegetable in its ability to raise the level of antioxidant enzymes in our bodies.

---

paprika-seared shrimp

6 servings

This has always been one of my favorites. My kids love it, too, and I like how quick it is to prepare. The paprika gives it that beautiful deep color and smoky flavor. When I was growing up, shrimp was very expensive, so my mother prepared it only on special occasions. Even though shrimp is so much more reasonably priced now, this still feels like a special-occasion meal and it's a real crowd-pleaser.—TRACY

2 teaspoons all-purpose flour

1 tablespoon paprika

1 teaspoon granulated sugar

Sea salt

Freshly ground black pepper

2 pounds large shrimp (15 to 20 per pound), peeled, deveined, and butterflied

2 tablespoons extra virgin olive oil

6 tablespoons (¾ stick) unsalted butter

1 tablespoon minced garlic

2 tablespoons chopped sun-dried tomatoes in oil

2 teaspoons capers, drained

½ cup plus 1 tablespoon dry white wine

1 tablespoon fresh lemon juice

1 tablespoon finely chopped Italian (flat-leaf) parsley

■ FROM THE MARKET

Shrimp (2 pounds large, 15 to 20 per pound)

Italian (flat-leaf) parsley (1 small bunch)

Garlic (3 large cloves)

Lemon (1)

Unsalted butter (6 tablespoons, or ¾ stick)

■ FROM THE PANTRY

All-purpose flour (2 teaspoons)

Paprika (1 tablespoon)

Granulated sugar (1 teaspoon)

Sea salt

Black pepper

Extra virgin olive oil (2 tablespoons)

Sun-dried tomatoes in oil (4 or 5)

Capers (2 teaspoons)

Dry white wine (½ cup plus 1 tablespoon)

Preheat the oven to 350°F.

In a small mixing bowl, combine the flour, paprika, sugar, ¼ teaspoon of salt, and ⅛ teaspoon of pepper. Lay the shrimp in a single layer on a rimmed baking sheet. Sprinkle the mixture on the shrimp, making sure to get both sides.

Heat 1 tablespoon of the oil in a large skillet over medium-high heat. When the oil is shimmering, place half the shrimp in one layer in the skillet, cut side down with tails sticking up. Let cook undisturbed for 1 to 2 minutes. Flip the shrimp and sear the other side, another 2 minutes. Transfer the shrimp to a small

shallow baking dish. Wipe the skillet clean with paper towels and repeat with
1 tablespoon of the oil and the remaining shrimp. Place the baking dish in the
oven and bake until lightly browned on the edges and opaque in the centers,
4 to 5 minutes.

While the shrimp are baking, wipe out the skillet with paper towels and return
it to the burner over low heat. Melt 1 tablespoon of the butter. Add the garlic
and stir for 30 seconds. Add the sun-dried tomatoes and capers, raise the heat
to medium-high, and sauté for 1 to 2 minutes, taking care not to burn the garlic.
Add the wine and lemon juice and bring to a boil. Reduce the heat to medium
and cook for an additional 4 minutes. Swirl in the remaining 5 tablespoons of
butter and season with salt and pepper. Pour the sauce over the shrimp, sprinkle
with the parsley, and serve.

panfried halibut
with chimichurri sauce

4 servings

Halibut is such a pleasing, light, flaky fish that we find it's popular with the whole family. Pairing it with a lemony chimichurri sauce is a perfect complement. This is such an easy dish to prepare, and beautiful to serve. The secret to this recipe is Wondra flour, which helps form that beautiful golden crust.

■ **FROM THE MARKET**

Halibut (4 skinless 6-ounce fillets)

Italian (flat-leaf) parsley (1 bunch)

Shallot (1 large)

Garlic (3 large cloves)

Lemons (2)

Wondra flour* (2 to 3 tablespoons)

*A fine, dust-free flour, perfect for creating a crispy layer on fish

■ **FROM THE PANTRY**

Extra virgin olive oil (⅓ cup plus 3 tablespoons)

Red wine vinegar (1 tablespoon)

Crushed red pepper flakes (½ teaspoon)

Sea salt

Black pepper

FOR THE CHIMICHURRI SAUCE

⅓ cup extra virgin olive oil

3 tablespoons fresh lemon juice

1 tablespoon red wine vinegar

1 tablespoon minced shallot

1 tablespoon minced garlic

½ teaspoon crushed red pepper flakes

Sea salt

Freshly ground black pepper

¾ cup finely chopped Italian (flat-leaf) parsley

FOR THE HALIBUT

Four 6-ounce skinless halibut fillets

3 tablespoons extra virgin olive oil

Sea salt

Freshly ground black pepper

2 to 3 tablespoons Wondra flour, or as needed

4 lemon wedges

FOR THE CHIMICHURRI SAUCE

In a small mixing bowl, combine ⅓ cup oil, the lemon juice, vinegar, shallot, garlic, and 1 tablespoon of water. Whisk until blended. Add the red pepper flakes, season with salt and pepper, and whisk again. Gently fold in the parsley and set aside.

FOR THE HALIBUT

Preheat the oven to 400°F.

Pat the halibut fillets dry. Generously coat them with 1 tablespoon of the oil and season them with salt and pepper. Sprinkle only the rounded top of each fillet with Wondra flour to coat.

Heat a large ovenproof skillet over high heat. Add the remaining 2 tablespoons of oil. When the pan is very hot, place the fillets flour-coated side down and cook until browned, about 3 minutes. (You can peek by lifting the corner of a fillet with a spatula.) Carefully flip the fillets to the other side and place the skillet in the oven. Cook until the centers are just opaque, 6 to 8 minutes.

Place the fillets on a platter and top with the chimichurri sauce, spooning about 1 tablespoon on each. Serve with lemon wedges and extra sauce passed separately.

classic sole meunière

4 servings

After just one bite of this decadent, buttery, velvety dish you will be instantly transported to a bistro on the Champs-Élysées, sipping Montrachet while watching *tout le monde* pass by.

Four 5-ounce skinless fillets of sole, grey or Dover

Kosher salt

Freshly ground black pepper

½ cup whole milk

½ cup all-purpose flour

6 tablespoons (¾ stick) unsalted butter

1 tablespoon capers, rinsed and drained

2 tablespoons fresh lemon juice

1 teaspoon grated lemon zest

1 tablespoon minced Italian (flat-leaf) parsley

1 lemon, cut into wedges

■ **FROM THE MARKET**

Grey sole or Dover sole (4 skinless 5-ounce fillets)

Italian (flat-leaf) parsley (1 small bunch)

Lemons (2)

Whole milk (½ cup)

Unsalted butter (6 tablespoons, or ¾ stick)

■ **FROM THE PANTRY**

Kosher salt

Black pepper

All-purpose flour (½ cup)

Capers (1 tablespoon)

Preheat the oven to 200°F.

Season each fillet with salt and pepper, making sure to season both sides.

Pour the milk into a wide, shallow dish. Put the flour in another wide dish and season with ½ teaspoon of salt and ⅛ teaspoon of pepper, mixing well. Place a fillet in the milk, then in the seasoned flour, coating both sides and gently shaking off any excess. Set aside on a baking sheet. Continue with the remaining fillets, placing them in a single layer.

Heat a large skillet over medium-high heat. Place 2 tablespoons of the butter in the pan and heat until the foam subsides. Gently place 2 fillets in the pan, rounded side down. Cook the fish for approximately 2 minutes, until golden brown. Carefully flip with a spatula, taking care not to break the fish. Cook on

the other side for an additional 1½ minutes. Transfer each fillet to an ovenproof plate; the fillets will now be rounded side up. Place the plates in the oven.

Wipe the pan with paper towels, add 2 more tablespoons of the butter, and repeat with the remaining fillets.

In a small saucepan over medium heat, melt the remaining 2 tablespoons of butter. When the butter begins to emit a nutty aroma, after about 2 minutes, add the capers and cook for 1 minute more. Add the lemon juice and zest, reduce the heat to low, and cook for 1 minute.

Remove the plates from the oven and spoon the sauce evenly over each fillet. Sprinkle with parsley and season with salt and pepper. Garnish with lemon wedges and serve.

teriyaki-glazed salmon

4 servings

We love this quick and easy dish. There is nothing like fresh wild salmon smothered in a sweet and salty glaze. After pan-searing, a brief time in the oven yields a crispy, caramelized perfection.

3 tablespoons low-sodium soy sauce

2 tablespoons sake

2 teaspoons mirin

1 teaspoon minced garlic

Four 6-ounce skinless salmon fillets

2 teaspoons canola oil

¾ cup Terrific Teriyaki Glaze (page 270, or your favorite store-bought)

In a wide, shallow dish, mix the soy sauce, sake, mirin, and garlic. Place the salmon fillets in the marinade and turn once, coating both sides. Cover and refrigerate for at least 30 minutes and up to 8 hours.

Set a rack in the middle of the oven and preheat the oven to 350°F.

Place a large, heavy-bottomed ovenproof skillet over medium-high heat. Remove the salmon from the marinade and dry with paper towels. Discard the marinade.

When the skillet is very hot, add the oil, using a pastry brush or paper towel to coat the entire bottom. Place the fillets in the pan, rounded side down. Cook for 1 minute. Flip with a metal spatula. Cook on the other side for 1 minute more. Turn off the heat. Spoon 2 to 3 tablespoons of teriyaki glaze on each fillet. Place the skillet in the oven. Cook about 5 minutes for a rare center, or 8 to 10 minutes for more well-done.

Arrange the salmon fillets on a platter and serve. Pass the remaining teriyaki glaze separately, if desired.

■ **FROM THE MARKET**

Salmon (4 skinless 6-ounce fillets)

Garlic (1 clove)

Premium Japanese sake (1 ounce)

■ **FROM THE PANTRY**

Low-sodium soy sauce (3 tablespoons)

Mirin (2 teaspoons)

Organic canola oil (2 teaspoons)

Terrific Teriyaki Glaze (¾ cup; page 270, or your favorite store-bought)

halibut puttanesca en papillote

4 servings

Our kids were not overly fond of fish until we began serving it in parchment paper pouches. They loved cutting through the paper to find their dinner inside. Besides offering a fun way of serving food, baking in parchment is actually one of the healthiest ways to cook fish. The fish steams in its own juices so it stays delectably moist, while the vegetables, olives, and capers meld into a flavor-packed broth. All that's needed is a crusty loaf of bread to sop it all up.

Organic olive oil cooking spray

Four 6-ounce skinless halibut or
    cod fillets

Kosher salt

Freshly ground black pepper

2 cups peeled and diced eggplant,
    cut into ½-inch cubes

2 cups diced zucchini, cut into
    ½-inch cubes

1 tablespoon minced garlic

20 pitted black olives, halved
    lengthwise

4 teaspoons capers, drained

8 anchovy fillets in oil (optional)

One 14.5-ounce can diced tomatoes,
    drained with juice reserved

4 tablespoons dry white wine

Pinch of crushed red pepper flakes,
    or to taste

Preheat the oven to 400°F. Prepare four pieces of parchment paper, 14 by 15 inches each; fold each piece in half and cut a half circle to form a full circle when open.

Spray one side of a parchment disk with a little oil. Place a piece of fish in the center of the parchment paper, about 1 inch away from the fold. Season with salt and black pepper. Top the fish with ½ cup of the eggplant and ½ cup of the zucchini. Add one quarter of the minced garlic, 10 olive halves, 1 teaspoon capers, 2 anchovy fillets (if desired), 3 heaping tablespoons tomatoes, and 1 tablespoon of the tomato juice. Top with 1 tablespoon wine and red pepper flakes.

To close the pouches, fold the edges of the parchment paper together to form a semicircle, and working from one end, begin tightly folding and crimping the edges together to form a seal.

Repeat with the remaining parchment and ingredients. Arrange the pouches on a rimmed baking sheet. Bake until the parchment puffs up, 15 to 20 minutes.

Serve the pouches on individual plates.

pan-roasted cod in spicy thai broth

4 servings

This dish is lovely to look at and delightful to eat. The broth is amber, with touches of green from spinach leaves floating on top. Best of all, it takes less than 30 minutes to prepare, so we often serve it when people drop by.

FOR THE BROTH

One 13- to 14-ounce can unsweetened coconut milk

¼ cup fresh lime juice

⅓ cup dry white wine

1½ tablespoons red curry paste

1 tablespoon minced garlic

1 tablespoon Thai fish sauce

1 tablespoon granulated sugar

1 teaspoon ground coriander

1 teaspoon finely grated fresh ginger

1 teaspoon tamarind paste

FOR THE FISH

1 tablespoon extra virgin olive oil

Four 6-ounce skinless cod fillets

2 ounces baby spinach leaves

■ **FROM THE MARKET**

Cod (4 skinless 6-ounce fillets)

Baby spinach leaves (2 ounces)

Fresh ginger (1 small knob)

Garlic (4 cloves)

Limes (3)

Unsweetened coconut milk (one 13- to 14-ounce can)

Red curry paste (1½ tablespoons)

Thai fish sauce (1 tablespoon)

Tamarind paste (1 teaspoon)

■ **FROM THE PANTRY**

Dry white wine (⅓ cup)

Granulated sugar (1 tablespoon)

Ground coriander (1 teaspoon)

Extra virgin olive oil (1 tablespoon)

Set a rack in the middle of the oven and preheat the oven to 400°F.

FOR THE BROTH

Combine the coconut milk, lime juice, wine, curry paste, garlic, fish sauce, sugar, coriander, ginger, and tamarind paste in a medium pot and bring to a boil. Reduce the heat to low and simmer for 8 minutes. Remove from the heat and set aside.

FOR THE FISH

Heat the oil in a large ovenproof nonstick skillet over high heat until shimmering. Add the cod and sear for 3 minutes on one side, then flip and sear on the other side for 2 minutes more. Place the pan in the oven and roast until opaque, about 8 minutes.

Place 8 spinach leaves in the bottom of each of four soup bowls. Add a fillet to each bowl and pour the broth over the fish. Garnish each bowl with 4 or 5 spinach leaves on top and serve.

sea scallop fricassee with tomatoes and corn

4 to 6 servings

The first time we tasted a seafood fricassee was in Paris and we loved the combination of flavors—garlicky, but bright and fresh. Our Parisian dish had teeny clams that are impossible to find in New York, so we substitute easily available sea scallops. The broth is so luscious, we serve this stew over pasta or polenta so not a smidgen gets lost.

■ FROM THE MARKET

Sea scallops
(1½ pounds)

Fresh corn (2 large ears)

Fresh tomatoes
(3 medium, about
1 pound)

Fresh basil (1 bunch)

Leeks (2 large)

Garlic (5 cloves)

Unsalted butter
(4 tablespoons, or ½ stick)

Clam juice
(one 8-ounce bottle)

■ FROM THE PANTRY

All-purpose flour
(⅓ cup)

Kosher salt

Black pepper

Extra virgin olive oil
(¼ cup)

Dry white wine (½ cup)

Crushed red pepper flakes
(⅛ teaspoon)

Pasta, rice, or polenta
(cooked, optional)

⅓ cup all-purpose flour

Kosher salt

Freshly ground black pepper

1½ pounds sea scallops, muscle removed

4 tablespoons extra virgin olive oil

4 tablespoons (½ stick) unsalted butter

1½ tablespoons minced garlic

1¼ cups thinly sliced leeks (2 large, white and pale green parts only), thoroughly rinsed and drained

½ cup dry white wine

¾ cup clam juice

⅛ teaspoon crushed red pepper flakes

1 cup fresh corn kernels, shaved from the cob

1½ cups finely chopped fresh tomatoes

⅔ cup tightly packed fresh basil leaves, cut into chiffonade

Cooked pasta, rice, or polenta for serving (optional)

In a large dish or platter, mix the flour with ¾ teaspoon of salt and ⅛ teaspoon of pepper. Gently turn the scallops in the seasoned flour until lightly coated.

Line a plate with paper towels.

Pour 3 tablespoons of the oil into a large skillet over medium-high heat. When the oil shimmers, add half the scallops in a single layer. Cook undisturbed until the scallops are lightly browned, about 4 minutes. Using tongs, flip the scallops. Cook until the other sides are brown, about 3 minutes more. Transfer the scallops to the paper towel–lined plate. Add the remaining 1 tablespoon of oil to the skillet. Cook the remaining scallops and set aside.

Discard any oil left in the skillet and wipe it clean with paper towels. Add 2 tablespoons of the butter and cook over medium heat until the butter sizzles. Stir in the garlic and leeks and cook for 1 minute, stirring constantly. Pour in the wine, increase the heat to high, and boil until the wine is reduced by a third, about 5 minutes.

Add the clam juice and red pepper flakes and cook for an additional 3 minutes. Stir in the corn, tomatoes, and the remaining 2 tablespoons of butter. Reduce the heat to low, and simmer until thickened and creamy, about 10 minutes. Season with ¼ teaspoon of salt and ⅛ teaspoon of pepper. Add the scallops and heat thoroughly, about 5 minutes. Sprinkle on the basil and serve over pasta, rice, or polenta if desired.

smoky sautéed shrimp

4 servings

The assertive spices in this dish turn up the heat, while the quick sautéing method keeps the shrimp wonderfully moist and tender. We like to serve it with rice, grits, polenta, or a crusty baguette to mop up the sizzling sauce.

½ cup extra virgin olive oil

4 large cloves garlic, sliced into thin slivers

1 teaspoon paprika

½ teaspoon smoked paprika

½ teaspoon ground cumin

¼ teaspoon ground chipotle chile pepper, or to taste

Kosher salt

Freshly ground black pepper

1½ pounds large shrimp (15 to 20 per pound), peeled and deveined

2 tablespoons finely chopped Italian (flat-leaf) parsley

½ lime

In a large skillet, heat the oil over medium heat until it shimmers. Add the garlic and cook until soft, about 2 minutes.

Add the paprika, smoked paprika, cumin, ground chipotle, ½ teaspoon of salt, and ⅛ teaspoon of pepper and stir. Raise the heat to medium-high and add the shrimp in one layer. Cook until the shrimp just turn pink, about 3 minutes, then flip the shrimp and cook until just opaque, about 2 minutes more; be careful not to overcook. Immediately remove the pan from the heat. Transfer the shrimp with the flavored oil to a serving dish, sprinkle with the parsley, squeeze on the lime juice, and serve.

■ **FROM THE MARKET**

Shrimp (1½ pounds large, 15 to 20 per pound)

Italian (flat-leaf) parsley (1 bunch)

Garlic (4 large cloves)

Lime (1)

■ **FROM THE PANTRY**

Extra virgin olive oil (½ cup)

Paprika (1 teaspoon)

Smoked paprika (½ teaspoon)

Ground cumin (½ teaspoon)

Ground chipotle chile pepper (¼ teaspoon, or to taste)

Kosher salt

Black pepper

vegetarian
and
meatless
mondays

pan-seared tofu teriyaki

supreme crispy quinoa vegetable burgers

savory mushroom cutlets

spanish tortilla with spinach and
manchego cheese

panfried tofu with chimichurri sauce

spinach and ricotta malfatti with
brown butter and sage

harvest vegetable bake

ISAAC

AT 13, TRACY INFORMED OUR MOTHER (CORKY) THAT SHE HAD DECIDED TO become a vegetarian. Vegetarianism at that time—especially for a 13-year-old—was not very common. Corky was accepting of this declaration, but in truth, she was a little taken aback by the break from family eating patterns. She said it was fine but explained to Tracy that she was in a family with five other people who eat meat and therefore she (Corky) was not going to make anything special—Tracy could "find her own foods to eat."

Finding her own foods lasted about a day. Corky proceeded to incorporate vegetarian meals into all of our diets with enthusiasm and vigor. Now our dinners included mushroom crêpes, spinach and ricotta malfatti, falafel and watercress salads. In time, Tracy gave up her vegetarianism—but we all continued to appreciate and embrace vegetarian meals.

Moving forward a generation, we each have a child or two who are vegetarians. Even without that impetus, however, we often opt for serving meatless meals—there are so many delicious and healthy choices. In addition to the wonderful pastas, there are super grains such as quinoa and bulgur, assorted beans, and amazing varieties of vegetables; all are terrific ingredients for creating satisfying and hearty meals that delight both vegetarians and meat eaters alike.

We are firm believers in Meatless Monday—the international movement to cut meat consumption in order to improve both our own health and the health of the planet. According to the Meatless Monday campaign, going meatless once a week can "help limit your carbon footprint and save precious resources like freshwater and fossil fuel." By eliminating meat from our diet for just one day a week we can make a real difference. Our vegetarian dinner options make Meatless Mondays—and really any day of the week—easy and delicious. And another benefit to eating vegetarian at least one day a week is that it's easy on the family budget.

pan-seared tofu teriyaki

4 servings

■ **FROM THE MARKET**

Extra firm organic tofu
(two 12- to 14-ounce
packages)

■ **FROM THE PANTRY**

Organic canola oil
(1 tablespoon)

Terrific Teriyaki Glaze
(¾ cup; page 270, or your
favorite store-bought)

In our experience, this recipe is the answer to people who say they don't
like tofu or don't know what to do with it. It's crispy and a tad sweet, so kids
love it, too. Pair it with a grain and a vegetable dish and you have a healthy,
delicious dinner.

Two 12- to 14-ounce packages extra
firm organic tofu, drained

1 tablespoon canola oil

¾ cup Terrific Teriyaki Glaze
(page 270, or your favorite
store-bought)

Set a rack in the middle of the oven and preheat the oven to 400°F.

Slice the tofu blocks in half horizontally to make them half as thick, then vertically, to make 4 equal-size rectangular tofu steaks from each package, for a total
of 8. Place the tofu in a single layer on several layers of paper towels on either a
plate or cutting board. Cover with more paper towels, place a plate or another
cutting board on top, and rest a weight, such as a small skillet, on top of that.
This will press the excess liquid from the tofu. Let the steaks drain for at least
10 minutes.

In a large nonstick skillet over medium-high heat, heat the oil until shimmering. Pat the tofu steaks dry and place them in the pan. Cook undisturbed until
golden, 4 to 5 minutes. Flip and cook until golden brown on the other side,
4 to 5 minutes more. Remove the pan from the heat.

In a casserole or baking pan large enough to hold the tofu in a single layer,
spread just enough teriyaki glaze to lightly coat the bottom (2 to 3 tablespoons).
Lay the tofu steaks on top and spoon on the remaining teriyaki glaze, coating
them completely.

Bake until browned and bubbly, 15 to 20 minutes. Serve hot.

supreme crispy quinoa vegetable burgers

4 servings

We have eaten so many veggie burgers over the years but never found one that we really loved, one that made us say, "This is a great burger!" We call these burgers "supreme" because they truly are. The beans and vegetables keep them moist on the inside, and the quinoa adds a mouthwatering crunch when you bite into them.

¼ cup quinoa, rinsed and drained

½ cup low-sodium vegetable broth

1 cup organic canned black beans, rinsed and drained

1 tablespoon finely chopped scallions

½ cup peeled and finely chopped carrots

¼ cup plain Breadcrumbs (page 264, or your favorite store-bought)

1 large clove garlic, minced

Kosher salt

Freshly ground black pepper

1 large egg

2 tablespoons extra virgin olive oil

4 multigrain hamburger buns

1 ripe avocado, thinly sliced (optional)

Your favorite burger toppings for serving

■ **FROM THE MARKET**

Scallions (1 small bunch)

Carrot (1 medium)

Avocado (1 ripe), optional

Garlic (1 large clove)

Large egg (1)

Multigrain hamburger buns (4)

■ **FROM THE PANTRY**

Quinoa (¼ cup)

Low-sodium vegetable broth (½ cup)

Organic black beans (one 15-ounce can)

Plain Breadcrumbs (¼ cup; page 264, or your favorite store-bought)

Kosher salt

Black pepper

Extra virgin olive oil (2 tablespoons)

Combine the quinoa and vegetable broth in a small saucepan and bring to a boil. Reduce to a simmer, cover, and cook until all the liquid is absorbed, about 10 minutes. Remove from the heat, set aside and let cool slightly.

Meanwhile, in a large mixing bowl, mash the beans with a potato masher, making sure to leave a few chunks. Add the scallions, carrots, breadcrumbs, garlic, ½ teaspoon of salt, and ⅛ teaspoon of pepper and mix well. Add the cooked quinoa and the egg and combine.

Using your hands, form the mixture into four individual patties and place on a platter.

(recipe continues)

ESMÉ

Heat a large nonstick skillet over medium-high heat. Add the oil and heat until shimmering. Reduce the heat to medium, place the patties in the pan, and cook until golden brown, about 5 minutes. Carefully flip and brown the other sides, about 5 minutes more. Assemble the burgers and buns on a platter. Top with slices of avocado, if desired, and serve with your favorite toppings.

Food for Thought

Quinoa has been called a "super grain" and it's the grain of the moment (even if technically it's not a grain). This isn't just hype. Quinoa is one of the most protein-rich foods we can eat, and that protein is complete in that it contains all nine essential amino acids. Quinoa also has twice as much fiber as most other grains.

savory mushroom cutlets

4 to 6 servings

■ **FROM THE MARKET**

White button mushrooms
(24 to 28, about 1 pound)

Scallions (4)

Large eggs (4)

Cheddar cheese (4 ounces)

Monterey Jack cheese
(4 ounces)

■ **FROM THE PANTRY**

Herb salt (1 teaspoon)

Black pepper

Plain Breadcrumbs
(1 cup plus more as needed;
page 264, or your favorite
store-bought)

Organic canola oil
(2 tablespoons)

Finding hearty vegetarian dishes that will appeal to meat eaters can be daunting. This mushroom cutlet recipe does just that—no one will miss the meat. I first discovered it in the late 1970s when I was a student in Northern California—already the vanguard for locally grown, healthy food. This recipe is so easy and so delicious—it soon became a favorite of all our families.—LORI

4 large eggs

1 teaspoon herb salt

Freshly ground black pepper

4 cups finely chopped white button mushrooms, stems trimmed

4 scallions, white and light green parts, finely chopped

1 cup plain Breadcrumbs plus more if needed (page 264, or your favorite store-bought)

1 cup shredded cheddar cheese

1 cup shredded Monterey Jack cheese

2 tablespoons canola oil

Soy sauce, hot sauce, steak sauce, and/or ketchup for serving

Preheat the oven to 300°F.

In a large mixing bowl, beat together the eggs, herb salt, and ⅛ teaspoon of pepper. Mix in the mushrooms and scallions. Slowly add ¾ cup of the breadcrumbs and the cheeses and mix well with a spoon or by hand just until it comes together well enough to be shaped; do not overmix.

Gently squeezing out any excess liquid, shape a handful of the mushroom mixture into a patty approximately ½ inch thick. Sprinkle with some of the remaining breadcrumbs to lightly coat. Place the formed patty on a baking sheet or platter. Repeat with the remaining mushroom mixture; you will have 8 to 10 patties.

Heat 1 tablespoon of the oil in a large nonstick skillet over medium-high heat until shimmering. Place half the patties in the pan and cook undisturbed until golden brown, about 4 minutes. Flip the patties and cook until the second side is golden, about 4 minutes more. Transfer the patties to a rimmed baking sheet and place it in the oven to keep them warm. Wipe the skillet clean with paper towels, add 1 tablespoon of oil, and cook the remaining patties.

Transfer to a platter and serve with your choice of soy sauce, hot sauce, steak sauce, or ketchup.

Food for Thought

Good news for people who don't love to eat onions or garlic. Scallions, which are much milder in flavor, provide so many of the same health benefits as their allium vegetable family members. Besides being a good source of antioxidant and anti-inflammatory compounds, they have been shown to have an antihistamine-like effect for those with allergies. And one single scallion stalk provides 43 percent of the daily-recommended dose of vitamin K, vital for bone density and strength.

spanish tortilla with spinach and manchego cheese

4 servings as a main course, 6 servings as a side

■ **FROM THE MARKET**

Yukon gold potatoes
(2 medium, about 8 ounces)

White onion (1 medium)

Baby spinach leaves
(2 ounces)

Italian (flat-leaf) parsley
(1 small bunch)

Fresh thyme (2 sprigs)

Unsalted butter
(3 tablespoons)

Large eggs (8)

Manchego cheese
(2 ounces)

■ **FROM THE PANTRY**

Kosher salt

Black pepper

This Spanish omelet is a great way to take familiar ingredients and turn them into something exotic. Perfect for a weeknight meal served with warm corn tortillas and guacamole. Or if you're entertaining, cut into bite-size wedges and offered as tapas with a selection of Mediterranean olives.

1¼ cups peeled and diced Yukon gold potatoes, cut into ½-inch cubes

2 or 3 tablespoons unsalted butter

8 large eggs

Kosher salt

Freshly ground black pepper

1 tablespoon finely chopped Italian (flat-leaf) parsley

1 teaspoon chopped fresh thyme leaves

1 medium white onion, halved lengthwise and thinly sliced crosswise (1¼ cups)

1 cup packed baby spinach leaves

½ cup shredded Manchego cheese

Line a plate with paper towels.

Place the potatoes in a medium microwave-safe bowl with a lid, and add 1 tablespoon of the butter. Cover the bowl and microwave on high for 3½ minutes. Remove the bowl (it will be hot) and shake to loosen the potatoes. Return the bowl to the microwave and cook until tender, about 3½ minutes more. Set aside.

If you don't want to use a microwave, place the potatoes in a small saucepan and add cold water to cover. Bring the water to a boil and cook partially covered for 5 to 7 minutes, until the potatoes are fork-tender. Remove from the heat, drain well, and return to the dry saucepan. Set aside. (You need only 2 tablespoons of butter in total if using this non-microwave method.)

In a mixing bowl, combine the eggs with 1 teaspoon of salt, $\frac{1}{8}$ teaspoon of pepper, the parsley, and thyme; whisk to blend.

Place a medium ovenproof nonstick skillet with a broiler-safe handle over medium heat. Add 2 tablespoons of butter. When it melts and starts to sizzle, add the potatoes in a single flat layer and cook undisturbed for 5 minutes. Flip the potatoes with a spatula and cook for an additional 3 to 5 minutes, stirring occasionally, until lightly browned. Transfer the potatoes with a slotted spoon to the paper towel–lined plate, leaving the remaining butter in the skillet.

Set a rack in the upper third of the oven and turn the oven on to broil.

Add the onion to the butter and sauté over medium heat until golden brown and tender, 4 to 6 minutes. Add the spinach and sauté for an additional 2 minutes, until wilted. Return the potatoes to the pan and pour the egg mixture over the vegetables. Stir quickly to mix all the ingredients together. Cook undisturbed until the edges begin to set, 4 to 5 minutes.

Run a rubber or silicone spatula around the rim of the pan to loosen the sides. Sprinkle the top of the tortilla with the cheese and place the pan under the broiler until the cheese is lightly browned, about $2\frac{1}{2}$ minutes. Remove the pan from the oven. Slide the tortilla onto a platter, browned side up. Let it cool for 5 minutes, then slice into wedges and serve.

panfried tofu
with chimichurri sauce

4 servings

■ FROM THE MARKET

Extra firm organic tofu
(two 12- to 14-ounce
packages)

Italian (flat-leaf) parsley
(1 bunch)

Shallot (1 large or
2 medium)

Garlic (3 cloves)

Lemons (2)

■ FROM THE PANTRY

Extra virgin olive oil
(⅓ cup)

Red wine vinegar
(1 tablespoon)

Crushed red pepper flakes
(½ teaspoon)

Sea salt

Black pepper

Organic canola oil
(1 tablespoon)

This is the vegetarian alternative to our halibut with chimichurri sauce. Sometimes we prepare both of these dishes for the same meal if we are feeding both fish eaters and vegetarians. This is a nice change of pace from the more frequently prepared soy- and teriyaki-based tofu dishes.

FOR THE CHIMICHURRI SAUCE

⅓ cup extra virgin olive oil

3 tablespoons freshly squeezed lemon juice

1 tablespoon red wine vinegar

1 tablespoon minced shallot

1 tablespoon minced garlic

¾ cup finely chopped Italian (flat-leaf) parsley

½ teaspoon crushed red pepper flakes

Sea salt

Freshly ground black pepper

FOR THE TOFU

Two 12- to 14-ounce packages extra firm organic tofu, drained

1 tablespoon canola oil

Preheat the oven to 400°F.

FOR THE CHIMICHURRI SAUCE

In a small mixing bowl, whisk together the olive oil, lemon juice, vinegar, and 1 tablespoon of water. Add the shallot and garlic and gently fold in the parsley. Add the red pepper flakes and season with salt and pepper. Mix well and set aside.

FOR THE TOFU

Slice the tofu blocks in half horizontally to make them half as thick, then vertically, to make 4 equal-size rectangular tofu steaks from each package, for a total of 8. Place the tofu in a single layer on several layers of paper towels on either a plate or cutting board. Cover with more paper towels, place a plate or another cutting board on top, and rest a weight, such as a small skillet, on top

of that. This will press the excess liquid from the tofu. Let the steaks drain for at least 10 minutes.

Season the tofu with salt and pepper. Heat a large nonstick skillet or grill pan over medium-high heat. Add the canola oil and heat until shimmering. Place the tofu steaks in the pan and cook undisturbed until golden, 4 to 5 minutes. Flip and cook on the other side for an additional 4 minutes.

Transfer the tofu steaks to a casserole or baking dish. Bake for 15 minutes, until the tofu is crisp and brown. Remove the casserole from the oven and top each tofu steak with 2 teaspoons of chimichurri sauce. Serve hot with the extra sauce passed separately.

spinach and ricotta malfatti with brown butter and sage

4 to 6 servings

The translation of *malfatti* is "poorly made," so there's no pressure for perfection. Through the years, we've discovered that no matter how we form these tasty dumplings, they're a huge hit. We think of them as ravioli without the pasta, and they're ever-so-light and scrumptious.

■ **FROM THE MARKET**

Fresh sage (1 bunch)

Large eggs (6)

Unsalted butter
(12 tablespoons, or 1½ sticks plus extra for the dish)

Fresh ricotta cheese
(1 pound)

Parmesan cheese
(8 ounces)

Frozen chopped spinach
(two 10-ounce packages)

■ **FROM THE PANTRY**

All-purpose flour (½ cup plus extra for dusting)

Kosher salt

Black pepper

Ground nutmeg
(¼ teaspoon)

FOR THE MALFATTI

Two 10-ounce packages frozen chopped spinach, thawed and drained

4 tablespoons (½ stick) unsalted butter, melted and cooled, plus extra for greasing the dish

1 pound fresh ricotta cheese

½ cup all-purpose flour plus extra for dusting

2 large eggs plus 4 large egg yolks, beaten

1 cup freshly grated Parmesan cheese

Kosher salt

Freshly ground black pepper

¼ teaspoon ground nutmeg

FOR THE SAGE BUTTER SAUCE

8 tablespoons (1 stick) unsalted butter

15 fresh sage leaves, torn into small pieces

Freshly ground black pepper

1 cup freshly grated Parmesan cheese

FOR THE MALFATTI

In a medium skillet over medium heat, cook the spinach, without adding water, for about 5 minutes. Allow the spinach to cool slightly, then squeeze it as dry as possible with your hands or by pressing the spinach with a spoon against the sides of a sieve.

In a large mixing bowl, combine the spinach, melted butter, ricotta, flour, eggs and egg yolks, 1 cup Parmesan cheese, 1 teaspoon of salt, ⅛ teaspoon of pepper, and nutmeg. Mix thoroughly and place the bowl in the refrigerator for 15 minutes.

(recipe continues)

Set a rack in the upper third of the oven and preheat the oven to 375°F. Butter a 9 by 13-inch baking dish.

Bring a large pot of water to a boil and add 1 tablespoon of salt. Reduce the heat to medium, bringing the water down to a low boil.

Meanwhile, lightly dust a baking sheet and a cutting board with flour. Remove the malfatti dough from the refrigerator. Scoop out 1 tablespoon of the mixture and form it into a small oval by rolling it on the floured board. Shake off the excess flour and place it on the baking sheet. Repeat with the remaining dough.

Drop about one third of the malfatti dumplings into the pot of low-boiling water (too many in the pot at the same time could cause them to fall apart). Cook until the dumplings float to the surface, about 4 minutes. Using a slotted spoon, quickly transfer each one to the baking dish. Repeat until all the malfatti are cooked and added to the dish. Set aside.

FOR THE SAGE BUTTER SAUCE

In a small saucepan, melt the butter over low heat. Add the sage and ⅛ teaspoon of pepper and stir until combined, about 1 minute. Pour the sauce over the dumplings. Sprinkle 1 cup of Parmesan cheese evenly on top. Place in the oven and bake until the cheese is melted, about 5 minutes. Serve immediately.

harvest vegetable bake

4 to 6 servings

Both the vegetarians and meat eaters in our family devour this dish. The combination of vegetables together with tofu and cheese makes it irresistible and totally satisfying. This is a wonderful dish to serve to friends as well—not only does it taste great, but it looks beautiful right from the oven, browned and bubbling.

One 12- to 14-ounce package extra firm organic tofu, drained and cut into ½-inch cubes

1 tablespoon unsalted butter

3 tablespoons extra virgin olive oil

½ cup finely chopped shallot

4 cloves garlic (2 cloves minced, 2 cloves sliced)

1 tablespoon dry sherry

½ cup dry white wine

1 cup low-sodium vegetable broth

1 teaspoon low-sodium soy sauce

Kosher salt

Freshly ground black pepper

1 cup sliced cremini or baby bella mushrooms

1 cup peeled and sliced carrots, cut into ¼-inch-thick rounds

2 cups sliced zucchini, cut into ⅓- to ¼-inch-thick rounds

2½ cups 1-inch broccoli florets

2 cups packed stemmed and roughly chopped Swiss chard

¾ cup shredded cheddar cheese

¾ cup shredded Monterey Jack cheese

Set a rack in the middle of the oven and preheat the oven to 350°F. Line a rimmed baking sheet with parchment paper.

Arrange the tofu in a single layer on the baking sheet and bake for 20 minutes, flipping once halfway through. Remove from the oven and set aside. Increase the oven temperature to 400°F.

Meanwhile, begin preparing the sauce and vegetables. In a small saucepan over medium heat, melt the butter. Add 1 tablespoon of the oil, the shallot, and the minced garlic. Stir occasionally until they become translucent and begin to brown, about 8 minutes. Add the sherry and white wine and cook for 2 minutes. Stir in the vegetable broth, soy sauce, ½ teaspoon of salt, and ⅛ teaspoon of pepper. Bring to a boil, then reduce the heat to low and simmer for 10 minutes. Set aside.

While the sauce simmers, pour the remaining 2 tablespoons of oil into a large skillet over medium heat. When the oil is shimmering, add the sliced garlic, the mushrooms, and carrots, and sauté for 2 minutes. Raise the heat to medium-high, add the zucchini and broccoli, and sauté for 6 minutes. Add the Swiss chard and stir all the vegetables continuously for 2 minutes more, until well combined and the Swiss chard has wilted.

Transfer the vegetables to a large casserole or baking dish. Add the tofu, pour the sauce over the casserole, and mix. Sprinkle the cheddar and Monterey Jack cheeses on top. Bake uncovered until the cheeses are browned and bubbling, 20 to 25 minutes. Serve hot.

pasta

FOR ALL OF US, PASTA IS ONE OF THE GREAT CULINARY JOYS IN LIFE. THERE IS so much to love about it—it's a comfort food that can also be quite exotic: it's versatile, inexpensive, and easy to prepare. A pasta dish can be a complete meal merely by including protein and vegetables.

Pasta itself is so simple: two ingredients, semolina or durum wheat flour and water. From this minimal beginning you can create a culinary tour de force with the creative use of ingredients, textures, and flavors. What's more, pasta is loved by young children, teenagers, and adults alike.

Growing up, we didn't eat pasta for dinner that often—there hadn't yet been the Italian food "renaissance," so eating "Italian" more typically meant pizza or Parmesan heroes at the local parlor. As for pasta, we were more likely to eat our grandmother's egg noodles with butter or *kasha varnishkes* (a Jewish dish with kasha and bow tie noodles) than any *cucina tipica* from Italy.

But there was one recipe that Corky made on Monday nights, which began our love affair with pasta. We sisters took ballet class on Mondays in a town that was an hour's drive from our home. Being a food aficionado and a multitasker, Corky located an authentic Italian butcher shop whose specialty was homemade sausage. She had her standing Monday order, a pound of regular sausage and two extra spicy links. At home, she'd produce the most succulent spaghetti with red sauce (as it was commonly called then) and sausages. Those meals were always a source of great anticipation, mixed with a little trepidation—would someone accidentally bite into one of those extra spicy sausages that were meant for our dad? And what would happen if we did?

For our own children, pasta dinners are a popular staple. We serve pasta with many meals, and it is a great way for the whole family to sit down together and enjoy the same food from the common pot. We have also found that pasta is a great starting point for our teenagers as they begin to cook for themselves. It's hard to slip up as long as you follow the golden rules of pasta: Do not overcook and do not oversauce.

Although pasta acquired a bad reputation during the "anticarb" years, we won't give it up—it's just too good. The key is to watch your serving sizes and not to eat it too frequently. We have all stayed fit and lean with pasta in our diets. A bowl of steaming, aromatic pasta is just too satisfying to pass up.

PASTA RULES

- Be sure to use plenty of water in a large pot to boil your pasta.
- Add 1 tablespoon of kosher salt to the water once it has boiled.
- Do not add oil to the water; if added, the sauce will slide off the pasta.
- Cook the pasta al dente, 1 minute less than the directions on the package.
- Always set aside some of your pasta water before you drain, to add to your sauce as needed.

orecchiette with sautéed artichoke hearts, broccoli, and sun-dried tomatoes

4 to 6 servings

Orecchiette is Italian for "little ears" and we have been making these little ears with broccoli and artichoke hearts for family get-togethers for so many years. We love how there is almost an equal ratio of green to pasta in this dish. The sun-dried tomatoes add a delightful sweet tanginess, and the red pepper flakes, a hint of spice. We tend to double the recipe because this simple yet satisfying dish holds up beautifully as leftovers.

■ FROM THE MARKET

Orecchiette pasta or farfalle (1 pound)

Broccoli (1½ pounds)

Italian (flat-leaf) parsley (1 small bunch)

Garlic (5 cloves)

Parmesan cheese (2 ounces)

Frozen artichoke hearts (one 9-ounce box)

■ FROM THE PANTRY

Kosher salt

Extra virgin olive oil (⅓ cup)

Crushed red pepper flakes (⅛ teaspoon)

Sun-dried tomatoes in oil (¼ cup)

Dry white wine (¼ cup)

Low-sodium vegetable broth (½ cup)

Black pepper

Kosher salt

⅓ cup extra virgin olive oil

5 cloves garlic, cut in thin slices

One 9-ounce box frozen artichoke hearts, thawed and sliced in half lengthwise

⅛ teaspoon crushed red pepper flakes, or to taste

¼ cup julienned sun-dried tomatoes in oil, drained

3 tablespoons finely chopped Italian (flat-leaf) parsley

5 cups 1-inch broccoli florets

1 pound orecchiette pasta

¼ cup dry white wine

½ cup low-sodium vegetable broth

⅓ cup freshly grated Parmesan cheese

Freshly ground black pepper

Bring a large pot of water to a boil over high heat and add 1 tablespoon of salt.

Meanwhile, heat the olive oil in a large skillet over medium-high heat. When the oil is shimmering, add the garlic and stir for 30 seconds. Add the artichoke hearts and sauté until they begin to turn golden brown, about 5 minutes. Add the red pepper flakes, sun-dried tomatoes, and 2 tablespoons of the parsley and cook for an additional 3 minutes. Remove from the heat and set aside.

Fill a large mixing bowl with water and ice and set aside.

Add the broccoli to the boiling water and blanch until the color brightens, 1 to 2 minutes. Using a slotted spoon, transfer the broccoli to the ice water to shock,

leaving the pot of water boiling for the pasta. Once the broccoli has cooled, drain it in a colander.

Add the pasta to the boiling water and cook until al dente, about 1 minute less than the directions on the package. Reserve ¼ cup of the pasta water and drain the pasta in a colander.

Return the skillet with the artichokes to medium-high heat, add the white wine and vegetable broth, and cook until it is hot, 2 to 3 minutes. Add the broccoli and cook, stirring, for an additional 3 to 4 minutes. Fold in the pasta, adding some of the reserved pasta water if the sauce seems dry, and toss until well combined. Stir in the Parmesan cheese and season with 1 teaspoon of salt and pepper to taste. Transfer the pasta to a serving bowl and sprinkle with the remaining 1 tablespoon of parsley. Serve hot.

spaghetti aglio e olio

4 servings

We love this traditional Italian pasta dish because it is so simple and inexpensive to prepare. Six ingredients, two pans, and less than 30 minutes to make, start to finish. Serve it with a salad and crusty bread as a main course, or pair it with a fish or chicken dish—either way it's so delectable.

Kosher salt

⅓ cup extra virgin olive oil

4 cloves garlic, minced

⅛ teaspoon crushed red pepper flakes, or to taste

¼ cup finley chopped Italian (flat-leaf) parsley

1 pound spaghetti

½ cup freshly grated Parmesan cheese

Freshly ground black pepper

■ **FROM THE MARKET**

Spaghetti (1 pound)

Italian (flat-leaf) parsley (1 bunch)

Garlic (4 cloves)

Parmesan cheese (2 ounces)

■ **FROM THE PANTRY**

Kosher salt

Extra virgin olive oil (⅓ cup)

Crushed red pepper flakes (⅛ teaspoon)

Black pepper

Bring a large pot of water to a boil over high heat and add 1 tablespoon of salt.

Meanwhile, in a large skillet over low heat, heat the oil. Add the garlic, red pepper flakes, and 1 tablespoon of the parsley. Stir until the garlic is very lightly browned, 2 to 3 minutes. Remove the pan from the heat and set aside.

Add the pasta to the boiling water and cook until al dente, about 1 minute less than the directions on the package. Reserve ¼ cup of the pasta water and drain the pasta in a colander.

Return the skillet to low heat. Add the pasta to the pan with 3 tablespoons of the reserved pasta water and cook, stirring, until the pasta is coated, 1 to 2 minutes. Transfer the pasta to a serving bowl, and sprinkle with the remaining parsley and ¼ cup of the Parmesan cheese. Season with salt and pepper and serve hot with the extra Parmesan cheese on the side.

conchiglie alla caprese
4 to 6 servings

Our brother, Michael, and his wife, Judith, served this meal at one of their first family dinner parties many years ago. On a warm summer evening we were all seated outside at their beautiful wooden farmhouse table. The August tomatoes had been picked that morning at the height of their ripeness. None of us had ever had fresh mozzarella before and it was such a treat. This meal could not be any easier to prepare but remains a family favorite. In the summer, try to find an assortment of heirloom tomatoes—they not only add to the flavor but also make this dish a beauty.

2½ cups chopped heirloom tomatoes, cut into ½-inch cubes

1½ cups diced fresh mozzarella cheese, cut into ½-inch cubes

¼ cup extra virgin olive oil

⅓ cup fresh basil leaves (about 10 large), cut into chiffonade

2 cloves garlic, minced

⅛ teaspoon crushed red pepper flakes

Sea salt

Freshly ground black pepper

Kosher salt

1 pound medium pasta shells (conchiglie)

■ **FROM THE MARKET**

Medium pasta shells, also called conchiglie (1 pound)

Ripe heirloom tomatoes (1½ pounds)

Fresh basil (1 bunch)

Garlic (2 cloves)

Fresh mozzarella cheese (8 ounces)

■ **FROM THE PANTRY**

Extra virgin olive oil (¼ cup)

Crushed red pepper flakes (⅛ teaspoon)

Sea salt

Black pepper

Kosher salt

In a large mixing bowl, mix together the tomatoes, mozzarella cheese, oil, basil, garlic, red pepper flakes, ½ teaspoon of sea salt, and black pepper to taste. Cover with plastic wrap and let the sauce marinate at room temperature while you prepare the pasta, or for up to 3 hours to enhance the flavors.

Bring a large pot of water to a boil over high heat. Add 1 tablespoon of kosher salt and the pasta. Cook until al dente, about 1 minute less than the directions on the package. Reserve ½ cup of the pasta water, then drain the pasta in a colander.

Add the pasta to the sauce. Add 2 tablespoons of the reserved pasta water, or as desired, to moisten the sauce. Season with sea salt and pepper. Serve hot or at room temperature.

creamy spinach pasta alfredo with crispy pancetta

4 to 6 servings

■ **FROM THE MARKET**

Fusilli pasta (1 pound)

Garlic (2 cloves)

Pancetta (8 ounces)

Heavy cream (¾ cup)

Unsalted butter
(4 tablespoons, or ½ stick)

Parmesan cheese
(2 ounces)

Frozen chopped spinach
(one 10-ounce package)

■ **FROM THE PANTRY**

Extra virgin olive oil
(3 tablespoons)

Kosher salt

Ground nutmeg (pinch)

Black pepper

This dish takes ordinary fettuccine Alfredo to new heights with the addition of creamed spinach and crispy bacon. Our kids love it because there's no need to eat an additional vegetable on the side—it's the perfect all-in-one meal. Just serve with garlic bread or a crispy Italian loaf.

3 tablespoons extra virgin olive oil

8 ounces pancetta, cut into ⅓-inch cubes

Kosher salt

1 pound fusilli pasta

2 cloves garlic, minced

One 10-ounce package frozen chopped spinach, thawed and squeezed to remove excess liquid

¾ cup heavy cream

Pinch of ground nutmeg

Freshly ground black pepper

4 tablespoons (½ stick) unsalted butter, cut into cubes

½ cup plus 1 tablespoon freshly grated Parmesan cheese

Bring a large pot of water to a boil over high heat.

Line a plate with paper towels.

In a large skillet, heat 1 tablespoon of oil over medium-high heat. Cook the pancetta until brown and crispy, stirring frequently, about 5 minutes, taking care not to burn. Using a slotted spoon, transfer the pancetta to the paper towel–lined plate to drain. Discard the fat in the skillet. Let the skillet cool slightly, then wipe it out with a paper towel.

Add 1 tablespoon of salt and the pasta to the pot of boiling water. Cook until al dente, about 1 minute less than the directions on the package. Reserve ½ cup of the pasta water and drain the pasta in a colander.

(recipe continues)

Heat the remaining 2 tablespoons of oil in the skillet over medium heat. Add the garlic and stir for 30 seconds. Add the spinach and mix well. Add the cream and stir until well heated, 2 to 3 minutes. Season with the nutmeg, ½ teaspoon of salt, and ⅛ teaspoon of pepper. Reduce the heat to low and add the cooked pasta. Stir in 3 tablespoons of the reserved pasta water. Add the butter and ¼ cup of the Parmesan cheese, stirring to make a creamy sauce. If the mixture seems dry, add additional pasta water.

Transfer the pasta to a serving bowl. Scatter the pancetta over the top and sprinkle with the remaining Parmesan cheese and freshly ground pepper. Serve hot.

trofie alla genovese

4 to 6 servings

We first had this dish on a trip to Italy and we were smitten on first taste. Although pasta with potatoes might seem counterintuitive, this perfect combination of flavors and textures is positively mouthwatering. The potatoes, green beans, and pasta are all cooked in the same pot, then tossed with the pesto sauce, making this dish incredibly simple to prepare.

Kosher salt

1 pound trofie or gemelli pasta

2 cups peeled and julienned Yukon gold potatoes, cut 1½ inches long

8 ounces haricots verts or young slender green beans, trimmed and cut into 1½-inch pieces

¾ cup Basil Pesto (page 267, or your favorite store-bought)

½ cup freshly grated Pecorino Romano cheese

¼ cup freshly grated Parmesan cheese

Freshly ground black pepper

■ FROM THE MARKET

Trofie or gemelli pasta (1 pound)

Yukon gold potatoes (8 ounces)

Haricots verts or young slender green beans (8 ounces)

Pecorino Romano cheese (2 ounces)

Parmesan cheese (1 ounce)

■ FROM THE PANTRY

Kosher salt

Basil Pesto (¾ cup; page 267, or your favorite store-bought)

Black pepper

Bring a large pot of water to a boil over high heat. Add 1 tablespoon of salt and the pasta.

If using trofie pasta, cook for 5 minutes. Add the potatoes and cook for 3 minutes more. Add the green beans and cook until the pasta is al dente and the potatoes are tender, an additional 5 to 6 minutes.

If using gemelli pasta, cook for 2 minutes. Add the potatoes and cook for 3 minutes more. Add the green beans and cook until the pasta is al dente and the potatoes are tender, an additional 4 to 5 minutes.

Reserve ½ cup of the pasta water and drain the pasta, potatoes, and green beans in a colander. Immediately transfer them to a large serving bowl. Add the pesto and toss, moistening with the reserved pasta water as desired. Sprinkle on the cheeses, season with salt and pepper, and toss again. Serve hot.

Food for Thought
Our kids love basil, so we use lots of it when making pesto and pastas. But there are reasons beyond taste for cooking with basil. Its oils can fight some antibiotic-resistant bacteria, as well as inhibit bacterial growth. Dietitians recommend adding basil to salad dressings to ensure the safety of the greens. And, unexpectedly, basil is an excellent source of iron.

fusilli with oven-roasted vegetables and parmesan

4 to 6 servings

■ **FROM THE MARKET**

Fusilli pasta (1 pound)

Zucchini (2 small)

Broccoli (1 head)

Snow peas (4 ounces)

Cremini or baby bella mushrooms (5 ounces)

Garlic (1 large clove)

Unsalted butter (1 tablespoon)

Parmesan cheese (4-ounce piece)

■ **FROM THE PANTRY**

Extra virgin olive oil (¼ cup plus 1 teaspoon)

Kosher salt

Black pepper

Dry white wine (⅓ cup)

Low-sodium vegetable broth (½ cup)

Roasted vegetables are the all-stars of our take on pasta primavera. The Parmesan shavings give each bite a delightfully savory taste.

2 cups quartered, sliced zucchini, ¼-inch pieces

¼ cup plus 1 teaspoon extra virgin olive oil

Kosher salt

Freshly ground black pepper

3 cups 1½-inch broccoli florets

1½ cups stemmed and sliced cremini or baby bella mushrooms, cut ⅓ inch thick

1 cup trimmed and diagonally halved snow peas

1 pound fusilli pasta

1 tablespoon unsalted butter

1 large clove garlic, minced

⅓ cup dry white wine

½ cup low-sodium vegetable broth

¾ cup shaved Parmesan cheese

Set oven racks in the upper and lower thirds of the oven and preheat the oven to 400°F.

In a medium mixing bowl, combine the zucchini, 2 teaspoons of the oil, ⅛ teaspoon of salt, and a pinch of pepper and toss to coat. Spread the zucchini on one side of a rimmed baking sheet in a single layer.

Using the same bowl, combine the broccoli, 1 tablespoon of the oil, ¼ teaspoon of salt, and ⅛ teaspoon of pepper and toss to coat. Spread the broccoli on the other side of the baking sheet in a single layer and set aside.

Using the same bowl, combine the mushrooms with 1 teaspoon of the oil, ⅛ teaspoon of salt, and a pinch of pepper and toss to coat. Place the mushrooms on one side of a second rimmed baking sheet in a single layer. Put the snow peas in the bowl, combine with 1 teaspoon of oil, a pinch of salt and pepper and toss to coat. Arrange them on the other side of the second baking sheet in a single layer.

Place both baking sheets in the oven (upper and lower racks) and roast for 10 minutes. Remove the pans from the oven; flip the vegetables with a spatula and rotate baking sheet positions. Roast the vegetables for 10 minutes more. Remove the mushrooms and snow peas from the oven (they will be lightly browned). Continue roasting the zucchini and broccoli; they will need 2 to 4 minutes more to brown.

Meanwhile, bring a large pot of water to a boil over high heat. Add 1 tablespoon of salt and the pasta. Cook until al dente, about 1 minute less than the directions on the package. Reserve ¼ cup of the pasta water, and drain the pasta in a colander.

In a large skillet over medium-low heat, melt the butter. Stir in the remaining 2 tablespoons of oil. Add the garlic and stir for about 30 seconds, being careful not to let it burn. Pour in the wine and vegetable broth and mix well. Increase the heat to medium-high and bring to a boil, then reduce the heat to low and cook, stirring occasionally, for 8 minutes.

Reduce the heat to a simmer and toss in the pasta. Mix thoroughly, coating the fusilli with the sauce. Stir in the roasted vegetables and add 2 tablespoons of the reserved pasta water, or as desired. Blend in the Parmesan cheese and mix well. Season with salt and pepper to taste. Serve hot.

Food for Thought

Even if you didn't listen when your mother told you to "eat your broccoli," it's not too late to reap this wonder vegetable's health benefits. Broccoli contains disease-fighting properties (such as phytochemicals and antioxidants), it's a great source of fiber, and it's high in calcium—perfect for those who avoid dairy.

cheese tortellini with butternut hash and toasted hazelnuts

4 servings

■ **FROM THE MARKET**

Cheese tortellini
(1½ pounds; we like tricolore)

Butternut squash
(1 pound whole or 8 to 9 ounces fresh peeled)

Garlic (1 clove)

Unsalted butter
(6 tablespoons, or ¾ stick)

Parmesan cheese
(2 ounces)

■ **FROM THE PANTRY***

Extra virgin olive oil
(1 tablespoon)

Kosher salt

Black pepper

Blanched raw hazelnuts
(⅓ cup)

Balsamic vinegar
(2 tablespoons)

*You will need parchment paper.

We cooked this tortellini with a brown butter sauce for a family dinner one evening. Before serving we gave it a taste, and although it was very good, we felt like something was missing. As we were trying to figure out what we should add, Sam walked into the kitchen and took a bite. He turned to us and said, "This would be really good with some butternut squash." He was right—adding the roasted squash makes this dish a standout.

2 cups peeled and diced butternut squash, cut into ½-inch cubes

1 tablespoon extra virgin olive oil

Kosher salt

Freshly ground black pepper

⅓ cup blanched raw hazelnuts

1½ pounds cheese tortellini

6 tablespoons (¾ stick) unsalted butter

1 clove garlic, minced

2 tablespoons balsamic vinegar

¼ cup freshly shredded Parmesan cheese

Set a rack in the middle of the oven and preheat the oven to 425°F. Line a rimmed baking sheet with parchment paper.

In a large mixing bowl, combine the squash, oil, ¼ teaspoon of salt, and a pinch of pepper. Spread the squash on the baking sheet. Roast until golden brown, about 25 minutes, flipping the squash halfway through the cooking time. Remove from the oven and set aside.

Meanwhile, place the hazelnuts in a small dry skillet over medium heat. Shake the pan and stir the nuts so that they do not burn. Cook until they begin to brown, 4 to 5 minutes. Transfer to a plate to cool. Chop the nuts roughly. Set aside.

Bring a large pot of water to a boil over high heat. Add 1 tablespoon of salt and the pasta. Cook until al dente, about 1 minute less than the directions on the package. Drain in a colander.

Meanwhile, melt the butter in a large skillet over medium heat, stirring now and then, until the butter turns brown and starts to emit a nutty aroma, 3 to 4 minutes. Add the garlic and cook until the butter bubbles and the garlic begins to brown. Turn off the heat and let cool for 1 minute. Add the vinegar, ½ teaspoon of salt, and ⅛ teaspoon of pepper.

Add the tortellini and butternut squash to the butter sauce and toss to coat. Transfer to a serving bowl and sprinkle with the chopped hazelnuts and Parmesan cheese. Serve hot.

Food for Thought
Butternut squash will give you all the
vitamin A you need in a day and more—over
457 percent of your daily value! It has more
than half your daily dose of vitamin C, and is
filled with healthy omega 3s.

penne alla sherry with shiitake mushrooms and spinach

4 to 6 servings

■ **FROM THE MARKET**

Ribbed penne pasta
(1 pound)

Baby spinach leaves
(4 ounces)

Shiitake mushrooms
(10 ounces)

Shallots (1 large)

Garlic (1 clove)

Heavy cream (⅓ cup plus
2 tablespoons)

■ **FROM THE PANTRY**

Kosher salt

Extra virgin olive oil
(3 tablespoons)

Crushed red pepper flakes
(⅛ teaspoon)

Dry sherry (¼ cup)

Low-sodium vegetable
broth (½ cup)

Canned crushed tomatoes
(one 14.5-ounce can)

Granulated sugar
(½ teaspoon)

Black pepper

This is a distant cousin of penne alla vodka. Instead of vodka we use sherry, we go light on the cream, and we add vegetables. The sherry, together with the mushrooms and spinach, give this dish a deliciously distinctive flavor.

Kosher salt

1 pound ribbed penne pasta

3 tablespoons extra virgin olive oil

1 clove garlic, minced

2 tablespoons finely chopped shallots

4 cups stemmed and sliced shiitake
mushrooms, cut ¼ inch thick

⅛ teaspoon crushed red pepper
flakes, or to taste

¼ cup dry sherry

½ cup low-sodium vegetable broth

1¼ cups canned crushed tomatoes
with juice

½ teaspoon granulated sugar

2 cups tightly packed fresh baby
spinach leaves

Freshly ground black pepper

⅓ cup plus 2 tablespoons heavy cream

Bring a large pot of water to a boil over high heat. Add 1 tablespoon of salt and the pasta. Cook until al dente, about 1 minute less than the directions on the package. Drain the pasta and set aside.

Heat the oil in a large skillet over medium heat. Add the garlic and shallots and sauté for 1 minute. Add the mushrooms and red pepper flakes and cook for 3 minutes, stirring frequently, until the mushrooms release their liquid. Allow the liquid to evaporate and the mushrooms to become lightly browned, another 2 to 3 minutes.

Stir in the sherry, scraping the bottom of the pan with a wooden spoon. Add the vegetable broth, tomatoes with their juice, and the sugar. Raise the heat to medium-high, bring to a boil, then reduce the heat to low and simmer for 10 minutes, stirring occasionally.

Add the spinach to the sauce and stir until it is soft, about 3 minutes. Season with ½ teaspoon of salt and ⅛ teaspoon of pepper. Add the cream and stir for 2 minutes.

Stir in the pasta and mix, thoroughly coating the pasta with the sauce. Adjust the salt and pepper to taste, transfer to a serving bowl, and serve hot.

linguine alle vongole

4 servings

■ **FROM THE MARKET**

Littleneck clams (3 dozen)

Linguine (1 pound)

Italian (flat-leaf) parsley
(1 bunch)

Garlic (6 large cloves)

Unsalted butter
(1 tablespoon)

■ **FROM THE PANTRY**

Dry white wine (1 cup)

Kosher salt

Extra virgin olive oil
(½ cup)

Crushed red pepper flakes
(½ teaspoon)

This dish conjures up summers on the Vineyard and mornings spent clamming in a quiet little cove near our house. There was no need to bring clamming rakes or shovels, only toes to unearth the clams buried in the sand. We'd go home with our catch and stash it in a bucket under the deck, later to scrub the clams and turn them into a memorable Vineyard meal.

1 cup dry white wine

3 dozen littleneck clams, well scrubbed

Kosher salt

1 pound linguine

½ cup extra virgin olive oil

6 large cloves garlic, minced

½ teaspoon crushed red pepper flakes, or to taste

1 tablespoon unsalted butter

¼ cup chopped Italian (flat-leaf) parsley

Pour ½ cup of the white wine into a large pot and add 18 of the clams. Cover and cook over high heat just until the clams open, about 5 minutes. With a slotted spoon, transfer the opened clams to a large mixing bowl, carefully leaving all the liquid in the pot. Add the remaining 18 clams to the pot and cook until they open, about 5 minutes more. Transfer these to the bowl. Reserve all the liquid that's left in the pot and let cool.

Line a sieve with cheesecloth or paper towels and set it over a medium mixing bowl. Pour the cooled cooking liquid through the sieve to strain it of sand and grit. Discard the sediment from the sieve and set the liquid aside.

Carefully remove the clams from their shells, discarding the shells and leaving all the clam liquid in the bowl to use later. Place the clams on a cutting board. Coarsely chop the clams and set aside.

Bring a large pot of water to a boil over high heat. Add 1 tablespoon of salt and the pasta. Cook until al dente, about 1 minute less than the directions on the package. Drain in a colander.

Meanwhile, heat the oil in a large skillet over medium-high heat until shimmering. Add the garlic and cook, stirring, until golden brown, about 1 minute. Add the red pepper flakes and cook for 1 minute more. Pour in the remaining ½ cup of wine and all the reserved clam liquids. Boil uncovered until reduced by half, about 8 minutes. Stir in the butter and, once it melts, add the clams, tossing them in the sauce. Stir in the pasta and mix until thoroughly coated, 2 to 3 minutes. Sprinkle with the parsley and serve.

Food for Thought

To clam lovers, the health benefits of these bivalves come as a welcome surprise. In addition to being high in omega-3 fatty acids, a mere 9 clams provide more iron than a T-bone steak, and a 3-ounce serving of clams contains as much protein as chicken—yet significantly more vitamins and minerals.

golden baked ziti
with bite-size turkey meatballs

6 servings

■ **FROM THE MARKET**

Ziti pasta (1 pound)

Italian (flat-leaf) parsley
(1 small bunch)

Fresh mozzarella cheese
(8 ounces)

Parmesan cheese (1 ounce)

■ **FROM THE PANTRY**

Kosher salt

■ **ADDITIONAL
   INGREDIENTS**

Bite-Size Turkey Meatballs
in sauce (page 54)

This dish comes out of the oven hissing and bubbling all the way to the table. The fresh mozzarella, bite-size meatballs, and homemade sauce make this a savory treat for the whole family.

Kosher salt

1 pound ziti pasta

Bite-Size Turkey Meatballs in sauce
   (page 54)

2 cups shredded fresh mozzarella
   cheese

¼ cup freshly grated Parmesan
   cheese

1 tablespoon chopped Italian
   (flat-leaf) parsley

Preheat the oven to 375°F.

Bring a large pot of water to a boil over high heat. Add 1 tablespoon of salt and the pasta. Cook until very al dente, about 3 minutes less than the directions on the package.

Meanwhile, place the meatballs and sauce in a large saucepan over medium-low heat and simmer until thoroughly heated.

Drain the pasta and transfer it to a 9 by 13-inch baking dish or other large casserole. Ladle the meatballs and sauce over the pasta. Stir gently to mix. Sprinkle the shredded mozzarella cheese over the top and finish with the grated Parmesan cheese.

Bake until the cheese is golden and bubbling, about 30 minutes. Sprinkle with the parsley and serve hot.

slow-cooked bolognese in 45 minutes

4 to 6 servings

■ **FROM THE MARKET**

Tagliatelle pasta (1 pound)

Carrot (1 medium)

Celery (1 stalk)

Italian (flat-leaf) parsley
(1 small bunch)

Fresh basil (1 small bunch)

Spanish onion (1 medium)

Garlic (2 cloves)

Ground beef sirloin
(90% lean; 8 ounces)

Ground beef chuck
(80% lean; 12 ounces)

Unsalted butter
(1 tablespoon)

Whole milk (1 cup)

Parmesan cheese (2 ounces)

■ **FROM THE PANTRY**

Extra virgin olive oil
(2 tablespoons)

Kosher salt

Black pepper

Dry white wine (1 cup)

Tomato paste (2 tablespoons)

Ground nutmeg
(⅛ teaspoon)

Dark brown sugar
(1 teaspoon)

Canned crushed tomatoes
(one 28-ounce can)

A great Bolognese doesn't need to simmer on your stovetop for hours and hours. Here is a sauce that has all of the deep rich flavors of your favorite restaurant's Bolognese—savory, meaty, and creamy—but it can be prepared in a fraction of the time.

2 tablespoons extra virgin olive oil

1 tablespoon unsalted butter

1 cup finely chopped Spanish onion

⅓ cup peeled and finely
    chopped carrots

⅓ cup finely chopped celery

2 cloves garlic, minced

8 ounces ground beef sirloin
    (90% lean)

12 ounces ground beef chuck
    (80% lean)

Kosher salt

Freshly ground black pepper

1 cup dry white wine

2 tablespoons tomato paste

⅛ teaspoon ground nutmeg

1 teaspoon dark brown sugar

1 cup whole milk

One 28-ounce can crushed tomatoes

2 tablespoons finely chopped Italian
    (flat-leaf) parsley

1 tablespoon finely chopped fresh basil

1 pound tagliatelle or other long pasta

½ cup freshly grated Parmesan
    cheese

Heat a large Dutch oven or stockpot over medium heat. Add the oil and butter and cook until the butter melts, about 1 minute. Add the onion, carrots, celery, and garlic. Cook, stirring occasionally, until soft, about 10 minutes.

Add the ground sirloin and chuck and increase the heat to medium-high. Stir, breaking up the meat with a wooden spoon, until browned, about 5 minutes. Add 1 teaspoon of salt, ¼ teaspoon of pepper, and the wine and cook for 2 minutes more. Add the tomato paste, nutmeg, and brown sugar and mix well. Reduce the heat to low, pour in the milk, and simmer for 5 minutes. Add the tomatoes, parsley, and basil and bring to a boil. Reduce the heat to low and simmer for 25 minutes more, stirring occasionally.

Bring a large pot of water to a boil over high heat. Add 1 tablespoon of salt and the pasta. Cook until al dente, about 1 minute less than the directions on the package. Reserve 1/4 cup of the pasta water and drain the pasta in a colander.

While the pasta is cooking, transfer half the Bolognese sauce to a large skillet set over low heat. Add the drained pasta to the sauce and mix thoroughly. Continue to add more sauce until you reach your desired sauce-to-pasta ratio. Incorporate about 2 tablespoons of the pasta water to loosen the sauce, if needed. Season with salt and pepper.

Transfer to a large serving bowl and serve with the grated Parmesan cheese on the side.

soups and chilis

creamless broccoli soup with whole
roasted garlic and frizzled leeks

butternut squash soup with
toasted pumpkin seeds

hearty lentil soup

provençal vegetable soup au pistou with
parmesan crisps

homestyle chicken and stelline soup

beer-infused chicken chili
with white beans

fully loaded vegetable chili

jalapeño, pork, and hominy chili

SOUP EPITOMIZES THE NOTION OF THE COMMON POT TO US: ALL MEMBERS of the family sitting together at the table, sharing the same food and conversations—basking in the feeling of being connected.

We have fond memories of when our mother made soup—matzo ball on Passover and chicken noodle when we were sick. We would have a hearty vegetable soup in the winter after we came indoors cold and tired from a day of sledding. Famished by being outdoors and enticed by the wonderful smells, we couldn't wait to peel off our layers of clothing and run to the kitchen table. Today, when we make soup for our families it reminds us of our mom—it is the quintessential comfort food.

Our kids consider it a special treat when we pair a piping hot bowl of soup with a salad and a crusty loaf of bread for dinner. The varieties are endless and soups are a good choice for the novice cook—they're difficult to overcook and it's hard to make mistakes. One of the magical properties of soup is that the longer you cook it the better it tastes, so weekends are ideal because there's plenty of time for the soup to simmer. We often make extra and freeze it—perfect for a meal on another day.

Chili, for us, falls into that same comfort group, although in reality it could be in a category all its own. We've talked to so many friends who have their own chili recipes and each one inevitably boasts that his or hers is the best. Chili is one of those dishes that can be adjusted to taste—meat or meatless, spicy or mild, one bean or multibean—it's up to the chef to choose.

One of the things we love most about chili is its versatility. Not only can it warm you up on a cold winter night, it's also great for feeding a large crowd at a big-game party.

creamless broccoli soup with whole roasted garlic and frizzled leeks

makes about 2 quarts (4 to 6 servings)

■ **FROM THE MARKET**

Broccoli (1½ pounds)

Fresh thyme (1 sprig)

Yukon gold potatoes
(3 large, about 1½ pounds)

Yellow onion (1 medium)

Leeks (4 large)

Garlic (1 large bulb)

■ **FROM THE PANTRY**

Extra virgin olive oil
(6 tablespoons plus more for
drizzling)

Kosher salt

Black pepper

Low-sodium vegetable
broth (1½ quarts)

Dry sherry (3 tablespoons)

Bay leaf (1)

Ground nutmeg (pinch)

This soup has such a full flavor and creamy consistency that people are amazed to learn that it is actually creamless. The whole roasted garlic lends it a rich and slightly sweet flavor, and the frizzled leeks add a savory crunch. We tend to make this soup on the weekend when we have a little more time in the kitchen—and then serve it during the week. The frizzled leeks are best when they are deliciously crisp, so we like to prepare them while heating up the soup, sprinkling them on top just before it is served.

FOR THE SOUP

1 large garlic bulb

2 tablespoons extra virgin olive oil plus
extra for roasting the garlic

Kosher salt

Freshly ground black pepper

1 medium yellow onion, chopped

2 cups chopped leeks (white and pale
green parts only), thoroughly rinsed
and drained

2½ cups peeled and diced Yukon gold
potatoes, cut into ½-inch cubes

6 cups coarsely chopped broccoli
florets and chopped peeled stalks

6 cups low-sodium vegetable broth

3 tablespoons dry sherry

1 bay leaf

1 sprig fresh thyme

1 pinch ground nutmeg

FOR FRIZZLED LEEKS

4 tablespoons extra virgin olive oil

2 large leeks (white and pale green
parts only), thoroughly rinsed and
drained, cut into 2- to 2½-inch-
long fine julienne

FOR THE SOUP

Preheat the oven to 425°F.

To roast the garlic bulb, cut ½ inch off the top of the bulb. Drizzle the top with a little oil and season with salt and pepper. Wrap the garlic in foil and place on a baking sheet. Roast until the garlic is tender, 40 to 45 minutes. (This can be done ahead of time and stored in the refrigerator.) Set aside.

In a large stockpot over medium-high heat, heat 2 tablespoons of oil. Add the onion and cook for 2 minutes, until softened. Add the chopped leeks and cook, stirring, until tender, about 5 minutes. Add the potatoes and cook for 1 minute. Add the broccoli, vegetable broth, sherry, bay leaf, thyme, 1 teaspoon of salt, and $\frac{1}{8}$ teaspoon of black pepper. Bring to a boil, then reduce the heat to low and simmer uncovered until the potatoes are tender and can be pierced easily with a knife, about 25 minutes.

While the soup is cooking, frizzle the leeks. Line a plate with paper towels. Heat $\frac{1}{4}$ cup of oil in a medium skillet over medium heat. When the oil is shimmering, add the julienned leeks and fry, stirring, until crispy and golden. Use a slotted spoon to transfer the leeks to the paper towel–lined plate to drain. Set aside.

Squeeze the roasted garlic pulp into the soup and stir. Discard the garlic skin. Cook the soup for an additional 5 minutes, stirring occasionally. Remove the stockpot from the heat and allow the soup to cool slightly. Discard the bay leaf and thyme.

Working in batches, ladle the soup into a blender (place a towel on the top when blending to avoid hot splashes) or food processor and blend on high until smooth. Pour the pureed soup into a clean pot. (As an alternative you can use a handheld immersion blender and blend the soup right in the pot.)

Return the soup to the heat and add a pinch of nutmeg, $\frac{1}{2}$ teaspoon of salt, and $\frac{1}{8}$ teaspoon of pepper or to taste. Stir to blend well and simmer until hot.

Ladle the soup into individual bowls and top each serving with a portion of the frizzled leeks. Serve hot.

butternut squash soup with toasted pumpkin seeds

makes about 2 quarts (4 to 6 servings)

■ **FROM THE MARKET**

Butternut squash
(2¾ pounds whole or 2¼
pounds peeled and seeded)

Carrot (1 medium)

Yellow onion (1 medium)

Garlic (2 cloves)

Fresh ginger (1 small knob)

Unsalted butter
(2 tablespoons)

■ **FROM THE PANTRY**

**Raw shelled pumpkin
seeds, also called pepitas**
(2 tablespoons)

**Organic olive oil cooking
spray**

Sea salt

Black pepper

**Low-sodium vegetable
broth** (1 quart)

Ground nutmeg (2 pinches)

Kosher salt

Balsamic Vinegar Glaze
(1 teaspoon; page 269, or
your favorite store-bought)

On a chilly fall evening, nothing beats a warm bowl of butternut squash soup. The toasted pumpkin seeds and balsamic vinegar ramp up the flavor, and because of the smooth, buttery texture of the squash, there is no need to add heavy cream.

2 tablespoons raw shelled pumpkin seeds (pepitas)

Organic olive oil cooking spray

Sea salt

Freshly ground black pepper

2 tablespoons unsalted butter

1 cup finely chopped yellow onion

½ cup peeled and chopped carrots

2 cloves garlic, minced

1 teaspoon finely grated fresh ginger

7 cups peeled, seeded, and diced butternut squash, cut into 1-inch cubes

4 cups low-sodium vegetable broth

2 pinches ground nutmeg

Kosher salt

1 teaspoon Balsamic Vinegar Glaze (page 269, or your favorite store-bought)

Preheat the oven to 350°F.

Spread the pumpkin seeds across a rimmed baking sheet in a single layer and spray lightly with the cooking oil. Sprinkle with sea salt and pepper. Bake until lightly toasted, about 10 minutes. Remove from the oven and set aside to cool.

In a large stockpot over medium heat, melt the butter. Add the onion and carrots and sauté until they begin to soften, about 5 minutes. Add the garlic and ginger and stir for 30 seconds. Add the butternut squash and cook, stirring frequently, for 5 minutes. Pour in the vegetable broth and bring to a boil. Reduce the heat to low and cook uncovered, stirring occasionally, until the vegetables are soft, 15 to 20 minutes.

Remove the stockpot from the heat and allow the soup to cool until no longer steaming. Working in batches, ladle the soup into a blender (place a towel on the top when blending to avoid hot splashes) or food processor and blend on high until smooth. Pour the pureed soup into a clean pot. (As an alternative you can use a handheld immersion blender and blend the soup right in the pot.)

Return the soup to the heat and add the nutmeg, 2 teaspoons of kosher salt, and black pepper to taste. Stir to blend well and simmer until hot. Ladle the soup into individual bowls and top each serving with 1 teaspoon of the toasted pumpkin seeds. Add a swirl of balsamic vinegar glaze, 1/8 to 1/4 teaspoon for each bowl, and serve.

hearty lentil soup

makes about 3 quarts (6 servings)

Lentils paired with tofu results in a dish that's chock-full of protein—a nutritional bounty for vegetarians. And it's so hearty that meat eaters like my husband love it, too.—DANA

2 tablespoons extra virgin olive oil

1 cup finely chopped yellow onion

1 cup peeled and diced carrots, cut into ¼-inch cubes

1 cup chopped celery

3 cloves garlic, minced

1 medium zucchini, quartered lengthwise and cut into ½-inch slices

1¾ cups brown lentils, rinsed

3 cups low-sodium vegetable broth

½ cup red wine

7 ounces extra firm organic tofu, cut into ¼-inch dice

¼ teaspoon dried oregano

Kosher salt

Freshly ground black pepper

1 Parmesan cheese rind (2-inch piece)

1 cup firmly packed baby spinach leaves

1½ teaspoons balsamic vinegar

■ **FROM THE MARKET**

Carrots (3 medium)

Celery (3 stalks)

Zucchini (1 medium)

Baby spinach leaves (2 ounces)

Yellow onion (1 medium)

Garlic (3 cloves)

Extra firm organic tofu (7 ounces)

Parmesan cheese rind (about 2 inches long)

■ **FROM THE PANTRY**

Extra virgin olive oil (2 tablespoons)

Brown lentils (1¾ cups)

Low-sodium vegetable broth (3 cups)

Red wine (½ cup)

Dried oregano (¼ teaspoon)

Kosher salt

Black pepper

Balsamic vinegar (1½ teaspoons)

In a large stockpot, heat the oil over medium heat. Stir in the onion, carrots, and celery. Sauté until the onion is translucent, about 5 minutes. Add the garlic and zucchini and cook for an additional 3 to 5 minutes, until the zucchini is just tender.

Add the lentils, vegetable broth, wine, and 6 cups of water and stir well. Add the tofu, oregano, 1½ teaspoons of salt, and ¼ teaspoon of pepper. Bring to a boil, then reduce the heat to a simmer and add the Parmesan cheese rind. Cover and cook for 50 minutes, stirring occasionally, until the lentils are tender and the soup is thickened.

Stir in the spinach and cook until wilted, 2 to 3 minutes. Discard the Parmesan cheese rind, stir in the vinegar, and season with ½ teaspoon of salt and ⅛ teaspoon of pepper, or to taste. Ladle the soup into individual bowls and serve hot.

provençal vegetable soup au pistou with parmesan crisps

makes about 4 quarts (8 servings)

■ **FROM THE MARKET**

Carrots (2 medium)

Celery (2 stalks)

Zucchini (1 small)

Green beans (8 ounces)

Fresh basil (1 large bunch)

Fresh thyme (1 sprig)

Leeks (3 medium)

Spanish onion (1 large)

Garlic (2 cloves)

Yukon gold potatoes
(2 large)

Parmesan cheese (8-ounce
chunk with rind, not
pregrated or preshredded)

■ **FROM THE PANTRY***

Extra virgin olive oil
(¼ cup plus 2 tablespoons)

Kosher salt

Black pepper

Low-sodium vegetable
broth (2 quarts)

Bay leaf (1)

Organic cannellini beans
(two 15-ounce cans)

Tomato paste
(1½ tablespoons)

*You will need
parchment paper.

This bountiful soup contains nearly your recommended daily servings of vegetables in a single bowl. Our Provençal soup has such hearty flavor and wonderful texture that we don't even include pasta. A large dollop of pistou on top adds a fabulous finishing touch.

FOR THE PARMESAN CRISPS

½ cup freshly shredded Parmesan
cheese (do not buy preshredded)

½ cup freshly grated Parmesan
cheese (do not buy pregrated)

FOR THE SOUP

2 tablespoons extra virgin olive oil

1 cup diced Spanish onion, cut into
¼-inch cubes

3 medium leeks (white and pale green
parts only), thoroughly rinsed and
drained, halved lengthwise, and
sliced ½ inch thick

2 medium carrots, peeled and cut into
½-inch dice

2 celery stalks, cut into ½-inch dice

2 cups peeled and diced Yukon gold
potatoes, cut into ½-inch cubes

1 small zucchini, cut into ½-inch dice

Kosher salt

Freshly ground black pepper

8 cups low-sodium vegetable broth

1 bay leaf

1 sprig fresh thyme

1 Parmesan cheese rind (2-inch piece)

8 ounces green beans, trimmed and
cut into 1-inch pieces

Two 15-ounce cans organic cannellini
beans, rinsed and drained

FOR THE PISTOU

2 cups packed fresh basil leaves

2 cloves garlic, halved

¼ cup extra virgin olive oil

1½ tablespoons tomato paste

1 cup freshly grated Parmesan cheese

Kosher salt

Freshly ground black pepper

Preheat the oven to 350°F. Line a rimmed baking sheet with parchment paper.
Line a platter with paper towels.

FOR THE PARMESAN CRISPS

In a mixing bowl, combine the shredded and grated Parmesan cheese. Drop 2-tablespoon mounds onto the baking sheet, pressing the cheese down and together to form 8 circles about 3 inches in diameter. Space the mounds about 3 inches apart. Bake until melted and light golden brown, about 7 minutes. Remove from the oven and set aside to cool for 5 minutes. Gently transfer to the paper towel–lined platter.

FOR THE SOUP

Heat 2 tablespoons of oil in a large stockpot over medium heat. Add the onion and leeks and cook, stirring occasionally, until translucent, about 10 minutes. Add the carrots, celery, potatoes, zucchini, 2 teaspoons of salt, and ¼ teaspoon of pepper. Cook for 5 minutes, stirring occasionally.

Pour in the vegetable broth and 2 cups of water, cover the pot, and bring to a boil. Add the bay leaf, thyme sprig, Parmesan cheese rind, and green beans. Reduce the heat to maintain a simmer and cook, partially covered, for 20 minutes.

Add the cannellini beans and cook for 15 minutes more. While the soup is simmering, prepare the pistou.

FOR THE PISTOU

Put the basil, garlic, 2 tablespoons of the oil, the tomato paste, and 1 cup Parmesan cheese into a food processor. Process until coarsely chopped. Scrape down the sides with a spatula and add the remaining 2 tablespoons of oil. Blend again to make a paste. Add ¼ teaspoon of salt and ⅛ teaspoon of pepper, pulse for 30 seconds more, and transfer to a mixing bowl.

Discard the thyme sprig, bay leaf, and Parmesan cheese rind from the soup. Ladle the soup into individual bowls. Top each serving with a generous spoonful of pistou and serve with a Parmesan crisp.

homestyle chicken and stelline soup

makes about 3 quarts (6 servings)

■ **FROM THE MARKET**

Bone-in, skin-on chicken breasts (2 whole or 4 halves)

Carrots (2 large)

Celery (3 stalks)

Italian (flat-leaf) parsley (1 bunch)

Russet potato (1 medium)

Leeks (2 large)

Stelline or pastina pasta (⅓ cup)

■ **FROM THE PANTRY**

Extra virgin olive oil (4 tablespoons)

Kosher salt

Black pepper

Low-sodium chicken broth (2½ quarts)

Some clichés are clichés because they are true, like this one: Chicken soup is the classic comfort food. Ours is chock-full of veggies, succulent chicken, and tiny pasta stars to add whimsy to the warmth.

2 whole or 4 split bone-in, skin-on chicken breasts

4 tablespoons extra virgin olive oil

Kosher salt

Freshly ground black pepper

⅓ cup stelline or pastina pasta

1 cup peeled and diced carrots, cut into ½-inch cubes

1 cup diced celery, cut into ½-inch cubes

1 russet potato, peeled and cut into ½-inch dice

2 cups chopped leeks (white and pale green parts only), thoroughly rinsed and drained

10 cups low-sodium chicken broth

¼ cup finely chopped Italian (flat-leaf) parsley

Preheat the oven to 350°F.

Rub the chicken breasts with 2 tablespoons of the oil and season liberally with salt and pepper. Place on a rimmed baking sheet and bake for 40 minutes. Let the chicken cool slightly. Discard the skin and bones. Shred the meat and set aside.

While the chicken is in the oven, bring a large pot of water to a boil over high heat. Add 1 tablespoon of kosher salt and the pasta. Cook until al dente, about 1 minute less than the directions on the package. Drain and set aside.

Next, in a large stockpot over medium heat, heat the remaining 2 tablespoons of oil until shimmering. Add the carrots, celery, potatoes, and leeks. Cook, stirring, until the vegetables are soft, about 10 minutes.

Add the chicken broth and bring to a boil. Reduce the heat to low and simmer for at least 30 minutes.

Add the shredded chicken and simmer for an additional 10 minutes. Add the pasta and season with ½ teaspoon of salt and ½ teaspoon of pepper.

Ladle the soup into individual bowls, sprinkle with parsley, and serve piping hot.

beer-infused chicken chili
with white beans

6 servings

■ **FROM THE MARKET**

Bone-in, skin-on chicken
breasts (4 large halves)

Spanish onion (1 large)

Garlic (3 large cloves)

Fresh cilantro
(1 small bunch)

Poblano peppers (2 large)

Jalapeño chile (1)

Limes (2)

Sharp cheddar cheese
(4 ounces)

Good-quality beer
(one 12-ounce bottle)

■ **FROM THE PANTRY**

Extra virgin olive oil
(2 tablespoons)

Kosher salt

Black pepper

Organic navy
or cannellini beans
(two 15-ounce cans)

Ground cumin (2 teaspoons)

Ground coriander
(1½ teaspoons)

Low-sodium chicken broth
(1 quart)

This is the perfect alternative to traditional chili, with all the flavors but none of the heaviness. The lime and cilantro give it a decisively fresh taste. We serve it with sharp cheddar cheese, but it's also great with chopped red onion and sour cream.

4 large bone-in, skin-on chicken
  breast halves

2 tablespoons extra virgin olive oil

Kosher salt

Freshly ground black pepper

Two 15-ounce cans organic white
  beans (navy or cannellini)

2 teaspoons ground cumin

1½ teaspoons ground coriander

1 large Spanish onion, chopped

2 cups seeded and diced poblano
  peppers, cut into ¼-inch cubes

1 jalapeño chile, seeded and
  finely diced

1 tablespoon minced garlic

4 cups low-sodium chicken broth

1 cup beer

3 tablespoons fresh lime juice

2 tablespoons chopped fresh cilantro

½ cup shredded sharp cheddar
  cheese

Preheat the oven to 350°F.

Rub the chicken breasts with 1 tablespoon of the oil and season liberally with salt and pepper. Place on a rimmed baking sheet and bake for 40 minutes. Let the chicken cool slightly. Discard the skin and bones. Shred the meat and set aside.

While the chicken is cooling, rinse and drain the beans in a colander. Put half the beans in a mixing bowl and smash them with a potato masher or fork until smooth. Add the remaining whole beans and set aside.

In a small mixing bowl, mix together the cumin, coriander, ½ teaspoon of salt, and ½ teaspoon of pepper.

Place a large saucepan over medium-high heat and add the remaining tablespoon of oil. When the oil is shimmering, add the onion, poblano, jalapeño, and garlic. Sauté until soft, 5 to 7 minutes. Stir in the spice mixture, cook for 1 minute, and remove from the heat.

Transfer 1 cup of the vegetables from the saucepan to a food processor or blender and add 1 cup of the chicken broth. Blend until pureed. Add the puree to the rest of the vegetables in the saucepan, turn the heat to medium, and stir. Add the beer and cook for 5 minutes.

Add the remaining 3 cups of chicken broth, the lime juice, cilantro, all the beans, the shredded chicken, ½ teaspoon of salt, and ⅛ teaspoon of pepper. Increase the heat to high, bring to a boil, then reduce the heat to medium-low and simmer, covered, for a minimum of 25 minutes and up to 1 hour (stirring occasionally) to intensify the flavor.

Ladle the chili into individual bowls and serve with the cheddar cheese.

Food for Thought
White beans, such as cannellini, great Northern, and navy, are higher in calcium than kale. One cup supplies 191 milligrams, which is 19 percent of the daily calcium requirement. They are also a good source of fiber, protein, zinc, copper, and magnesium. White beans are low on the glycemic index and so offer major weight-loss benefits, along with delivering a hefty supply of antioxidants that fight off disease and help maintain health.

fully loaded vegetable chili

6 to 8 servings

(continued on next page)

This vegetable chili has all of the smoky seasonings of a conventional beef chili, and the addition of the ancient grain bulgur gives a pleasing meat-like heartiness and texture. Don't be put off by the long list of ingredients; this dish is actually a cinch to prepare.

■ FROM THE MARKET

Carrots (2 large)

Celery (1 large stalk)

Red Pepper (1 small)

Yellow onions (2 medium)

Garlic (3 cloves)

Sharp cheddar or Monterey Jack cheese (4 ounces)

Frozen corn kernels (½ cup)

■ FROM THE PANTRY

Chili powder (3 tablespoons)

Dried oregano (1 teaspoon)

Crushed red pepper flakes (½ teaspoon)

Paprika (1½ teaspoons)

Cayenne pepper (⅛ teaspoon)

Ground coriander (1 teaspoon)

Ground cumin (1 teaspoon)

Kosher salt

Black pepper

Organic black beans (one 15-ounce can)

Organic kidney beans (one 15-ounce can)

(continued on next page)

FOR THE SEASONING MIX

3 tablespoons chili powder

1 teaspoon dried oregano

½ teaspoon crushed red pepper flakes, or to taste

1½ teaspoons paprika

⅛ teaspoon cayenne pepper

1 teaspoon ground coriander

1 teaspoon ground cumin

Kosher salt

Freshly ground black pepper

FOR THE CHILI

One 15-ounce can organic black beans

One 15-ounce can organic kidney beans

2 tablespoons extra virgin olive oil

2 cups chopped yellow onion

3 cloves garlic, minced

1 cup peeled and chopped carrots

½ cup chopped celery

½ cup chopped red bell pepper

2 tablespoons tomato paste

One 28-ounce can crushed tomatoes with juice

2 cups low-sodium vegetable broth

1 tablespoon low-sodium soy sauce

1 bay leaf

¾ cup bulgur

½ cup frozen corn kernels

½ cup shredded sharp cheddar or Monterey Jack cheese, or as needed

FOR THE SEASONING MIX

Place the chili powder, oregano, red pepper flakes, paprika, cayenne pepper, coriander, cumin, 1½ teaspoons of salt, and ⅛ teaspoon of black pepper in a small mixing bowl and stir to blend. Set aside.

FOR THE CHILI

In a colander, combine the black beans and kidney beans. Rinse, drain, and set aside.

In a large pot, heat the oil over medium heat. Add the onion and sauté for 1 minute. Add the garlic, carrots, celery, and red bell pepper. Sauté until softened, about 10 minutes.

Add the tomato paste, 2 cups of water, and the seasoning mix; stir until well blended. Add the tomatoes, vegetable broth, soy sauce, and bay leaf, and mix well. Increase the heat to high and bring to a boil. Stir in the bulgur and reduce the heat to low. Simmer partially covered, stirring occasionally, until the bulgur is tender, about 20 minutes.

Stir in the beans and the corn and simmer, partially covered, for an additional 10 minutes. Remove and discard the bay leaf.

Ladle the chili into individual bowls and top each with 1 tablespoon of shredded cheese. Serve hot.

> **Food for Thought**
> Bulgur, a 4,000-year-old Mediterranean grain made from whole wheat, is a rich source of protein. It is lower in calories than quinoa and most other whole grains, and packed with fiber. This nutty grain also is low on the glycemic index, so it's a healthy substitute for rice or potatoes.

(From the Pantry continued)

Extra virgin olive oil (2 tablespoons)

Tomato paste (2 tablespoons)

Crushed tomatoes (one 28-ounce can)

Low-sodium vegetable broth (2 cups)

Low-sodium soy sauce (1 tablespoon)

Bay leaf (1)

Bulgur (¾ cup)

jalapeño, pork, and hominy chili

4 servings

■ **FROM THE MARKET**

Ground pork (1 pound)

Fresh cilantro (1 bunch)

White onion (1 large)

Jalapeño chiles
(2 for mild, 3 for hot;
each about 3 inches long)

Garlic (3 cloves)

Ricotta salata cheese
(2 ounces)

Corn tortillas (12)

Canned hominy
(yellow or white; one
15-ounce can)

■ **FROM THE PANTRY**

Raw shelled pumpkin
seeds, also called pepitas
(⅓ cup)

Organic olive oil cooking
spray

Sea salt

Low-sodium chicken broth
(1¾ cups)

Extra virgin olive oil
(3 tablespoons)

Smoked paprika
(½ teaspoon)

Ground cumin (1 teaspoon)

Ground chipotle chile
pepper (½ teaspoon)

Kosher salt

Not even a sprinkling of gorgeously fresh cilantro and oven-toasted pumpkin seeds can turn this dish into a beauty prize winner, yet this chili makes up for its looks with its wonderfully zesty flavor.

⅓ cup raw shelled pumpkin seeds (pepitas)

Organic olive oil cooking spray

Sea salt

1 large white onion, quartered

2 or 3 large fresh jalapeño chiles, including seeds, quartered (2 for mild, 3 for hot)

3 cloves garlic, halved

1¾ cups low-sodium chicken broth

3 tablespoons extra virgin olive oil

1 pound ground pork

½ teaspoon smoked paprika

1 teaspoon ground cumin

½ teaspoon ground chipotle chile pepper

Kosher salt

One 15-ounce can yellow or white hominy, rinsed and drained

⅓ cup plus ¼ cup chopped fresh cilantro

½ cup crumbled ricotta salata cheese

12 corn tortillas

Preheat the oven to 350°F.

Spread the pumpkin seeds across a rimmed baking sheet in a single layer and spray lightly with the cooking oil. Sprinkle with sea salt. Bake until lightly toasted, 8 to 10 minutes. Remove from the oven and set aside to cool.

Place the onion, jalapeños, garlic, and ¼ cup of the chicken broth in a food processor or blender and puree until smooth. Set aside.

In a medium saucepan over high heat, heat 1 tablespoon of the oil until shimmering. Add the pork and cook until no longer pink, using a fork to

break up the clumps, about 5 minutes. Using a slotted spoon, transfer the pork to a mixing bowl.

Pour out all but 1 tablespoon of the fat from the saucepan. Add the remaining 2 tablespoons of oil and heat until shimmering. Slowly and carefully add the puree, smoked paprika, cumin, chipotle, and 1 teaspoon of salt. Cook, stirring, until the mixture thickens and most of the liquid evaporates, about 12 minutes. Add the pork, hominy, ⅓ cup of the cilantro, and the remaining 1½ cups of chicken broth. Simmer for 15 minutes. Transfer to a warm serving bowl and garnish with the remaining ¼ cup of cilantro, the ricotta salata cheese, and the pumpkin seeds.

Place the tortillas, 6 at a time, between two damp microwave-safe paper towels and microwave just until heated, 30 to 40 seconds. Serve warm with the chili.

salads

pollan signature salad

mixed lettuce salad with three vinegars

chopped italian salad with chicken milanese

jicama and boston lettuce salad
with lime vinaigrette

shredded kale salad with toasted hazelnuts

vegetarian caesar salad

mediterranean salad with seared tuna

arugula salad with shaved parmesan

shaved brussels sprouts salad with
pecorino cheese

SALADS USED TO BE PRETTY UNIMPRESSIVE FARE: A WEDGE OF ICEBERG lettuce with a generous dollop of fluorescent orange goo and, if you were lucky, a sprinkling of bacon bits. Far from being the humdrum side dish of yesteryear, salad has evolved into an all-star. With prewashed organic greens so readily available in markets these days, salad is the perfect quick accompaniment to any dinner. We also love to serve up a big salad as a main course by adding a grilled piece of chicken, fish, or tofu. Even without the bacon bits, salads can be kid friendly, too. Our children love to pick fresh vegetables from the family garden and visit the farmers' market to choose fruits and veggies in season and create their own salads.

We encourage you to include vegetables grown locally; if the sugar snap peas look better than the radishes called for in the recipe, feel free to swap them out. We also suggest you avoid commercially prepared dressings. Believe it or not, creating your own is not complex chemistry. It is quick and easy and the flavor is worth the whisking time. Though we have paired a specific and different dressing with each salad, the Pollan Signature Salad Dressing (page 262) works beautifully with all of them. To cut down on prep time, we make up a jar of it on Sunday night and use it throughout the week.

Oh, one more thing. Make sure your greens are completely dry so the dressing will cling to the leaves.

pollan signature salad

6 servings

We serve this salad at all our large family gatherings. Light, crisp, both vinegary and sweet, our signature salad is a delicious addition to any meal.

■ **FROM THE MARKET**

Organic mesclun or mixed baby greens
(5 to 7 ounces)

Bosc pear (1)

Parmesan cheese
(2 ounces)

■ **FROM THE PANTRY**

White balsamic vinegar
(⅓ cup)

Raspberry vinegar, champagne vinegar, or sherry vinegar
(1 tablespoon)

Dijon mustard
(1½ teaspoons)

Grapeseed oil (⅓ cup)

Extra virgin olive oil
(2 tablespoons)

Sea salt

Black pepper

Caramelized Walnuts
(½ cup; page 263, or your favorite store-bought)

FOR THE DRESSING

⅓ cup white balsamic vinegar

1 tablespoon raspberry vinegar, champagne vinegar, or sherry vinegar

1½ teaspoons Dijon mustard

⅓ cup grapeseed oil

2 tablespoons extra virgin olive oil

Sea salt

Freshly ground black pepper

FOR THE SALAD

5 to 7 ounces mesclun or mixed baby greens

½ cup chopped Caramelized Walnuts (page 263, or your favorite store-bought)

½ Bosc pear (cut lengthwise), cored, and thinly sliced

⅓ cup shaved Parmesan cheese

FOR THE DRESSING

In a glass jar with a lid or in a small mixing bowl, combine the vinegars, mustard, grapeseed oil, olive oil, ⅛ teaspoon of salt, and pepper to taste. Shake the jar vigorously or whisk in the bowl to emulsify.

FOR THE SALAD

Place the mesclun in a large salad bowl. Pour on half the dressing and toss the greens to coat. Add the walnuts, pear, and more dressing to taste (taking care not to overdress) and toss again. Top with the Parmesan cheese shavings and serve.

Food for Thought

Walnuts are the healthiest tree nuts around—they have close to twice as much antioxidants as other nuts! What's more, they are an excellent source of essential omega-3 fatty acids, which is great news for people who don't eat heart-healthy fish.

mixed lettuce salad
with three vinegars

4 to 6 servings

■ **FROM THE MARKET**

Butter lettuce
(2 small heads)

Romaine lettuce heart (1)

Avocado (1 ripe)

French breakfast radishes
or round red radishes (6)

Fresh mint (1 small bunch)

Red onion (1 small)

Garlic (1 small clove)

Ricotta salata cheese
(2 ounces)

Whole-grain Dijon mustard
(1 teaspoon)

■ **FROM THE PANTRY**

Raw pine nuts (¼ cup)

Mayonnaise (1 teaspoon)

Champagne vinegar
(1 tablespoon)

Red wine vinegar
(1 tablespoon)

Apple cider vinegar
(1 tablespoon)

Grapeseed oil (½ cup)

Maple syrup (¼ teaspoon)

Low-sodium soy sauce
(¼ teaspoon)

Sea salt

Black pepper

Three vinegars might seem like overkill, but the complexity of flavor they impart is what makes this wonderfully fresh spring salad so unique. If you can't find French breakfast radishes at your local farmers' market, any peppery radish works well.

¼ cup raw pine nuts

FOR THE DRESSING

1 teaspoon whole-grain Dijon mustard

1 teaspoon mayonnaise

½ teaspoon finely chopped red onion

1 small clove garlic, minced

1 tablespoon champagne vinegar

1 tablespoon red wine vinegar

1 tablespoon apple cider vinegar

½ cup grapeseed oil

¼ teaspoon maple syrup

¼ teaspoon low-sodium soy sauce

Sea salt

Freshly ground black pepper

FOR THE SALAD

2 small heads butter lettuce, torn into bite-size pieces

1 romaine lettuce heart, torn into bite-size pieces

1 ripe avocado, cut in half, pitted, peeled, and sliced into small wedges

6 French breakfast radishes or round red radishes, trimmed and thinly sliced

¼ cup finely grated ricotta salata cheese

2 tablespoons finely chopped mint leaves

Set a small dry nonstick skillet over medium heat. Add the pine nuts and shake the pan occasionally until they begin to brown and give off a toasty aroma, about 3 minutes. Transfer to a plate and set aside.

FOR THE DRESSING
In a small mixing bowl, combine the mustard, mayonnaise, onion, and garlic. Slowly whisk in the champagne vinegar, red wine vinegar, and apple cider

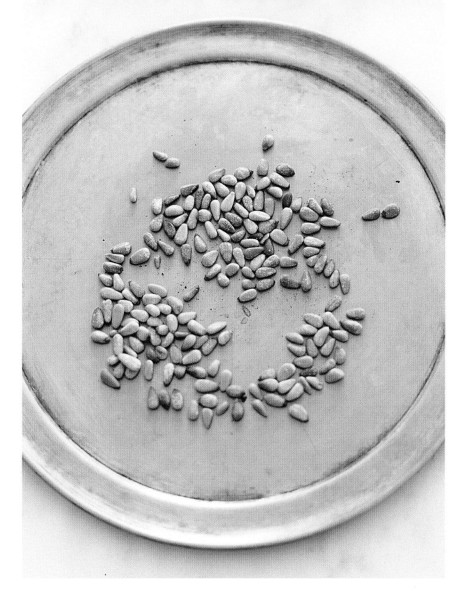

vinegar. Gradually add the oil, continuing to whisk until completely emulsified. Add the maple syrup and soy sauce. Whisk until thoroughly combined and season with salt and pepper to taste.

FOR THE SALAD
Put the butter lettuce and romaine lettuce in a large salad bowl. Pour half the dressing over the greens and toss. Add more dressing to taste and toss again. Place the salad greens on individual plates; arrange slices of avocado and radish on top. Sprinkle each with pine nuts, ricotta salata cheese, and mint and serve.

chopped italian salad with chicken milanese

4 to 6 servings

We love chopped salads and are always looking for new ways to prepare them. We took the traditional Milanese ingredients—chicken and arugula—added crunchy vegetables, cheese, and nuts, and created a delicious salad that can be served as a main course.

FOR THE DRESSING

1 teaspoon Dijon mustard

1 clove garlic, minced

3 tablespoons red wine vinegar

½ cup extra virgin olive oil

Sea salt

Freshly ground black pepper

FOR THE SALAD

¼ cup raw pine nuts

Kosher salt

8 ounces green beans

4 cooked breaded chicken cutlets (page 40), at room temperature

4 cups chopped butter lettuce, ½-inch pieces

4 cups chopped arugula, ½-inch pieces

2 cups chopped radicchio, ½-inch pieces

½ cup peeled and chopped carrots

½ cup grape or cherry tomatoes, halved

½ cup mini mozzarella balls, or 4-ounce ball fresh mozzarella cheese, cut into ½-inch dice

½ cup Croutons (page 264, or your favorite store-bought)

FOR THE DRESSING

In a small mixing bowl, whisk together the mustard, garlic, and vinegar. Slowly pour in the oil in a steady stream, whisking until completely emulsified. Add sea salt and pepper to taste. Set aside.

(recipe continues)

■ **FROM THE MARKET**

Butter lettuce (1 head)

Arugula (1 bunch or 5 ounces)

Radicchio (1 head)

Green beans (8 ounces)

Carrot (1)

Grape or cherry tomatoes (1 pint)

Garlic (1 clove)

Mini mozzarella balls (½ cup) **or** fresh mozzarella cheese (one 4-ounce ball)

■ **FROM THE PANTRY**

Dijon mustard (1 teaspoon)

Red wine vinegar (3 tablespoons)

Extra virgin olive oil (½ cup)

Sea salt

Black pepper

Raw pine nuts (¼ cup)

Kosher salt

Croutons (½ cup; page 264, or your favorite store-bought)

■ **ADDITIONAL INGREDIENTS**

Breaded chicken cutlets (4 cutlets; page 40)

FOR THE SALAD

Set a small dry nonstick skillet over medium heat. Add the pine nuts and shake the pan occasionally until they begin to brown and give off a toasty aroma, about 3 minutes. Transfer to a plate and set aside.

In a small saucepan, bring 4 cups of water to a boil and add 1 teaspoon of kosher salt. Meanwhile, fill a mixing bowl with cold water and ice. Add the green beans to the boiling water and cook until just tender, 3 to 4 minutes. Drain and immediately transfer the beans to the bowl of ice water to stop the cooking. Once cooled, drain well. Slice the beans into ½-inch pieces and set aside.

Cut the chicken cutlets into ½-inch-thick strips. Cut each strip into 1-inch-long pieces. Set aside.

In a large salad bowl, combine the lettuce, arugula, radicchio, green beans, carrots, tomatoes, mozzarella cheese, pine nuts, and croutons. If the dressing has separated, whisk again to reemulsify it. Pour the dressing over the greens and toss. Lay the chicken pieces on top of the salad and serve.

jicama and boston lettuce salad with lime vinaigrette

4 to 6 servings

A simple, crisp salad is the perfect companion to assertively seasoned dishes. Here, the jicama supplies the crunch, while the ricotta salata balances the tartness of the limes.

2 heads Boston lettuce

2 tablespoons fresh lime juice

¼ cup grapeseed oil

2 tablespoons extra virgin olive oil

1 tablespoon apple cider vinegar

1 teaspoon Dijon mustard

Sea salt

Freshly ground black pepper

1 medium jicama, peeled and cut into 2-inch-long julienne

½ cup shaved ricotta salata cheese

3 tablespoons finely chopped cilantro

■ **FROM THE MARKET**

Boston lettuce (2 heads)

Jicama (1 medium)

Fresh cilantro (1 bunch)

Lime (1)

Ricotta salata cheese (2 ounces)

■ **FROM THE PANTRY**

Grapeseed oil (¼ cup)

Extra virgin olive oil (2 tablespoons)

Apple cider vinegar (1 tablespoon)

Dijon mustard (1 teaspoon)

Sea salt

Black pepper

Tear the lettuce into bite-size pieces and place in a large mixing bowl.

In a glass jar with a lid or in a small mixing bowl, combine the lime juice, grapeseed oil, olive oil, vinegar, mustard, and salt and pepper to taste. Shake the jar vigorously or whisk in the bowl to emulsify.

Add the dressing to the greens, reserving some for drizzling, and toss to coat lightly.

Arrange the salad on individual plates. Place the jicama and ricotta salata cheese on top and drizzle with a bit more dressing. Sprinkle with the cilantro, season with salt and pepper, and serve.

Food for Thought

Jicama contains no fat, no cholesterol, and very few calories yet it offers a significant amount of vitamin C, potassium, and is one of the highest sources of dietary fiber. The fiber is inulin, which acts as a prebiotic, promoting helpful bacteria in the gut.

Food for Thought

In recent years kale has suffered from overexposure as the superfood du jour. But kale truly is a nutritional powerhouse, boasting incredibly high levels of vitamins, minerals, and antioxidants (1 cup has 180 percent of the daily requirement of vitamin A, 200 percent of vitamin C, and 1020 percent—yes, you read that right—of vitamin K!). Just as remarkable—kale, calorie for calorie, has more iron than beef.

shredded kale salad
with toasted hazelnuts

4 to 6 servings

■ **FROM THE MARKET**

Tuscan kale, also known as cavolo nero, dinosaur kale, or lacinato (1 bunch, about 1 pound)

Garlic (2 cloves)

Dried currants (3 tablespoons)

Ricotta salata cheese (2 ounces)

■ **FROM THE PANTRY**

Balsamic vinegar (1 tablespoon)

Blanched raw hazelnuts (¼ cup)

Extra virgin olive oil (¼ cup)

Balsamic Vinegar Glaze (¼ cup; page 269, or your favorite store-bought)

Sea salt

Black pepper

Kale is ubiquitous of late, but with good reason—it is healthy and delicious. Here, lightly cooking the raw kale removes its toughness.

3 tablespoons dried currants

1 tablespoon balsamic vinegar

¼ cup blanched raw hazelnuts

1 pound Tuscan kale, washed and very thoroughly dried

¼ cup extra virgin olive oil

2 cloves garlic, minced

¼ cup Balsamic Vinegar Glaze (page 269, or your favorite store-bought)

Sea salt

Freshly ground black pepper

½ cup shredded ricotta salata cheese

Put the currants into a small mixing bowl with the balsamic vinegar and 1 tablespoon of hot water and set aside to soak.

Meanwhile, place the hazelnuts in a small dry skillet over medium heat. Cook until they begin to brown, shaking the pan and stirring so they do not burn, 4 to 5 minutes. Let the nuts cool, chop roughly, and set aside.

To prepare the kale, cut out and discard the center stems, keeping long half-leaves. Stack together 4 to 5 leaves at a time and slice into chiffonade until you have 5 tightly packed cups of long, thin strips.

Heat the oil in a large skillet over medium heat. When the oil is shimmering, add the garlic and stir for 30 seconds. Add the kale and stir for an additional 30 seconds until just warm and barely soft. Immediately transfer the kale to a mixing bowl and place it in the refrigerator until just cooled, 4 to 5 minutes.

When cool, transfer the kale to a salad bowl and toss with the balsamic vinegar glaze. Drain the currants, add them along with the hazelnuts, and toss. Season with salt and pepper, sprinkle on the ricotta salata cheese, and serve.

vegetarian caesar salad

6 servings

We have always loved a classic Caesar salad, but many of our kids do not eat anchovies. We find that capers are the perfect replacement, providing a salty-briny kick—you won't even miss the anchovies.

2 tablespoons mayonnaise

2 teaspoons Dijon mustard

1 large clove garlic, minced

Sea salt

Freshly ground black pepper

⅓ cup extra virgin olive oil

2 tablespoons fresh lemon juice

½ teaspoon steak sauce or organic vegetarian Worcestershire sauce

1 teaspoon capers plus ¼ teaspoon of the liquid

3 romaine lettuce hearts, chilled

½ cup freshly grated Parmesan cheese

1 cup Croutons (page 264, or your favorite store-bought)

In a large salad bowl, whisk together the mayonnaise, mustard, garlic, ⅛ teaspoon of salt, and ⅛ teaspoon of pepper. Very slowly pour the oil into the bowl, continuously whisking until the mixture has emulsified. Whisk in the lemon juice and steak sauce and stir in the capers and their liquid. Remove approximately half the dressing and set aside.

Tear the lettuce into bite-size pieces and place it in the salad bowl on top of the dressing. Sprinkle with half the Parmesan cheese and half the croutons. Toss until the lettuce is coated. Add more dressing to taste. Sprinkle with the remaining cheese and croutons and serve.

■ **FROM THE MARKET**

Romaine lettuce hearts (3)

Garlic (1 large clove)

Lemon (1)

Parmesan cheese (2 ounces)

Steak sauce, or organic vegetarian Worcestershire sauce (½ teaspoon)

■ **FROM THE PANTRY**

Mayonnaise (2 tablespoons)

Dijon mustard (2 teaspoons)

Sea salt

Black pepper

Extra virgin olive oil (⅓ cup)

Capers (1 teaspoon)

Croutons (1 cup; page 264, or your favorite store-bought)

mediterranean salad
with seared tuna

4 servings

■ **FROM THE MARKET**

Sushi-grade ahi tuna
(four 4-ounce steaks,
at least 1 inch thick)

Romaine lettuce (3 hearts)

Italian (flat-leaf) parsley
(1 bunch)

Fresh lemon thyme or, if not
available, fresh thyme (2 sprigs)

Green beans (4 ounces)

Persian cucumbers (3 small) or
seedless cucumber (1 large)

Grape tomatoes (½ pint)

Red onion (1 medium)

Small red or white potatoes
(12 ounces)

Shallot (1)

Garlic (1 clove)

Lemon (1)

Assorted pitted Mediterranean
olives, such as kalamata,
lugano, or gaeta (8 ounces)

■ **FROM THE PANTRY**

Dijon mustard (1 teaspoon)

Dried oregano (¼ teaspoon)

Red wine vinegar
(2 tablespoons)

Extra virgin olive oil
(½ cup plus 2 teaspoons)

Kosher salt

Black pepper

This salad is a complete meal replete with heart-healthy ingredients and delicious fresh and savory flavors. To get the full spectrum of the Mediterranean
diet, we love to pair this with a glass of red wine.

FOR THE DRESSING

1 teaspoon Dijon mustard

1 clove garlic, minced

½ teaspoon finely chopped shallot

¼ teaspoon dried oregano

¼ teaspoon fresh lemon thyme,
or fresh thyme

2 tablespoons red wine vinegar

1 tablespoon fresh lemon juice

½ cup extra virgin olive oil

Kosher salt

Freshly ground black pepper

FOR THE TUNA AND SALAD

Four 4-ounce sushi-grade ahi tuna
steaks, at least 1 inch thick

Kosher salt

Freshly ground black pepper

2 cups sliced Persian or seedless
cucumbers, cut ½ inch thick

1 cup sliced red onion, halved
lengthwise and thinly sliced
crosswise

3 teaspoons chopped Italian
(flat-leaf) parsley

12 ounces small red or white potatoes,
halved

1 cup sliced green beans, trimmed and
halved crosswise

2 teaspoons extra virgin olive oil

3 Romaine lettuce hearts, torn or
chopped into bite-size pieces

1 cup grape tomatoes

1 cup assorted pitted
Mediterranean olives

FOR THE DRESSING

In a small mixing bowl, combine the mustard, garlic, shallot, oregano, and thyme.
Add the vinegar and lemon juice, and whisk to blend. Pour in ½ cup of oil in a
slow stream and continue to whisk until emulsified. Add ¼ teaspoon of salt and
pepper to taste.

(recipe continues)

FOR THE TUNA AND SALAD

Season the tuna steaks generously with salt, pepper, and 1 tablespoon of the salad dressing. Cover and refrigerate for at least 30 minutes or up to 1 hour.

In a small mixing bowl, combine the cucumbers, onion, 1 teaspoon of the parsley, and 1 tablespoon of the dressing. Mix well and set aside.

Place the potatoes in a large pot; add water to cover by 2 inches and 1 teaspoon of salt. Bring the water to a boil and cook for 10 to 15 minutes, until the potatoes are fork-tender. Remove the potatoes with a slotted spoon (leave the water boiling) and place them in a small mixing bowl. Spoon on 1 tablespoon of the dressing, add 1 teaspoon of the parsley, and season with salt and pepper. Mix well and set aside.

Fill a mixing bowl with water and ice cubes. Add the green beans to the boiling water and cook until tender, about 4 minutes. Drain the beans and transfer to the bowl of ice water until cool. Drain again and dry on paper towels.

Remove the tuna from the refrigerator. Set a medium skillet over high heat. Add 2 teaspoons of oil and heat until smoking hot. Place the tuna in the pan and sear for 1½ minutes on one side. Flip and cook for an additional 1½ minutes (for rare). Transfer to a cutting board and allow the tuna to rest for 5 minutes. Using a thin, sharp knife, cut it against the grain into ½-inch slices.

If the dressing has separated, whisk again to reemulsify. Place the lettuce, green beans, and the remaining dressing in a large salad bowl and toss. Arrange the greens on individual plates and top each with potatoes, cucumbers and their dressing, tomatoes, and olives. Place a sliced tuna steak on top of each salad. Sprinkle with the remaining 1 teaspoon of parsley and season with salt and pepper to taste.

TIP: You can prepare your dressing up to 2 days ahead. Whisk it to reemulsify before using, or shake well if stored in a jar.

arugula salad
with shaved parmesan

6 servings

We always wondered why this Italian classic tasted so much better at the restaurant than it did at home—then a favorite waiter let us in on the secret. Apply the olive oil and lemon juice directly to the leaves rather than whisking up a traditional dressing. We have no idea why it works, it just does.

5 ounces arugula

3 tablespoons extra virgin olive oil

1½ tablespoons fresh lemon juice

Sea salt

Freshly ground black pepper

12 to 18 thin shavings Parmesan cheese

■ FROM THE MARKET

Arugula (5 ounces)

Lemon (1)

Parmesan cheese (3 ounces)

■ FROM THE PANTRY

Extra virgin olive oil (3 tablespoons)

Sea salt

Black pepper

Place the arugula in a salad bowl. Pour the oil over the leaves and toss. (We like to use clean hands, but salad tongs work just as well.) Add the lemon juice and toss again. Sprinkle with ⅛ teaspoon of salt and pepper to taste and add the Parmesan cheese shavings. Toss once more and serve.

shaved brussels sprouts salad with pecorino cheese

6 servings

This delightfully different salad features raw Brussels sprouts sliced whisper-thin. We add salty Pecorino Romano cheese and crisp apple and toss with a tangy citrus vinaigrette to finish this light, fresh, and so tasty salad.

1 tablespoon fresh lemon juice

1½ tablespoons fresh orange juice

½ teaspoon finely grated lemon zest

½ teaspoon finely grated orange zest

1 teaspoon Dijon mustard

2 tablespoons sherry vinegar

¼ cup extra virgin olive oil

Kosher salt

Freshly ground black pepper

1½ pounds Brussels sprouts, trimmed and very thinly sliced with a mandoline or a knife

1 small or ½ large red-skinned apple (Pink Lady or Gala), cut into 1-inch-long julienne

½ cup shaved Pecorino Romano cheese

■ **FROM THE MARKET**

Brussels sprouts
(1½ pounds)

Lemon (1)

Orange (1)

Crisp red-skinned apple
such as Pink Lady or
Gala (1)

Pecorino Romano cheese
(2 ounces)

■ **FROM THE PANTRY**

Dijon mustard (1 teaspoon)

Sherry vinegar
(2 tablespoons)

Extra virgin olive oil
(¼ cup)

Kosher salt

Black pepper

In a glass jar with a lid or in a small mixing bowl, combine the lemon and orange juices, lemon and orange zests, mustard, vinegar, oil, ¼ teaspoon of salt, and pepper to taste. Shake the jar vigorously or whisk in the bowl to emulsify.

In a salad bowl, combine the Brussels sprouts and apples. Add the dressing and toss gently. Top with the Pecorino Romano cheese shavings. Season with salt and pepper and serve.

vegetables and
sides

rich and creamy polenta

orzo-rice pilaf

farro-vegetable pilaf

toasted quinoa and vegetable pilaf

brown rice and barley with frizzled kale

crispy parmesan-zucchini chips

creamed spinach gratin with
toasted breadcrumbs

mixed spring vegetable medley

chickpea salad with fresh
herbs and manchego cheese

french lentil salad with a touch of heat

spicy chunky guacamole

healthy green goddess dip with crudités

mashed potato casserole with spinach,
carrots, and gruyère

cheezy grits

jalapeño-flecked golden cornbread

golden baby artichokes with lemon zest

crispy garlic bread

ROASTED VEGETABLES

roasted broccoli with crisp garlic

brussels sprouts with pine nuts
and dried cranberries

crispy paprika-roasted potatoes

roasted balsamic haricots verts with
slivered almonds

crunchy oven-roasted fries

maple-balsamic root vegetable "fries"

roasted zucchini and cremini mushrooms with
toasted parmesan

cauliflower with toasted breadcrumbs
and parmesan

asparagus with parmesan and frizzled shallots

roasted corn on the cob with herbs and spices

WE LOVE AND EXALT VEGETABLES AND GRAINS. WITH THE STUNNING ARRAY OF produce sold at farmers' markets and the vast choices now available at grocery stores, vegetables can easily take a top spot on the dinner plate no matter the time of year. The same can be said for grains and starches. Whereas rice and potatoes were the standard dinnertime sides not so long ago, today we can choose from so many delicious and nutritious varieties: quinoa, farro, bulgur, barley, sweet potatoes, parsnips—the list goes on.

Back in the 1970s our dinners were well known among our friends for including unusual vegetables, which was quite uncommon for the times. No one else we knew had artichokes with lemon-butter sauce, asparagus hollandaise, or pommes Anna—the classic French layered potato dish. These exotic and tasty vegetable dishes were often the highlight of the meal.

Today we've branched out even further; we cook with kale, Swiss chard, jicama, celery root, Brussels sprouts, cremini mushrooms—always trying new recipes and combinations. We often create a meal by seeing first what looks enticing at the farmers' market, or because we have a hankering for a certain grain or legume. We then construct the rest of the dinner around the sides.

We've devoted a whole section on roasting vegetables. The big secret: it's the simplest, most time-efficient method for preparing vegetables—pop them in the oven and forget about them while you prepare the rest of your meal. And roasting brings out a completely different flavor in vegetables. We add slight variations to each of these dishes, which take them to a whole new level.

Finally, a note on purchasing organic versus conventionally grown produce: We believe it's important to reduce our exposure to pesticides in produce as much as we possibly can—but sometimes organic varieties are just not affordable or readily available. We follow the Environmental Working Group's annual Dirty Dozen and Clean Fifteen lists (http://www.ewg.org/foodnews/index.php), which help us determine when to insist on organic and when conventionally grown fruits and vegetables can suffice.

rich and creamy polenta

4 to 6 servings

■ **FROM THE MARKET**
Mascarpone cheese
(4 ounces)

■ **FROM THE PANTRY**
Yellow cornmeal (1 cup)
Kosher salt
Black pepper

The simplicity of this recipe belies the deliciousness and versatility of polenta. It's the perfect companion to any saucy dish—we love it with our Hunter's Chicken Stew or Smoky Sautéed Shrimp—and leftover polenta can be fried, baked, or turned into pancakes.

1 cup yellow cornmeal

½ cup mascarpone cheese

Kosher salt

Freshly ground black pepper

Thoroughly whisk the cornmeal with 1 cup of cold water in a small mixing bowl.

In a large pot, bring 3 cups of water to a boil over high heat. Very slowly add the cornmeal and water mixture, stirring constantly to prevent lumps from forming. Cook for 5 minutes, stirring constantly. Reduce the heat to low. Simmer, stirring until thickened, about 10 minutes.

Stir in the mascarpone cheese, 1½ teaspoons of salt, and ¼ teaspoon of pepper and cook for an additional 5 minutes. Transfer the polenta to a bowl and serve.

TIP: To clean the pot, fill it with ice-cold water and leave it soaking for half an hour. Any polenta attached to the pot will just lift off.

orzo-rice pilaf

4 servings

This is a super way to rev up a simple rice side dish. The orzo pasta and nuts give it a great texture and the zest adds a subtle lemony flavor.

1 tablespoon raw pine nuts or slivered
    raw almonds

2 tablespoons unsalted butter

½ cup orzo pasta

1 small clove garlic, minced

1 cup long-grain white rice

Kosher salt

Finely grated zest of 1 lemon

1 tablespoon finely chopped Italian
    (flat-leaf) parsley

Freshly ground black pepper

■ **FROM THE MARKET**

Orzo pasta (½ cup)

Italian (flat-leaf) parsley
(1 small bunch)

Garlic (1 small clove)

Lemon (1)

Unsalted butter
(2 tablespoons)

■ **FROM THE PANTRY**

Raw pine nuts or slivered
raw almonds (1 tablespoon)

Long-grain white rice
(1 cup)

Kosher salt

Black pepper

Set a small dry nonstick skillet over medium heat. Add the pine nuts and shake the pan occasionally until they begin to brown and give off a toasty aroma, about 3 minutes. Transfer to a plate and set aside.

In a medium saucepan over medium heat, melt the butter. Stir in the orzo and let it brown for 3 minutes. Add the garlic and stir for an additional 2 minutes. Add the rice and mix until the rice and orzo are coated with butter. Add 1 teaspoon of salt and 4 cups of water. Cover the pot and bring to a boil. Reduce the heat to low and simmer until all the water is absorbed, about 15 minutes.

Fluff the pilaf with a fork. Add the toasted nuts, lemon zest, and parsley and season with salt and pepper. Toss together and serve warm.

farro-vegetable pilaf

4 to 6 servings

Farro has a nutty, full-bodied flavor and a dense, chewy texture. It readily adopts the flavors of any ingredients it is combined with.

1½ cups semipearled farro, rinsed and drained

Sea salt

4 tablespoons extra virgin olive oil

½ cup finely chopped red onion

2 tablespoons balsamic vinegar

½ cup finely chopped red bell pepper

¾ cup peeled and finely chopped carrots

2 scallions, finely chopped

¼ cup finely sliced fresh chives

Freshly ground black pepper

¼ cup finely chopped Italian (flat-leaf) parsley

In a medium saucepan, combine the farro, 1 teaspoon of salt, and 4 cups of water. Place over high heat and bring to a boil. Stir once and reduce the heat to low. Simmer, covered, until the farro is tender but not soft, about 20 minutes. Drain well and transfer to a mixing bowl.

Meanwhile, heat 2 tablespoons of the oil in a small skillet over medium heat until shimmering. Add the onion and cook, stirring, until it becomes translucent, 5 to 6 minutes. Remove the pan from the heat and add the remaining 2 tablespoons of oil and the vinegar; stir well. Pour over the cooked farro and toss to evenly coat.

Add the red pepper, carrots, scallions, chives, ½ teaspoon of salt, ⅛ teaspoon of pepper, and the parsley and stir to combine. Allow the dish to sit for at least 15 minutes so that the dressing is absorbed. Season with additional salt and pepper and serve warm or at room temperature.

Food for Thought
Farro, an ancient whole grain, is a terrific source of vitamins and is loaded with fiber. Even better, farro has the most protein of any grain—7 grams per serving!

■ **FROM THE MARKET**

Semipearled farro (1½ cups)

Red bell pepper (1 small)

Carrots (2 small)

Italian (flat-leaf) parsley (1 bunch)

Fresh chives (1 small bunch)

Scallions (2)

Red onion (1 medium)

■ **FROM THE PANTRY**

Sea salt

Extra virgin olive oil (4 tablespoons)

Balsamic vinegar (2 tablespoons)

Black pepper

toasted quinoa and vegetable pilaf

6 servings

■ **FROM THE MARKET**

Carrot (1)

Italian (flat-leaf) parsley
(1 small bunch)

Yellow onion (1 medium)

Garlic (1 clove)

Lemon (1)

Frozen petite peas (¼ cup)

■ **FROM THE PANTRY**

Extra virgin olive oil
(1 tablespoon)

Quinoa (1½ cups)

Low-sodium vegetable
broth (2 cups)

Kosher salt

Black pepper

Quinoa may be the trendiest food of the moment, but its origins date back 3,000 to 4,000 years, when it was first cultivated in the Andes region. This super food is super tasty, with a crunchy, nutty texture that pairs beautifully with vegetarian dishes as well as with poultry, meat, or fish.

1 tablespoon extra virgin olive oil

1 cup finely chopped yellow onion

1 clove garlic, minced

½ cup peeled and finely chopped carrots

1½ cups quinoa, rinsed and thoroughly drained

2 cups low-sodium vegetable broth

1 teaspoon finely grated lemon zest

¼ cup frozen petite peas

2 teaspoons fresh lemon juice

Kosher salt

Freshly ground black pepper

1 tablespoon finely chopped Italian (flat-leaf) parsley

In a medium saucepan over medium heat, heat the oil until shimmering. Add the onion, garlic, and carrots and sauté until soft, 8 to 10 minutes. Add the quinoa and stir frequently until the quinoa becomes lightly browned, 3 to 5 minutes. Add the vegetable broth, 1 cup of water, and the lemon zest and bring to a boil. Reduce the heat to low, add the peas, and cover.

Simmer until the quinoa is soft and the liquid has been absorbed, 15 to 20 minutes. Remove the pan from the heat and lay a clean dish towel under the lid for 10 minutes.

Fluff the quinoa with a fork and stir in the lemon juice, 1 teaspoon of salt, and pepper to taste. Sprinkle with the parsley and serve.

brown rice and barley
with frizzled kale

4 to 6 servings

We love when we can combine vegetables with a grain—it makes healthy dinner preparation that much quicker.

1 tablespoon unsalted butter

2 tablespoons extra virgin olive oil

¼ cup finely chopped shallots

½ cup finely chopped yellow onion

2 cloves garlic, minced

Kosher salt

Freshly ground black pepper

1½ cups long- or medium-grain brown rice

½ cup pearl barley

2 cups low-sodium vegetable broth

4 cups roughly chopped stemmed Tuscan kale leaves, thoroughly dried

■ **FROM THE MARKET**

Tuscan kale, also known as cavolo nero, dinosaur kale, or lacinato (1 bunch, about 1 pound)

Yellow onion (1 small)

Shallots (2)

Garlic (2 cloves)

Unsalted butter (1 tablespoon)

■ **FROM THE PANTRY**

Extra virgin olive oil (2 tablespoons)

Kosher salt

Black pepper

Brown rice, long- or medium-grain (1½ cups)

Pearl barley (½ cup)

Low-sodium vegetable broth (2 cups)

In a large saucepan over medium heat, add the butter and 1 tablespoon of the oil. When the butter has melted, add the shallots, onion, garlic, ½ teaspoon of salt, and ¼ teaspoon of pepper. Cook, stirring frequently, until soft, about 5 minutes.

Stir in the rice and barley and cook for an additional 2 minutes. Stir in the vegetable broth and 1 cup of water. Bring to a boil, reduce the heat to low, cover, and cook until all the liquid has been absorbed, about 45 minutes. Remove from the heat and let stand for 5 minutes.

Meanwhile, prepare the frizzled kale. Line a plate with paper towels. Heat the remaining 1 tablespoon of oil in a large skillet over medium-high heat. When the oil is shimmering, add the kale and cook until it begins to crisp, about 5 minutes. Transfer to the paper towel–lined plate to drain.

Put the brown rice and barley into a serving bowl, fluff with a fork, and season with salt and pepper. Top with the crispy kale, toss together, and serve.

crispy parmesan-zucchini chips

4 to 6 servings

■ **FROM THE MARKET**

Zucchini (4 medium)

Italian (flat-leaf) parsley
(1 small bunch)

Garlic (1 large clove)

Parmesan cheese
(2 ounces)

■ **FROM THE PANTRY***

Plain Breadcrumbs
(⅓ cup; page 264, or your
favorite store-bought)

Sea salt

Black pepper

Organic olive oil cooking
spray or extra virgin olive
oil (1 tablespoon)

*You will need
parchment paper.

Fried zucchini is delicious, but it's not the healthiest choice. This lighter alternative rivals the crunchiness and taste of the original, and it couldn't be easier to make.

⅓ cup freshly grated Parmesan cheese

⅓ cup plain Breadcrumbs (page 264, or your favorite store-bought)

1 large clove garlic, minced

1 tablespoon finely chopped Italian (flat-leaf) parsley

Sea salt

Freshly ground black pepper

4 medium zucchini, trimmed and sliced into ¼-inch-thick rounds

Organic olive oil cooking spray or 1 tablespoon olive oil

Preheat the oven to 450°F. Line two rimmed baking sheets with parchment paper.

In a shallow dish, combine the Parmesan cheese, breadcrumbs, garlic, and parsley. Season with salt and pepper.

Spray the zucchini slices on both sides with the cooking spray, or toss with the oil. Dip the zucchini into the seasoned breadcrumbs, making sure each slice is coated on both sides. Place the slices on the baking sheets.

Bake until the zucchini slices are nicely browned, 10 to 15 minutes. Flip the rounds and bake for an additional 10 to 15 minutes. Sprinkle with additional salt if desired and serve hot.

creamed spinach gratin
with toasted breadcrumbs

8 servings

■ **FROM THE MARKET**

Yellow onions (2 medium)

Garlic (2 cloves)

Half-and-half (1 cup)

Whole milk (2 cups)

Unsalted butter
(4 tablespoons, or ½ stick)

Parmesan cheese
(4 ounces)

Gruyère cheese (3 ounces)

Frozen chopped spinach
(five 10-ounce packages)

■ **FROM THE PANTRY**

Plain Breadcrumbs
(½ cup; page 264, or your
favorite store-bought)

Kosher salt

Black pepper

All-purpose flour (¼ cup)

Ground nutmeg
(¼ teaspoon)

In our childhood, one of our favorite vegetable sides was store-bought frozen spinach soufflé. Our homemade creamed spinach recipe surpasses the one from our youth. It is creamy on the inside, and slightly crunchy on top. This is a staple at our holiday dinners—but it is great any day of the week, and better yet, reheated the next day.

Five 10-ounce packages frozen chopped spinach, thawed

4 tablespoons (½ stick) unsalted butter

½ cup plain Breadcrumbs (page 264, or your favorite store-bought)

Kosher salt

Freshly ground black pepper

2 cups finely chopped yellow onion

2 cloves garlic, minced

¼ cup all-purpose flour

1 cup half-and-half

2 cups whole milk

1 cup shredded Parmesan cheese

¼ teaspoon ground nutmeg

¾ cup shredded Gruyère cheese

Set a rack in the middle of the oven and preheat the oven to 425°F.

Squeeze out all the liquid from the spinach. Set the spinach aside.

In a large skillet over medium-high heat, melt 1 tablespoon of the butter. Add the breadcrumbs and a pinch each of salt and pepper and stir until golden brown, about 2 minutes. Transfer the breadcrumbs to a mixing bowl and set aside.

Wipe out the skillet with a paper towel. Melt the remaining 3 tablespoons of butter over medium heat. Add the onion and garlic and cook, stirring, until the onion is translucent but not brown, 6 to 7 minutes.

Add the flour and stir continuously until combined, about 1 minute. Pour in the half-and-half and milk and stir until the mixture thickens, 7 to 8 minutes.

Add the spinach and mix well. Fold in ½ cup of the Parmesan cheese and season with the nutmeg, 1 teaspoon of salt, and ¼ teaspoon of pepper.

Transfer the mixture to a 9 by 13-inch baking dish or other large casserole. Scatter the remaining ½ cup of Parmesan cheese and all of the Gruyère cheese evenly over the top and sprinkle with the toasted breadcrumbs. Bake until the cheese is melted and the top is golden, about 20 minutes. Serve hot.

Food for Thought

The very thing that makes you cry when you cut into onions is a compound that helps regulate blood sugar. This, along with the other nutrients in onions, also helps lower high blood pressure, lower bad cholesterol, and boost good cholesterol. What's more, the quercetin in onions has potent anticancer, anti-inflammatory, anti-bacterial, and antiviral qualities.

mixed spring vegetable medley

4 to 6 servings

■ **FROM THE MARKET**

Broccoli (1 small head)

Carrots (7 small)

Green beans (12 ounces)

Fresh chives (1 small bunch)

Unsalted butter
(2 tablespoons)

■ **FROM THE PANTRY**

Sea salt

Black pepper

Steaming the vegetables before sautéing allows them to stay crisp and bright. The delicate flavor of the chives combines beautifully with the butter to create a simple yet elegant side dish. Feel free to substitute cauliflower, zucchini, or sugar snap peas.

7 small carrots, peeled and cut on the diagonal into 1-inch slices

12 ounces green beans, trimmed and cut in half on the diagonal

1 small head broccoli, cut into 1-inch florets

2 tablespoons unsalted butter

1 tablespoon finely sliced chives

Sea salt

Freshly ground black pepper

Fill a large pot with water so that it just barely reaches the bottom of a steamer basket or colander. Place over high heat and bring to a boil. Put the carrots and green beans in the steamer and cover. After 3 minutes, add the broccoli and cook for an additional 3 minutes or until all the vegetables are fork-tender. Remove from the pot and set aside, reserving the water.

Melt the butter in a large skillet over medium heat. Add the chives and cook for 30 seconds. Add the steamed vegetables, mixing until they are coated. Stir in 2 tablespoons of water from the pot and season with salt and pepper. Serve immediately.

STEPHEN

chickpea salad with fresh herbs and manchego cheese

6 servings

Refreshing, light, and citrusy, this salad is so simple to make. The fresh herbs and lemon give the chickpeas and Manchego cheese such vibrancy, and the arugula adds a delicious peppery bite. This dish becomes even more flavorful when you prepare it a day or two ahead.

■ FROM THE MARKET

Arugula (3 to 4 ounces)

Italian (flat-leaf) parsley
(1 bunch)

Fresh basil (1 bunch)

Fresh mint (1 small bunch)

Red onion (1 small)

Garlic (1 clove)

Lemon (1)

Manchego cheese
(3 ounces)

■ FROM THE PANTRY

Canned organic chickpeas
(two 15-ounce cans)

Sea salt

Black pepper

Red wine vinegar
(1 tablespoon)

Dijon mustard (1 teaspoon)

Extra virgin olive oil
(2 tablespoons)

Two 15-ounce cans organic chickpeas

⅓ cup finely chopped red onion

½ teaspoon minced garlic

3 tablespoons finely chopped Italian
(flat-leaf) parsley

3 tablespoons finely chopped
fresh basil

1 tablespoon finely chopped
fresh mint

½ teaspoon finely grated lemon zest

Sea salt

Freshly ground black pepper

1 tablespoon red wine vinegar

1 teaspoon Dijon mustard

2 tablespoons lemon juice

2 tablespoons extra virgin olive oil

½ cup diced Manchego cheese, cut
into ⅓-inch cubes

3 to 4 ounces arugula

Rinse and drain the chickpeas and put them in a medium mixing bowl. Add the onion, garlic, parsley, basil, mint, lemon zest, ½ teaspoon of salt, and ¼ teaspoon of pepper. Mix well.

In a small mixing bowl, whisk together the vinegar, mustard, lemon juice, and oil. Pour over the chickpeas and stir to mix well. Add the Manchego cheese and toss until all the ingredients are combined. (The salad can be made ahead up to this point and refrigerated.)

Before serving, arrange a bed of arugula in a wide, shallow serving bowl and mound the chickpea salad on top.

french lentil salad with a touch of heat

4 servings

One of our favorite French restaurants is in the Caribbean and it is known for its irresistible lentil salad. The recipe was a closely guarded secret that we tried for years to replicate. Finally, we think we've succeeded.

1 cup French lentils, rinsed and drained

1 bay leaf

2 sprigs fresh thyme

5 tablespoons extra virgin olive oil

⅓ cup peeled and finely chopped carrots

1 clove garlic, minced

1 teaspoon very thinly sliced fresh red finger chile or seeded jalapeño chile

1 teaspoon Dijon mustard

2 tablespoons red wine vinegar

¼ cup finely chopped red onion

Sea salt

Freshly ground black pepper

1 tablespoon finely chopped Italian (flat-leaf) parsley

■ **FROM THE MARKET**

Carrot (1)

Italian (flat-leaf) parsley (1 small bunch)

Fresh thyme (2 sprigs)

Red finger chile (1 small)*

Red onion (1 small)

Garlic (1 clove)

*You can substitute a jalapeño chile.

■ **FROM THE PANTRY**

French lentils (1 cup)

Bay leaf (1)

Extra virgin olive oil (5 tablespoons)

Dijon mustard (1 teaspoon)

Red wine vinegar (2 tablespoons)

Sea salt

Black pepper

In a medium saucepan, combine the lentils, 2½ cups of water, the bay leaf, and thyme. Bring to a boil over high heat, reduce the heat to low, and simmer, covered, until the lentils are tender, about 20 minutes, being careful not to overcook them. Drain the lentils, remove the bay leaf and thyme, put them into a mixing bowl, and set aside to cool.

Meanwhile, in a small skillet, heat 1 tablespoon of the oil over medium-low heat until shimmering. Add the carrots, garlic, and ½ teaspoon of the chile. Cook, stirring, until the mixture is soft, 2 to 4 minutes. Set aside.

In a small mixing bowl, whisk together the Dijon mustard, vinegar, and the remaining 4 tablespoons of oil. Set aside.

Stir the cooked vegetables, onion, and the remaining ½ teaspoon of the chile (or to taste) into the bowl of lentils. Stir in the vinaigrette, ¼ teaspoon of salt, and ¼ teaspoon of pepper. Garnish with parsley and serve.

spicy chunky guacamole
4 to 6 servings

■ **FROM THE MARKET**

Ripe avocados (3)

Tomato (1 small)

Fresh cilantro
(1 small bunch; optional)

Jalapeño chile (1)

Red onion (1 small)

Garlic (1 clove)

Lime (1)

■ **FROM THE PANTRY**

Sea salt

Black pepper

Guacamole is terrific with chips, but we also like it as a side with many dishes—fish tacos, burgers, and Spanish tortillas. It's simple to customize this recipe: You can make it as mild or as spicy as you like, and if you don't like cilantro, you can just omit it.

3 ripe avocados

¼ cup chopped tomato

1 tablespoon chopped red onion

1 clove garlic, minced

2 teaspoons chopped cilantro (optional)

1 tablespoon fresh lime juice

½ teaspoon finely chopped jalapeño chile, or to taste

Sea salt

Freshly ground black pepper

Cut the avocados in half and remove the pits (set one pit aside for later). Scoop the avocado flesh into a mixing bowl and smash it with a fork, making sure to leave some lumps. Add the tomato and mix gently. Add the onion, garlic, cilantro (if desired), lime juice, jalapeño, ½ teaspoon of salt, and black pepper to taste. Stir lightly to blend.

Transfer the guacamole to a serving bowl. Place the reserved avocado pit on top (to help prevent the guacamole from turning brown) and cover tightly with plastic wrap, pressing the wrap onto the surface of the guacamole. Refrigerate until ready to serve.

> **Food for Thought**
> Avocados are loaded with healthy essential fats. And research shows that lycopene and beta-carotene are more efficiently absorbed when eaten along with avocados, which means that guacamole with tomatoes and cilantro is not only full of flavor, it is bursting with important health benefits, too.

healthy green goddess dip with crudités

4 to 6 servings

When the kids were small, the easiest way for us to entice them to eat all of their veggies was to put out a big platter of raw carrots, cucumbers, and celery with this tasty green goddess dip. As everyone has matured, so have their palates, and their taste in vegetables has grown more eclectic (jicama, radishes, and sugar snap peas), but this dip remains a family favorite.

2 to 3 pounds assorted vegetables, such as carrot, celery, and jicama sticks; red and yellow pepper strips; cauliflower and broccoli florets; cucumber and radish rounds; grape tomatoes; and sugar snap peas

½ of a ripe avocado

½ cup plain Greek yogurt (we like 2%)

¼ cup mayonnaise

1 tablespoon white wine vinegar

2 teaspoons lemon juice

1 teaspoon finely chopped shallot

1 clove garlic, minced

1 teaspoon finely chopped chives

1 teaspoon finely chopped dill

1 teaspoon finely chopped tarragon

1 teaspoon capers, drained

1 teaspoon Dijon mustard

Sea salt

Freshly ground black pepper

Arrange the cut vegetables on a platter.

Combine the avocado, yogurt, mayonnaise, vinegar, lemon juice, shallot, garlic, chives, dill, tarragon, capers, mustard, and ⅛ teaspoon of salt in a food processor or blender. Blend until completely smooth. Transfer to a small serving bowl and season with pepper. Serve with the vegetable platter.

■ **FROM THE MARKET**

Assorted vegetables such as carrot, celery, and jicama sticks; red and yellow pepper strips; cauliflower and broccoli florets; cucumber and radish rounds; grape tomatoes; and sugar snap peas (2 to 3 pounds)

Ripe avocado (1)

Fresh chives (1 small bunch)

Fresh dill (2 sprigs)

Fresh tarragon (2 sprigs)

Shallot (1)

Garlic (1 clove)

Lemon (1)

Plain Greek yogurt (½ cup; we like 2%)

■ **FROM THE PANTRY**

Mayonnaise (¼ cup)

White wine vinegar (1 tablespoon)

Capers (1 teaspoon)

Dijon mustard (1 teaspoon)

Sea salt

Black pepper

mashed potato casserole
with spinach, carrots, and gruyère

6 servings

■ **FROM THE MARKET**

Russet potatoes (2 pounds)

Carrots (2 medium)

Whole milk (½ cup)

Unsalted butter
(2 tablespoons plus
1 teaspoon)

Gruyère cheese (4 ounces)

Parmesan cheese (1 ounce)

Frozen chopped spinach
(5 ounces)

■ **FROM THE PANTRY**

Kosher salt

Black pepper

We have a list of "oldies but goodies," recipes that are still favorites after many years. This delicious casserole rates high on that list.

2 tablespoons unsalted butter plus
    1 teaspoon to coat dish

4 cups peeled and diced russet
    potatoes, cut into 1-inch cubes

2 carrots, peeled, halved lengthwise,
    and cut into ¼-inch half-moons

Kosher salt

5 ounces frozen chopped spinach,
    thawed and drained

½ cup whole milk

Freshly ground black pepper

4 ounces Gruyère cheese, very
    thinly sliced

4 tablespoons freshly grated
    Parmesan cheese

Preheat the oven to 425°F. Butter a 9-inch baking dish or casserole.

Place the potatoes and carrots in a large pot; add water to cover by 2 inches and 1 tablespoon of salt. Bring to a boil and cook, partially covered, for 15 minutes. Add the spinach and cook until the potatoes can be pierced with a knife and the carrots are tender, 10 to 15 minutes more.

Drain the vegetables in a colander and return them to the pot. Turn the heat to low and stir to thoroughly dry the potatoes, about 5 minutes. Spoon them into a large mixing bowl and mash with a potato masher.

Combine the milk and the butter in a small saucepan and place over low heat. When the butter has melted, slowly stir this mixture into the potatoes. Add 2 teaspoons of salt and ¼ teaspoon of pepper and continue mashing until the vegetables are completely smooth.

Spread the vegetables in the baking dish. Cover with the Gruyère cheese, sprinkle with the Parmesan cheese and bake until the cheeses begin to brown, 20 to 25 minutes. Serve hot.

cheezy grits

4 to 6 servings

Whether they're hominy, stone ground, or just plain grits, the South's time-honored contribution to comfort food is one of our favorite sides at dinner.

Kosher salt

1 cup stone-ground or old-fashioned grits (not instant)

1 tablespoon unsalted butter

1¼ cups grated sharp cheddar cheese

½ cup freshly grated Parmesan cheese

Freshly ground black pepper

Pinch of ground nutmeg

Pinch of cayenne pepper

Fill a medium pot with 4 cups of water. Bring to a boil, add 1 teaspoon of salt, and very slowly stir in the grits. Reduce the heat to low and stir to make sure the grits don't stick to the bottom of the pot. Continue cooking, stirring frequently, until the water is absorbed and the grits are thick and soft, about 15 minutes.

Stir in the butter, cheddar cheese, Parmesan cheese, and a pinch each of black pepper, nutmeg, and cayenne. Mix until smooth and well blended. Remove from the heat and serve.

If you are not immediately serving the grits, after removing them from the heat, place a piece of wax paper directly on the surface to prevent a crust from forming. The grits may be kept warm this way for 20 to 30 minutes.

■ **FROM THE MARKET**

Stone-ground or old-fashioned (not instant) grits (1 cup)

Unsalted butter (1 tablespoon)

Sharp cheddar cheese (5 ounces)

Parmesan cheese (2 ounces)

■ **FROM THE PANTRY**

Kosher salt

Black pepper

Ground nutmeg (pinch)

Cayenne pepper (pinch)

jalapeño-flecked golden cornbread

8 to 10 servings

Our deliciously buttery cornbread has just a hint of heat and is a golden, moist perfection.

Organic olive oil cooking spray

1½ cups all-purpose flour

1 cup yellow cornmeal

2 teaspoons baking powder

¼ teaspoon baking soda

Kosher salt

¾ cup shredded sharp cheddar cheese

3 tablespoons light brown sugar

½ cup frozen corn kernels, thawed, or kernels from cooked fresh corn

1 cup buttermilk

2 large eggs

¼ cup seeded and finely chopped jalapeño chile

8 tablespoons (1 stick) butter, melted

Set a rack in the middle of the oven and preheat the oven to 400°F. Lightly spray an 8-inch square baking dish with cooking spray.

In a medium mixing bowl, combine the flour, cornmeal, baking powder, baking soda, ½ teaspoon of salt, and ½ cup of the cheddar cheese. Set aside.

In a blender or food processor, combine the brown sugar, corn, buttermilk, and eggs. Blend until smooth, 8 to 10 seconds. Pour the puree into the dry ingredients and mix with a wooden spoon or rubber spatula until just mixed through. Add the jalapeño. Slowly add the melted butter and stir until incorporated.

Pour the batter into the baking dish and sprinkle with the remaining ¼ cup of cheddar cheese. Bake until golden brown and a toothpick comes out clean, about 20 minutes.

Cool for 10 minutes. Loosen the sides of the pan with a knife. Invert the cornbread onto a cooling rack, then flip onto a platter and serve.

golden baby artichokes
with lemon zest

4 servings

We have a number of men in our lives who just refuse to eat artichokes—the thistles, the choke, scraping the meager "meat" off the leaves with your teeth—frankly, they think it's too much work for too little reward. Our golden sautéed baby artichokes are the answer. No one can resist these delectably satisfying whole bites.

¼ cup plus 1 teaspoon fresh
    lemon juice

2 pounds baby artichokes (about 9)

3 tablespoons extra virgin olive oil

3 small cloves garlic, sliced

1 teaspoon finely grated lemon zest

1 tablespoon finely chopped Italian
    (flat-leaf) parsley

Sea salt

Freshly ground black pepper

■ **FROM THE MARKET**

Baby artichokes
(2 pounds, about 9)

Italian (flat-leaf) parsley
(1 small bunch)

Garlic (3 small cloves)

Lemons (2)

■ **FROM THE PANTRY**

Extra virgin olive oil
(3 tablespoons)

Sea salt

Black pepper

Fill a large mixing bowl with cold water and add ¼ cup of the lemon juice. Peel off all the dark outer leaves of each artichoke until you reach the pale green inner leaves. (You might be tempted to leave some, but they will be too tough to eat.) Cut off the bottom ¼ inch of the stem, leaving the rest intact. With a vegetable peeler, remove the dark outer layer of the stem until you reach a pale green layer. Cut 1 inch off the top of the artichoke. Quarter the artichoke lengthwise and put it in the bowl of lemon water to keep it from turning brown. Repeat with the remaining artichokes.

Fill a large stockpot with water and bring to a boil. Drain the artichokes and add them to the pot. Boil until tender when pierced with a fork, 5 to 7 minutes. Drain in a colander and set aside.

Place a large skillet over medium-high heat and pour in the oil. When it is shimmering, add the artichokes and cook for 5 minutes. Add the garlic and

continue to cook, flipping the artichokes occasionally, until golden brown, 10 to 12 minutes more.

Sprinkle on the remaining teaspoon of lemon juice, the lemon zest, and parsley. Season with salt and pepper. Stir well and cook for 1 minute more. Serve hot.

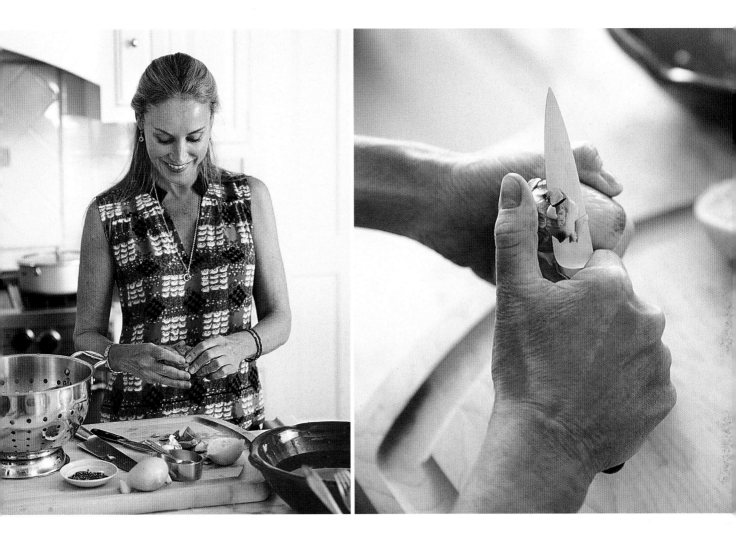

Food for Thought

The delectable artichoke holds an impressive source of nutrients. Artichokes have more antioxidants than any other vegetable, are loaded with vitamins and minerals, help to reduce bad cholesterol, are low in calories, and are fat free. And one artichoke has more fiber than a cup of prunes!

crispy garlic bread

6 servings

■ **FROM THE MARKET**

French or Italian bread
(1 long loaf)

Garlic (4 large cloves)

■ **FROM THE PANTRY**

Extra virgin olive oil
(⅓ cup)

Paprika (½ to 1 teaspoon)

This is a staple at big Pollan family get-togethers. Bread, olive oil, and garlic . . . need we say more?

1 long loaf French or Italian bread	⅓ cup extra virgin olive oil
4 large cloves garlic, minced	½ to 1 teaspoon paprika

Preheat the oven to 350°F.

Slice the bread in half horizontally. In a small mixing bowl, combine the garlic and oil. Using a pastry brush, spread the mixture onto the cut sides of the bread. Sprinkle a light dusting of paprika on the top of both halves.

With a serrated knife, make 1½-inch-wide cuts into the bread halves but do not cut all the way through. Place the two halves back together and wrap the bread in foil. Bake for 20 minutes.

Open the foil and arrange the two halves side by side. Cook for an additional 4 to 5 minutes, until the top is lightly browned and toasty. Cut the pieces all the way through and serve.

ROASTED VEGETABLES

IF YOU DON'T HAVE ALL OF THE INGREDIENTS FOR ANY ONE OF THESE ROASTING recipes, simply toss any vegetable you do have with olive oil, salt, and freshly ground black pepper and spread them on a rimmed baking sheet. Roast in a preheated 400°F or 425°F oven for 20 to 30 minutes, until nicely browned, flipping the vegetables once midway. The vegetables will caramelize and acquire a sweet and nutty flavor.

roasted broccoli with crisp garlic

4 servings

■ **FROM THE MARKET**

Broccoli (1 large head)

Garlic (2 large cloves)

■ **FROM THE PANTRY**

Extra virgin olive oil
(3 tablespoons)

Sea salt

Black pepper

1 large head broccoli, cut into medium florets

3 tablespoons extra virgin olive oil

2 large cloves garlic, sliced

Sea salt

Freshly ground black pepper

Preheat the oven to 400°F.

In a large mixing bowl, combine the broccoli, oil, garlic, ½ teaspoon of salt, and ⅛ teaspoon of pepper. Mix well with a wooden spoon until the broccoli is evenly coated with the oil.

Spread the broccoli and garlic on a rimmed baking sheet or in a large roasting pan. Roast until tender and beginning to brown on the edges, about 20 minutes. Season with salt and pepper. Serve hot.

brussels sprouts with pine nuts and dried cranberries

6 servings

2 pounds Brussels sprouts, trimmed and halved lengthwise

2 tablespoons extra virgin olive oil

Sea salt

Freshly ground black pepper

1 tablespoon raw pine nuts

1 tablespoon dried cranberries

■ FROM THE MARKET

Brussels sprouts (2 pounds)

Dried cranberries
(1 tablespoon)

■ FROM THE PANTRY

Extra virgin olive oil
(2 tablespoons)

Sea salt

Black pepper

Raw pine nuts
(1 tablespoon)

Preheat the oven to 425°F.

In a large mixing bowl, combine the Brussels sprouts, oil, ½ teaspoon of salt, and ¼ teaspoon of pepper. Mix well until the Brussels sprouts are evenly coated with the oil.

Spread the Brussels sprouts on a rimmed baking sheet and roast for 20 minutes. Flip them with a spatula and roast for another 15 minutes. Sprinkle with the pine nuts and cranberries and return them to the oven for an additional 5 minutes. The Brussels sprouts will be crisp and browned. Serve warm.

Food for Thought
Brussels sprouts are perfect little packages of vitamins, minerals, and cancer-fighting antioxidants. They contain the highest level of cancer preventive glucosinolates of all vegetables. An added benefit is that they are a potent natural detoxifier. Plus, they are very low in calories (only about 38 calories in 1 cup raw) and high in fiber (4 grams per cup).

crispy paprika-roasted potatoes

4 to 6 servings

1 tablespoon all-purpose flour

1½ teaspoons paprika

Sea salt

Freshly ground black pepper

2 pounds small potatoes (fingerlings or red or yellow new potatoes), scrubbed but not peeled, cut in half or 1-inch pieces

3 tablespoons extra virgin olive oil

■ FROM THE MARKET

Small potatoes such as fingerlings or red or yellow new potatoes (2 pounds)

■ FROM THE PANTRY

All-purpose flour (1 tablespoon)

Paprika (1½ teaspoons)

Sea salt

Black pepper

Extra virgin olive oil (3 tablespoons)

Preheat the oven to 425°F. Line a platter or serving bowl with paper towels.

In a small mixing bowl, mix the flour, paprika, 1 teaspoon of salt, and ¼ teaspoon of pepper. Set aside.

Place the potatoes in a large pot and add enough cold water to cover. Set over high heat, cover the pot, and bring to a boil. Cook, partially covered, until just fork-tender, about 10 minutes (do not overcook).

While the potatoes are boiling, pour the oil into a large baking dish or rimmed baking sheet. Place it in the hot oven.

Once the potatoes are cooked, drain them in a colander and return them to the pot. Pour the seasoned flour over the potatoes (no need to stir). Put the lid on the pot and, holding the cover securely in place with pot holders, shake vigorously until the potato edges become slightly ragged and the potatoes are coated with the flour.

Carefully remove the hot baking dish from the oven. Pour the potatoes in with care, because the oil will spatter. Use a wooden spoon to spread the potatoes into a single layer; there is no need to stir.

Roast undisturbed until the bottoms are golden brown, about 20 minutes. Flip the potatoes and roast for an additional 20 minutes. Transfer to the paper towel–lined platter and drain any excess oil. Remove the paper towels and serve hot.

roasted balsamic haricots verts with slivered almonds

4 to 6 servings

■ **FROM THE MARKET**

Haricots verts (or green beans) (1 pound)

■ **FROM THE PANTRY***

Extra virgin olive oil (2 tablespoons)

Sea salt

Black pepper

Balsamic Vinegar Glaze (2 teaspoons; page 269, or your favorite store-bought)

Slivered raw almonds (¼ cup)

*You will need parchment paper.

1 pound haricots verts (or green beans), ends trimmed

2 tablespoons extra virgin olive oil

Sea salt

Freshly ground black pepper

2 teaspoons Balsamic Vinegar Glaze (page 269, or your favorite store-bought)

¼ cup raw slivered almonds

Preheat the oven to 400°F. Line a rimmed baking sheet with parchment paper.

In a medium mixing bowl, combine the haricots verts with the oil, ½ teaspoon of salt, and ⅛ teaspoon of pepper. Mix well.

Arrange the haricots verts on the baking sheet in a single layer. Roast until lightly browned, about 15 minutes.

Remove the baking sheet from the oven, flip the haricots verts, and drizzle with the vinegar glaze. Scatter the almonds over the beans and return the baking sheet to the oven. Roast until the almonds begin to brown, about 5 minutes more. Serve warm.

crunchy oven-roasted fries

4 to 6 servings

Kosher salt

3 large russet potatoes

2 tablespoons extra virgin olive oil

Sea salt

■ **FROM THE MARKET**

Russet potatoes
(3 large, about 2 pounds)

■ **FROM THE PANTRY***

Kosher salt

Extra virgin olive oil
(2 tablespoons)

Sea salt

*You will need
parchment paper.

Preheat the oven to 450°F. Line a rimmed baking sheet with parchment paper. Fill a large mixing bowl with cold water and add 1 tablespoon of kosher salt.

Peel the potatoes and cut them into ¼-inch-thick strips, about 3 inches long. Soak the cut potatoes in the salted water for 10 minutes. Drain the potatoes and dry them completely with a clean dish towel.

Place the potatoes in a clean large mixing bowl and add the oil and ½ teaspoon of sea salt. Toss to coat them completely.

Arrange the potato strips on the parchment paper–lined baking sheet, spreading them to lie flat in a single layer. Roast for 20 minutes, until the bottoms begin to brown. Flip the potatoes with a spatula, rotate the pan in the oven, and roast until golden brown, about 10 minutes more.

Sprinkle with ½ teaspoon of sea salt and serve hot.

maple-balsamic root vegetable "fries"

4 to 6 servings

■ **FROM THE MARKET**

Carrots (3 large)

Celery root (1 medium, about 12 ounces)

Parsnips (2 medium, about 10 ounces)

Golden beets (2 medium, about 8 ounces)

Fresh thyme (1 small bunch)

■ **FROM THE PANTRY***

Extra virgin olive oil (2 tablespoons)

Pure maple syrup (1 tablespoon)

Balsamic vinegar (½ teaspoon)

Sea salt

Black pepper

*You will need two sheets of parchment paper.

3 large carrots, peeled and cut into ¼-inch-thick sticks, 2 to 3 inches long

1 medium celery root, peeled and cut into ¼-inch-thick sticks, 2 to 3 inches long

2 medium parsnips, peeled and cut into ¼-inch-thick sticks, 2 to 3 inches long

2 medium golden beets, peeled and each cut into 8 wedges

5 sprigs fresh thyme

2 tablespoons extra virgin olive oil

1 tablespoon pure maple syrup

½ teaspoon balsamic vinegar

Sea salt

Freshly ground black pepper

Set racks in the upper and lower thirds of the oven and preheat the oven to 425°F. Line two rimmed baking sheets with parchment paper.

In a large mixing bowl, combine the carrots, celery root, parsnips, beets, and thyme sprigs. Add the oil and mix to thoroughly coat the vegetables.

In a small mixing bowl, combine the maple syrup, vinegar, ½ teaspoon of salt, and ⅛ teaspoon of pepper; mix well. Pour the mixture on the vegetables and toss to coat.

Arrange the vegetables in single layers on the two baking sheets. Roast on separate racks for 20 minutes.

Remove them from the oven and, using a spatula, flip the vegetables. Return the sheets to the oven, switching their positions (upper rack and lower rack). Roast until the vegetables are light brown and caramelized, an additional 15 to 20 minutes.

Discard the thyme sprigs, season with salt and pepper, and serve.

roasted zucchini and cremini mushrooms with toasted parmesan

4 to 6 servings

■ FROM THE MARKET

Zucchini (4 small or
3 medium)

Cremini or baby bella
mushrooms (16 small)

Parmesan cheese
(2 ounces)

■ FROM THE PANTRY

Extra virgin olive oil
(1 tablespoon)

Kosher salt

Black pepper

4 small (or 3 medium) zucchini,
trimmed and cut into ½-inch-thick
rounds

16 small cremini or baby bella
mushrooms, stemmed

1 tablespoon extra virgin olive oil

Kosher salt

Freshly ground black pepper

½ cup freshly grated Parmesan
cheese

Set a rack in the middle of the oven and preheat the oven to 400°F. Place a wire
cooling rack on a rimmed baking sheet.

In a large mixing bowl, combine the zucchini, mushrooms, oil, ½ teaspoon of
salt, and ⅛ teaspoon of pepper. Toss until evenly coated.

Put the Parmesan cheese in a shallow bowl. Dip each vegetable piece, one at a
time, into the cheese, pressing to coat both the tops and bottoms.

Place the zucchini flat and mushrooms dome side up on the wire rack. Roast
until the cheese is golden brown, about 20 minutes. Arrange the vegetables on
a platter, alternating zucchini and mushrooms. Serve warm.

cauliflower with toasted breadcrumbs and parmesan

4 to 6 servings

1 head cauliflower, cut into
   2-inch florets

2½ tablespoons extra virgin olive oil

Sea salt

Freshly ground black pepper

1 large clove garlic, minced

¼ cup plain Breadcrumbs (page 264,
   or your favorite store-bought)

1 tablespoon plus 1 teaspoon chopped
   Italian (flat-leaf) parsley

¼ cup freshly grated Parmesan
   cheese

■ **FROM THE MARKET**

Cauliflower (1 head)

Italian (flat-leaf) parsley
(1 small bunch)

Garlic (1 large clove)

Parmesan cheese (1 ounce)

■ **FROM THE PANTRY**

Extra virgin olive oil
(2½ tablespoons)

Sea salt

Black pepper

Plain Breadcrumbs (¼ cup;
page 264, or your favorite
store-bought)

Preheat the oven to 425°F.

Place the cauliflower on a rimmed baking sheet. Add 1½ tablespoons of the oil, ½ teaspoon of salt, and ⅛ teaspoon of pepper and toss to coat. Spread the florets in a single layer on the baking sheet. Roast for 15 minutes.

Meanwhile, in a small skillet over medium-low heat, combine the remaining 1 tablespoon of oil and the garlic. Cook, stirring, until fragrant, 2 to 3 minutes. Add the breadcrumbs and 1 tablespoon of parsley. Continue to cook until the breadcrumbs turn golden, about 3 minutes. Set aside to cool for 3 to 4 minutes, then add the Parmesan cheese.

After the cauliflower has roasted for 15 minutes, remove the baking sheet from the oven; flip the cauliflower and sprinkle on the breadcrumb-cheese mixture. Return the cauliflower to the oven and roast until golden brown, an additional 10 to 15 minutes.

Season with salt and pepper, sprinkle with the remaining chopped parsley, and serve.

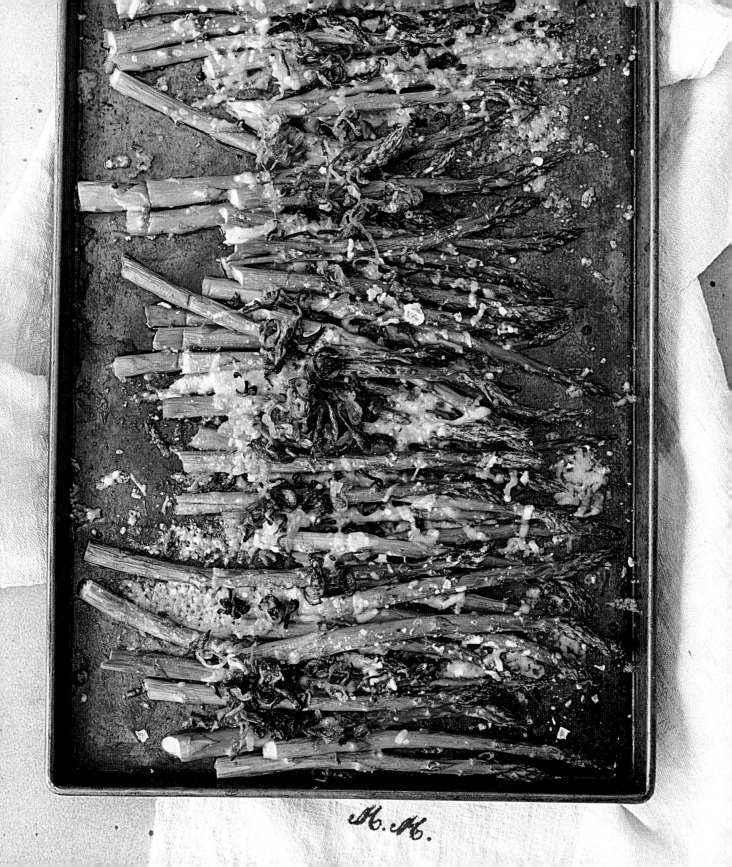

asparagus with parmesan and frizzled shallots

6 servings

■ FROM THE MARKET

Asparagus (2 pounds)

Shallots (5 large)

Parmesan cheese
(2 ounces)

■ FROM THE PANTRY

Extra virgin olive oil
(1½ tablespoons)

Safflower oil (¼ cup)

Kosher salt

Black pepper

2 pounds asparagus

1½ tablespoons extra virgin olive oil

Kosher salt

Freshly ground black pepper

¼ cup safflower oil

2 cups very thinly sliced shallots,
separated into rings

½ cup shredded Parmesan cheese

Preheat the oven to 400°F. Line a plate with paper towels.

Remove the coarse ends of the asparagus by bending each spear at the bottom until it snaps at its natural breaking point. Discard the ends and place the stalks on a rimmed baking sheet. Drizzle with the olive oil, season with ½ teaspoon of salt and ⅛ teaspoon of pepper, and toss to coat. Arrange the asparagus in a single layer on the baking sheet.

Roast the asparagus until tender, 15 to 20 minutes for thick asparagus, 12 to 15 minutes for thin.

Meanwhile, heat the safflower oil in a medium nonstick skillet over medium heat until shimmering. Add the shallots and sauté until they are golden brown and crispy, 10 to 12 minutes, taking care not to burn. Using a slotted spoon, transfer to the paper towel–lined plate and set aside.

Sprinkle the asparagus with the Parmesan cheese, place back in the oven, and roast until the cheese has melted, 3 to 5 minutes. Arrange the asparagus on a serving platter and scatter with the frizzled shallots. Serve hot.

Food for Thought
Just 6 spears of asparagus give you 50 percent of your daily potassium requirement, and–pregnant women take note–33 percent of your daily folic acid needs.

---

roasted corn on the cob with herbs and spices

6 servings

6 ears fresh corn, husks and silk removed

½ teaspoon herbes de Provence, or a mix of dried herbs

⅛ teaspoon cayenne pepper

½ teaspoon paprika

Sea salt

Freshly ground black pepper

2 tablespoons unsalted butter, at room temperature

■ FROM THE MARKET

Fresh corn (6 ears)

Unsalted butter (2 tablespoons)

■ FROM THE PANTRY

Herbes de Provence (½ teaspoon) or a mix of dried herbs

Cayenne pepper (⅛ teaspoon)

Paprika (½ teaspoon)

Sea salt

Black pepper

Preheat the oven to 400°F. Tear off six sheets of aluminum foil, each big enough to wrap an ear of corn.

In a small mixing bowl, combine the herbs, cayenne pepper, paprika, ½ teaspoon of salt, and ⅛ teaspoon of pepper.

Place each ear on a sheet of aluminum foil. Spread all over with butter and sprinkle on the seasoning mix to lightly coat. Tightly wrap the corn in the foil and place on the middle rack of the oven. Roast for 25 minutes. Serve hot.

TIP: To remove silk from an ear of corn, wipe the ear with a dampened paper towel.

it's easier than you think

homemade sauces,
dressings, and other
culinary basics made easy

pollan signature salad dressing

caramelized walnuts

breadcrumbs

croutons

basil pesto

perfect marinara sauce

balsamic vinegar glaze

terrific teriyaki glaze

GROCERY AISLES ARE CHOCK-FULL OF PACKAGED SAUCES AND DRESSINGS, and although their convenience is tempting, these kitchen fundamentals are much easier to prepare than you think, and when homemade, they take all dishes up a few notches. By making and storing these basics, you'll not only save money, you'll also lose calories, additives, preservatives, fat, salt, and sugar. Once you start making these tastier, healthier versions yourself, you won't go back.

We like to make these recipes ahead in double or triple batches—and then freeze or store in convenient serving-size containers to be used at future meals. Or, if you are preparing immediately for one of our recipes, double up and save a batch to store in your pantry, refrigerator, or freezer. Below we tell you how to store them. Remember to label and date them before storing.

POLLAN SIGNATURE SALAD DRESSING— Make a double batch to use throughout the week. If not using right away, store it in the refrigerator in a mason jar. Take it out of the refrigerator as you are preparing your meal and let it come to room temperature. Shake well before using.

CARAMELIZED WALNUTS— Once cool, store in an airtight container for 3 to 4 weeks.

BREADCRUMBS— Keep in the freezer in a large plastic bag or an airtight container for up to 6 months. There is no need to thaw before you use them.

CROUTONS— Let them cool completely before storing in an airtight container or plastic bag. They last 1 to 2 weeks unrefrigerated and 4 to 6 months in the freezer.

BASIL PESTO— This will last for 5 to 7 days in the refrigerator and up to 6 months in the freezer. We like to freeze pesto sauce in an ice cube tray and then just pop out the desired amount as needed.

PERFECT MARINARA SAUCE— Divide this sauce into separate serving-size containers and freeze for 4 to 6 months.

BALSAMIC VINEGAR GLAZE — Let cool and store in an airtight container in the refrigerator for up to 2 months. Bring to room temperature before using, as it may solidify slightly.

TERRIFIC TERIYAKI GLAZE — Store in an airtight jar or container in the refrigerator for up to 1 week or freeze for up to 1 month. If it thickens too much, add a little hot water to loosen.

pollan signature salad dressing

makes about ¾ cup

■ **FROM THE PANTRY**

White balsamic vinegar
(⅓ cup)

Raspberry vinegar,
champagne vinegar,
or sherry vinegar
(1 tablespoon)

Dijon mustard
(1½ teaspoons)

Grapeseed oil (⅓ cup)

Extra virgin olive oil
(2 tablespoons)

Sea salt

Black pepper

⅓ cup white balsamic vinegar

1 tablespoon raspberry vinegar,
champagne vinegar, or sherry
vinegar

1½ teaspoons Dijon mustard

⅓ cup grapeseed oil

2 tablespoons extra virgin olive oil

Sea salt

Freshly ground black pepper

In a glass jar with a tightly fitting lid or in a mixing bowl, combine the vinegars, mustard, oils, ⅛ teaspoon of salt, and a pinch of pepper. Shake the jar vigorously or whisk to emulsify. Store in the refrigerator for up to 1 week.

caramelized walnuts

makes 1 cup

1 cup raw walnut halves   3 tablespoons granulated sugar

■ FROM THE PANTRY*

Raw walnut halves (1 cup)

Granulated sugar
(3 tablespoons)

*You will need wax paper or
parchment paper.

Line a plate or work surface with wax or parchment paper.

Place a large nonstick skillet over medium-high heat. Add the walnuts and sugar and stir continuously with a wooden spoon. After about 3 minutes the sugar will begin to melt. Keep stirring until the sugar turns caramel brown and the nuts are golden and toasted, an additional 1 to 2 minutes. Remove from the heat immediately (they can burn quickly) and spread on the wax or parchment paper, using the wooden spoon to separate them at once. Let cool completely.

Break the walnuts apart with your fingers. Store in an airtight container and they will last for 3 to 4 weeks.

TIP: To clean the candy coating off your skillet, simply add water to it, bring the water to a boil, and stir with your wooden spoon. The caramelized sugar will dissolve.

breadcrumbs

■ **FROM THE PANTRY**

Leftover bread of any kind, such as peasant loaf, baguette, white, or whole wheat

Leftover bread

Preheat the oven to 350°F.

Tear or cut bread into 2-inch chunks. Place the bread on a rimmed baking sheet and toast in the oven for 10 to 15 minutes, until most of the cubes are hard and crispy. Transfer to a food processor or blender. Process until the crumbs reach your desired coarseness.

Store in an airtight container or sealed freezer bag. The breadcrumbs will last in the freezer for months. No need to thaw before using.

croutons

4 cups

■ **FROM THE MARKET**

Bread, peasant, baguette, or multigrain (½ loaf; fresh or day-old)

Garlic (2 cloves)

■ **FROM THE PANTRY**

Extra virgin olive oil (2 tablespoons)

½ loaf bread (peasant, baguette, or multigrain, fresh or day-old), cut into 1-inch cubes (about 4 cups)

2 tablespoons extra virgin olive oil

2 cloves garlic, minced

Preheat the oven to 350°F.

In a large mixing bowl, combine the bread, oil, and garlic and mix together (hands work best for this) until the bread is coated. Spread the bread out on a rimmed baking sheet and bake until golden brown and toasted, about 25 minutes, flipping with a spatula halfway through.

Allow to cool to room temperature. Croutons may be stored in a sealed plastic bag or airtight container for up to 2 weeks or frozen for 4 to 6 months.

basil pesto

makes about 2 cups

2 large cloves garlic, lightly crushed

2 cups tightly packed fresh basil leaves

3 tablespoons raw pine nuts

Kosher salt

Freshly ground black pepper

½ cup extra virgin olive oil plus
   2 to 3 tablespoons if storing

½ cup freshly grated Parmesan
   cheese

2 tablespoons freshly grated
   Pecorino Romano cheese

■ FROM THE MARKET

Fresh basil leaves
(1 large bunch)

Garlic (2 large cloves)

Parmesan cheese
(2 ounces)

Pecorino Romano cheese
(1 ounce)

■ FROM THE PANTRY

Raw pine nuts
(3 tablespoons)

Kosher salt

Black pepper

Extra virgin olive oil
(½ cup plus 2 to
3 tablespoons if storing)

In a food processor or blender, combine the garlic, basil leaves, pine nuts, 1 teaspoon of salt, ⅛ teaspoon of pepper, and ½ cup of the oil. Pulse until coarsely chopped. Scrape down the sides with a rubber spatula, add the Parmesan and Pecorino Romano cheeses, and pulse again until smooth and evenly blended, 3 to 4 minutes.

If storing for later use, transfer the pesto to an airtight container and layer with a coating of 2 to 3 tablespoons of oil. Refrigerate until needed, 5 to 7 days, or freeze for up to 6 months.

perfect marinara sauce

makes about 6 cups

¼ cup extra virgin olive oil

1 medium Spanish or yellow onion,
chopped

2 cloves garlic, minced

½ carrot, peeled and finely chopped

Two 28-ounce cans crushed tomatoes
with juice

6 fresh basil leaves, torn

2 teaspoons chopped Italian
(flat-leaf) parsley

1 tablespoon tomato paste

¼ teaspoon garlic powder

1 teaspoon granulated sugar

Kosher salt

Freshly ground black pepper

½ cup red wine

Heat the oil in a large saucepan over medium heat. Add the onion and garlic and sauté until the onion is translucent, about 10 minutes.

Add the carrot and cook until tender, 5 to 7 minutes.

Pour in the tomatoes and their juice and stir. Add the basil, parsley, tomato paste, garlic powder, sugar, 1 teaspoon of salt, ½ teaspoon of pepper, and the wine. Increase the heat to high and stir for 5 minutes.

Reduce the heat to low and simmer for a minimum of 30 minutes or up to 1 hour, stirring every so often; the longer it cooks, the better it tastes. This may be frozen for 4 to 6 months.

balsamic vinegar glaze

makes ⅓ to ½ cup

1 cup good-quality balsamic vinegar   1 teaspoon dark brown sugar

■ FROM THE PANTRY

Balsamic vinegar,
good-quality (1 cup)

Dark brown sugar
(1 teaspoon)

In a nonreactive saucepan, bring the vinegar to a boil over medium-high heat. Stir in the sugar and reduce the heat to low. Simmer uncovered until the vinegar is reduced by half, is syrupy, and coats the back of a spoon when stirred, 15 to 20 minutes. Be careful not to cook for too long or the glaze may burn.

The glaze will continue to thicken as it cools. Once cool, pour it into an airtight container and store in the refrigerator for up to 2 months.

terrific teriyaki glaze

makes ¾ cup

■ **FROM THE MARKET**

Fresh ginger (1 knob)

Garlic (2 small cloves)

■ **FROM THE PANTRY**

Sesame seeds (1 teaspoon; optional)

Cornstarch (1 teaspoon)

Low-sodium soy sauce (½ cup)

Mirin (2 tablespoons)

Dark brown sugar (2 tablespoons)

Sesame oil (1 teaspoon)

1 teaspoon sesame seeds (optional)

1 teaspoon cornstarch

½ cup low-sodium soy sauce

2 tablespoons mirin

2 tablespoons dark brown sugar

1 teaspoon minced garlic

1 teaspoon finely grated fresh ginger

1 teaspoon sesame oil

If using sesame seeds, cook them in a small dry skillet over medium heat, shaking the pan occasionally, until they begin to darken and give off a toasty aroma, 2 to 3 minutes. Transfer the seeds to a small plate and set aside.

In a small mixing bowl, mix the cornstarch with 2 teaspoons of warm water. Set aside.

In a small saucepan, combine the soy sauce, mirin, brown sugar, garlic, ginger, and ⅓ cup of water. Place over medium-high heat and stir occasionally until the sauce comes to a low boil. Reduce the heat to medium and add the dissolved cornstarch. Continue stirring until the sauce thickens, about 5 minutes. Remove from the heat and add the sesame oil and the sesame seeds, if desired.

Use with your favorite teriyaki recipe. Store in the refrigerator for up to 1 week or freeze for up to 1 month.

desserts

grandma mary's grand marnier
orange cake

grandma mary's mandelbrot cookies

aunt joyce's chocolate walnut
meringue cookies

sam's applesauce spice cookies

aquinnah and schuyler's chocolate cream pie
with chocolate graham cracker crust

jack's brownie cookie ice cream
sandwiches

esmé's s'mores cookies

savannah's fudge and pecan-filled
vanilla cookies

hallie's mixed berry pie

mack and cam's mini pecan tarts

micaela's nirvana bars

isaac's mexican wedding cookies

nana fox's oatmeal cookies

raspberry pudding cake

streusel-topped apple cake

crispy crunchy apple crumble

key lime pie with walnut
oatmeal crust

caramelized peaches à la
mode with raspberry sauce

nectarine blueberry cobbler
with praline crumble

NOTHING COMPARES TO THE LUSCIOUS, ENVELOPING AROMAS OF HOMEMADE desserts; the smells of cinnamon, warm fruit, caramelized sugar, melting chocolate, or toasted nuts emanating from the kitchen sets mouths to watering.

Each one of us made our first forays into cooking and into the kitchen through baking. For children, baking dessert has immediate appeal: It's a science project, it's an art project, and it's a little bit of alchemy. Mix a bunch of seemingly random ingredients and what comes out of the oven is crunchy or moist, sweet and delicious.

Baking is how each of us came to love the kitchen and it's how all of our children have begun to embrace the joys of cooking. Our grandmothers taught us how to make their favorite desserts, beginning with Tzena, then Mary, and now Corky, each with a gathering of children mixing and measuring alongside them.

Some of the recipes that follow go back three or four generations and they have stood the test of time. Other recipes are more recent creations. Each of the grandchildren has contributed one of their favorites to this section, either a recipe that they have conceived or one that they have updated and improved on, to make it his or her own.

grandma mary's grand marnier orange cake

makes one 10-inch Bundt cake (10 to 12 servings)

■ **FROM THE MARKET**

Juice orange (1)

Unsalted butter
(½ pound, or 2 sticks, plus
extra for greasing pan)

Large eggs (3)

Plain 2% Greek yogurt
(1 cup)

**Grand Marnier or other
orange liqueur** (⅓ cup or
2 mini bottles)

■ **FROM THE PANTRY***

Sliced blanched almonds
(3 tablespoons)

All-purpose flour (2 cups)

Baking soda (1 teaspoon)

Baking powder (1 teaspoon)

Granulated sugar (1½ cups)

Raw walnuts (1¼ cups)

*You will need
 parchment paper.

This was our Grandmother Mary's sophisticated version of the traditional Jewish nut cake—but just as easy to make. I was a waitress for many summers on Martha's Vineyard, and one summer I was also a dessert "chef"—this cake would sell out immediately whenever I baked it. I have fine-tuned Mary's recipe over the years—replacing the sour cream with Greek yogurt, doubling the nuts, and cooking the glaze.—LORI

½ pound (2 sticks) unsalted butter, at room temperature, plus extra for greasing pan

3 tablespoons sliced blanched almonds

2 cups all-purpose flour

1 teaspoon baking soda

1 teaspoon baking powder

1½ cups granulated sugar

3 large eggs, separated

1 cup plain 2% Greek yogurt

1 tablespoon finely grated orange zest

1 cup chopped raw walnuts

⅓ cup Grand Marnier or other orange liqueur

¼ cup freshly squeezed orange juice

Set a rack in the middle of the oven and preheat the oven to 350°F. Butter a 10-inch Bundt or tube pan.

Spread the almonds on a rimmed baking sheet. Bake until they are toasted and fragrant, 3 to 5 minutes. Let cool on the pan. Leave the oven on.

In a medium mixing bowl, sift together the flour, baking soda, and baking powder. Set aside. In a large mixing bowl, using a wooden spoon, cream the butter and 1 cup of the sugar until light and fluffy. Add the egg yolks and beat until blended. Alternate adding thirds of the flour mixture and the yogurt and mix until smooth. Stir in the orange zest and walnuts.

(recipe continues)

Using an electric hand mixer or a stand mixer, whisk the egg whites until they are stiff but not dry, about 2 minutes. Gently fold the egg whites into the batter until incorporated.

Pour the batter into the pan, smoothing the top. Bake, rotating the pan halfway through, until the cake is golden brown and a cake tester inserted in the center of the cake comes out clean, 45 to 50 minutes. Allow the cake to cool in the pan for 7 to 10 minutes.

While the cake is cooling, combine the Grand Marnier and orange juice in a small saucepan over medium heat and bring to a simmer. Add the remaining $1/2$ cup of sugar and stir for 2 minutes, until well blended. Remove from the heat.

Line a rimmed baking sheet with parchment paper and place a wire cooling rack on top.

Invert the cake onto the wire cooling rack and spoon half the glaze over the top of the cake. Sprinkle the sliced almonds on top, then spoon on the remaining glaze. Transfer the cake to a serving plate and spoon any glaze drippings that have pooled on the parchment paper back onto the cake.

grandma mary's mandelbrot cookies

makes about 4 dozen cookies

This is our favorite recipe of our grandmother's and the first one she taught us to make. Yiddish for "almond bread," mandelbrot is the Jewish version of biscotti. Because these cookies are twice-baked, they are crisp and crunchy—and highly addictive. Delicious served with coffee, tea, and dessert wine for dunking—or as Grandma Mary sometimes did, eaten for breakfast.

1 cup blanched slivered almonds

1 cup plus 1 tablespoon chopped raw walnuts

3¼ cups all-purpose flour plus extra for flouring the work surface

1 teaspoon baking powder

¼ teaspoon kosher salt

4 large eggs

1¼ cups plus 2 tablespoons granulated sugar

½ cup canola oil

1 teaspoon pure vanilla extract

½ teaspoon almond extract

¾ teaspoon ground cinnamon

1 cup golden raisins

1 large egg white

■ **FROM THE MARKET**

Large eggs (5)

Golden raisins (1 cup)

Almond extract (½ teaspoon)

■ **FROM THE PANTRY***

Blanched slivered almonds (1 cup)

Raw walnuts (1¼ cups plus 2 tablespoons)

All-purpose flour (3¼ cups plus extra for flouring the work surface)

Baking powder (1 teaspoon)

Kosher salt

Granulated sugar (1¼ cups plus 2 tablespoons)

Organic canola oil (½ cup)

Pure vanilla extract (1 teaspoon)

Ground cinnamon (¾ teaspoon)

*You will need parchment paper.

Set a rack in the middle of the oven and preheat the oven to 350°F.

Spread the almonds and 1 cup of the walnuts on a rimmed baking sheet. Bake until they are toasted and fragrant, 5 to 7 minutes. Let cool on the pan. Leave the oven on.

In a medium mixing bowl, sift together 3 cups of the flour, the baking powder, and salt. Set aside. In a large mixing bowl, whisk together the 4 eggs and 1¼ cups of the sugar. Whisk in the oil, vanilla, almond extract, and ¼ teaspoon of the cinnamon. Gradually stir in the flour mixture, blending with a wooden spoon. Fold in the toasted nuts and the raisins. The dough should be soft and workable but not sticky. If it is sticky, add more flour, a tablespoon at a time, not to exceed ¼ cup. (You can also cover and refrigerate the dough for 20 minutes

to 1 hour to make it more workable. If you do, turn off the oven now and turn it back on when you are about to shape the dough.)

Finely chop the remaining 1 tablespoon of walnuts. Put them in a small mixing bowl and add the remaining 2 tablespoons of sugar and ½ teaspoon of ground cinnamon.

Line a rimmed baking sheet with parchment paper.

Transfer the dough to a floured work surface and divide it into thirds. Dampen your hands with cold water and shape each piece into a log about 3 inches wide and 12 inches long. Place the logs on the parchment paper–lined baking sheet, leaving 3 inches between them. Use your hands to even the sides of the logs, creating long rectangles.

Whisk the egg white in a small mixing bowl to make an egg wash. Brush the egg wash onto the top of each log. Sprinkle each with a third of the cinnamon sugar–walnut blend, about 1 tablespoon each.

Bake until golden and firm to the touch, about 35 minutes. Remove from the oven but leave the oven on. Let the loaves cool slightly, only 3 to 5 minutes. (Do not let the loaves cool too long or the slices will crumble when you cut them.)

Transfer the loaves to a cutting board. Using a serrated knife, cut each on the diagonal into ½-inch slices. Arrange the cookies in a single layer on two ungreased rimmed baking sheets, cut side down.

Set racks in the upper and lower thirds of the oven and place one pan on each. Bake until lightly toasted, 5 to 7 minutes. Flip the pieces and rotate the sheets top to bottom and front to back to ensure even baking. Bake for an additional 5 to 7 minutes, until toasted on the second side.

Transfer the cookies to wire cooling racks and let them cool completely. Store in an airtight container.

aunt joyce's chocolate walnut meringue cookies

makes 1½ dozen cookies

■ **FROM THE MARKET**

Large eggs (2)

Cream of tartar
(⅛ teaspoon)

■ **FROM THE PANTRY***

Semisweet chocolate chips
(1 cup)

Kosher salt

Pure vanilla extract
(1 teaspoon)

Granulated sugar (½ cup)

Raw walnuts (1¼ cups)

*You will need
parchment paper.

Our Aunt Joyce has an insatiable sweet tooth and is a fabulous baker. When it came time to gather our favorite dessert recipes, we naturally turned to her. Her meringue cookies are a cinch to make. They are light, chocolaty, and deliciously nutty.

1 cup semisweet chocolate chips

2 large egg whites, at room temperature

⅛ teaspoon kosher salt

⅛ teaspoon cream of tartar

1 teaspoon pure vanilla extract

½ cup granulated sugar

1 cup chopped raw walnuts

Set racks in the upper and lower thirds of the oven and preheat the oven to 325°F. Line two baking sheets with parchment paper.

Place the chocolate chips in a small microwave-safe bowl. Melt the chocolate for 15 seconds at a time until soft. (Or use a double boiler.) Stir until smooth. Cool the chocolate until lukewarm, about 10 minutes.

Using an electric hand mixer or a stand mixer, beat the egg whites and salt until frothy. Add the cream of tartar and vanilla and beat again until soft peaks form. Continue beating, adding the sugar gradually, about 1 tablespoon at a time, until the mixture holds stiff peaks.

Using a rubber spatula, gently fold the melted chocolate into the egg whites. Gradually add the walnuts and fold until just combined.

Drop the batter onto the baking sheets by rounded teaspoonfuls, 2 inches apart. Bake for 14 to 16 minutes until the tops have cracked and the centers look somewhat dry. Allow the cookies to cool on the baking sheets for 10 minutes, then transfer them to a wire cooling rack to finish cooling. Store in an airtight container.

sam's applesauce spice cookies

makes 20 cookies

When I was in elementary school, once a week my second-grade teacher would assign "make your own homework," an opportunity to do or create pretty much anything. At first this free-form assignment seemed daunting, but I struck gold when I developed this recipe for delicious, soft, and cakey applesauce cookies, and was soon making a batch a week for my classmates. They remain an easy A and my go-to cookie for any occasion.—SAM

FOR THE COOKIES

8 tablespoons (1 stick) unsalted butter, at room temperature

1 cup lightly packed dark brown sugar

1 large egg

1 teaspoon pure vanilla extract

1 cup organic unsweetened applesauce

2 cups all-purpose flour

1 teaspoon baking soda

¼ teaspoon kosher salt

1 teaspoon ground nutmeg

1 teaspoon ground cloves

1 teaspoon ground cinnamon

FOR THE SPICE GLAZE

1 cup confectioners' sugar

¼ teaspoon ground cinnamon

■ **FROM THE MARKET**

Unsalted butter
(8 tablespoons, or 1 stick)

Large egg (1)

Organic unsweetened
applesauce (1 cup)

Ground cloves (1 teaspoon)

■ **FROM THE PANTRY***

Dark brown sugar (1 cup)

Pure vanilla extract
(1 teaspoon)

All-purpose flour (2 cups)

Baking soda (1 teaspoon)

Kosher salt

Ground nutmeg (1 teaspoon)

Ground cinnamon
(1¼ teaspoons)

Confectioners' sugar (1 cup)

*You will need
parchment paper.

FOR THE COOKIES

Set a rack in the middle of the oven and preheat the oven to 350°F. Line a baking sheet with parchment paper.

Put the butter and brown sugar into a large mixing bowl. Using an electric hand mixer or a fork, cream until smooth. Add the egg and vanilla and beat until light and fluffy. Mix in the applesauce.

In a separate mixing bowl, combine the flour, baking soda, salt, nutmeg, cloves, and 1 teaspoon cinnamon. Add to the wet ingredients and mix until well blended.

(recipe continues)

Drop rounded tablespoons of batter onto the baking sheet about 1½ inches apart. Bake, rotating the sheet halfway through, until lightly browned around the edges, 10 to 12 minutes.

FOR THE SPICE GLAZE
While the cookies are baking, combine the confectioners' sugar and 2 tablespoons of warm water in a small mixing bowl; mix to dissolve any lumps. Add ¼ teaspoon of cinnamon and mix again until completely smooth.

Line a baking sheet with aluminum foil and place a wire cooling rack on the foil (to catch the drippings from the glaze). Transfer the cookies to the cooling rack.

Using a pastry brush, brush the glaze over the entire surface of each cookie while they are still warm. Once the cookies have cooled completely and the glaze has dried, store them in an airtight container.

aquinnah and schuyler's chocolate cream pie with chocolate graham cracker crust

makes one 9-inch pie (6 to 8 servings)

■ **FROM THE MARKET**

Unsalted butter
(½ pound, or 2 sticks,
plus 5 tablespoons)

Large eggs (4)

Heavy cream (¾ cup)

Chocolate graham crackers
(10 to 12 full cracker sheets)
or chocolate bear or bunny
grahams (5½ ounces)

**Semisweet baking
chocolate** (4½ ounces)

■ **FROM THE PANTRY**

Granulated sugar
(3 tablespoons)

Kosher salt

Confectioners' sugar
(2 cups)

Pure vanilla extract
(2 teaspoons)

The first thing Grammy, Corky, taught us how to bake was her chocolate cream pie. We come from a family of chocolate fanatics, so this recipe is definitely a favorite. Our Thanksgiving dinners are never complete without this treat. Most chocolate cream pies have bittersweet chocolate, but we use semisweet to give it a lighter, more sugary taste.—AQUINNAH AND SCHUYLER

FOR THE CRUST

1½ cups finely crushed chocolate
graham crackers (10 to 12 full
sheets) or chocolate bear or bunny
grahams (5½ ounces)

2 tablespoons granulated sugar

¼ teaspoon kosher salt

5 tablespoons unsalted butter, melted

FOR THE FILLING

4 large eggs (see Raw Egg Warning,
page 287)

½ pound (2 sticks) unsalted butter,
at room temperature

4 ounces semisweet baking chocolate
(4 squares), melted and cooled

2 cups sifted confectioners' sugar

2 teaspoons pure vanilla extract

FOR THE TOPPING

¾ cup very cold heavy cream

1 tablespoon granulated sugar

½ ounce semisweet baking chocolate
(½ square), shaved into strips with a
vegetable peeler

Set a rack in the middle of the oven and preheat the oven to 350°F.

FOR THE CRUST

Mix the graham cracker crumbs, 2 tablespoons of sugar, the salt, and 5 tablespoons of butter in a mixing bowl until well blended. Press evenly on the bottom and sides of a 9-inch pie pan. Bake, rotating the pan halfway through, until dry to the touch, 8 to 10 minutes. Remove from the oven and set aside to cool.

FOR THE FILLING

Place the eggs in a mixing bowl and, using a stand mixer or an electric hand mixer, beat until the yolks and whites are combined. Mix in ½ pound of butter and the cooled melted chocolate. Very slowly add the confectioners' sugar and mix to combine. Raise the speed to high and beat for 2 minutes, until thoroughly blended. Add the vanilla and continue beating on high speed for an additional 3 minutes or until the mixture thickens. Spoon the filling into the pie shell and refrigerate.

FOR THE TOPPING

Pour the heavy cream into a mixing bowl and, using a stand mixer or an electric hand mixer, beat on high speed until soft peaks appear. Add 1 tablespoon of sugar and continue beating on high speed until firm peaks form. Refrigerate until needed.

When you're ready to serve, spread the whipped cream on top of the pie and garnish with the shaved chocolate.

TIP: To speed up the whipping process, place the bowl and the beaters in the freezer 30 minutes or so before making the whipped cream.

RAW EGG WARNING: To reduce the slight risk of salmonella or other food-borne illness we recommend you use only fresh, properly refrigerated, clean grade A or AA eggs with intact shells, and avoid contact between the yolks or whites and the outer shell.

jack's brownie cookie ice cream sandwiches

makes 2 dozen cookies or 12 sandwiches

There is nothing like finding homemade treats in your freezer. I love to bake these brownie sandwich cookies because of their versatility and unmatchable deliciousness. Almost anything tastes good sandwiched between these rich, strongly chocolaty cookies—whipped cream, buttercream, raspberry jam, hazelnut spread—allowing me to experiment or to stick with the classic ice cream sandwich on hot summer days.—JACK

½ cup all-purpose flour

¼ teaspoon baking powder

2 tablespoons Dutch process cocoa powder

1½ cups good-quality semisweet chocolate chips

4 tablespoons (½ stick) unsalted butter, at room temperature

½ cup granulated sugar

¼ cup packed light brown sugar

1½ teaspoons pure vanilla extract

2 teaspoons Kahlúa, or 1 teaspoon instant espresso mixed with one teaspoon hot water

2 large eggs

¼ teaspoon kosher salt

1½ cups vanilla ice cream or vanilla frozen yogurt

■ **FROM THE MARKET**

Large eggs (2)

Unsalted butter (4 tablespoons, or ½ stick)

Dutch process cocoa powder (2 tablespoons)

Vanilla ice cream or frozen yogurt (1½ cups)

Kahlúa or other coffee liqueur (2 teaspoons), or instant espresso powder (1 teaspoon)

■ **FROM THE PANTRY***

All-purpose flour (½ cup)

Baking powder (¼ teaspoon)

Semisweet chocolate chips, good-quality (1½ cups)

Granulated sugar (½ cup)

Light brown sugar (¼ cup)

Pure vanilla extract (1½ teaspoons)

Kosher salt

*You will need parchment paper.

In a medium mixing bowl, sift together the flour, baking powder, and cocoa powder. Mix well and set aside.

Melt the chocolate chips in the microwave, 15 seconds at a time, for about 2 minutes total. (You can also use a double boiler or a metal or glass bowl set over simmering water.) Pour the melted chocolate into a large mixing bowl and add the butter, granulated sugar, brown sugar, vanilla, and Kahlúa. Mix well. Allow to cool slightly, 3 to 5 minutes.

(recipe continues)

In a small mixing bowl, gently whisk the eggs together. Add the eggs and salt to the chocolate mixture and stir until blended. Fold in the dry ingredients, mixing well. Cover and refrigerate until the dough is chilled and firm enough to shape into balls, at least 30 minutes.

Set racks in the upper and lower thirds of the oven and preheat the oven to 350°F. Line two baking sheets with parchment paper.

Form the dough into 1½- to 2-inch balls and place on the baking sheets about 2 inches apart. Press down on each ball with the palm of your hand to form a disk about ⅓ inch thick. Bake until the tops are cracked but the cookies are still soft, 12 to 13 minutes. To ensure even baking, rotate the pans top to bottom and front to back halfway through.

Allow the cookies to cool on the baking sheets for about 5 minutes, then transfer them to a wire cooling rack to finish cooling.

When the cookies are completely cool, spread a small scoop of ice cream onto the bottom of one cookie and top with another cookie, pressing down to make a sandwich. Stack the cookie sandwiches in an airtight container with a sheet of parchment or wax paper between the layers of sandwiches and freeze for at least an hour to allow the sandwiches to firm up before serving. These will last for weeks in the freezer.

esmé's s'mores cookies

makes about 1½ dozen large cookies

When I was nine, I decided to start a cookie business called Cookie Crazie. All of the proceeds went to the Michael J. Fox Foundation, my dad's Parkinson's foundation. Hands down, our best seller was this recipe that I invented. I am allergic to peanuts and tree nuts, so this recipe is completely nut free. If you have a nut allergy, make sure to buy nut-free chocolate and nut-free graham crackers. Enjoy!—ESMÉ

6 full graham cracker sheets

½ pound (2 sticks) butter, at room temperature

¾ cup granulated sugar

¾ cup firmly packed light brown sugar

1 teaspoon pure vanilla extract

2 large eggs

2¼ cups all-purpose flour

1 teaspoon baking soda

½ teaspoon kosher salt

2 cups milk chocolate chips

60 (about ¾ cup) mini marshmallows

Two 1.55-ounce milk chocolate bars, separated into 24 squares, then halved

■ FROM THE MARKET

Graham crackers
(6 full cracker sheets)

Unsalted butter
(½ pound, or 2 sticks)

Large eggs (2)

Milk chocolate chips
(one 11.5-ounce bag)

Milk chocolate bars
(two 1.55-ounce bars)

Mini marshmallows
(60, or about ¾ cup)

■ FROM THE PANTRY*

Granulated sugar (¾ cup)

Light brown sugar (¾ cup)

Pure vanilla extract
(1 teaspoon)

All-purpose flour (2¼ cups)

Baking soda (1 teaspoon)

Kosher salt

*You will need parchment paper if you don't have a silicone baking mat.

Set a rack in the middle of the oven and preheat the oven to 375°F. Line a baking sheet with a silicone baking mat (preferred) or parchment paper.

Place the graham crackers in a plastic bag and crush with a rolling pin or wooden spoon into coarse crumbs. Set aside.

Using a stand mixer or an electric hand mixer, beat together the butter, granulated sugar, brown sugar, and vanilla until creamy, about 1 minute. Add the eggs and beat well, about 1 minute more.

In another mixing bowl, stir together the flour, baking soda, and salt. Add the dry ingredients to the wet and beat until well blended, about 1 minute.

(recipe continues)

Stir in the chocolate chips with a wooden spoon. Add the graham cracker crumbs and combine.

Using a ¼-cup dry measuring cup, drop mounds of the dough onto the lined baking sheet about 2 inches apart (using half the dough). Bake, rotating the sheet halfway through, until golden brown and firm on the surface but with slightly soft centers, about 12 minutes. Remove from the oven and immediately

push 3 marshmallows into the middle of each cookie in a large open triangle.
Insert 2 or 3 chocolate pieces in the center of each triangle.

Transfer the cookies to a wire cooling rack. Let the cookie sheet cool slightly,
then repeat with the remaining dough, marshmallows, and chocolate pieces.
Store in an airtight container.

savannah's fudge and pecan-filled vanilla cookies

makes 3 dozen cookies

■ **FROM THE MARKET**

Unsalted butter
(8 tablespoons, or 1 stick)

Large egg (1)

■ **FROM THE PANTRY**

All-purpose flour (1½ cups)

Baking soda (¼ teaspoon)

Baking powder
(¼ teaspoon)

Kosher salt

Granulated sugar (1 cup)

Pure vanilla extract
(1½ teaspoons)

Raw pecan halves (1 cup)

Semisweet chocolate chips
(1 cup)

Sweetened condensed milk
(½ of a 14-ounce can)

Confectioners' sugar for
dusting

My friend Carolyn and I enjoyed baking these cookies before basketball practice—and feasting on them when we got home. I decided one day to bake them myself and realized that I didn't have all the ingredients I needed—so I improvised. The original chocolate cookies with cherries were transformed into delicious vanilla cookies filled with fudge and pecans. I love the texture. They are perfectly crunchy, but when you bite into the middle, they are soft and chewy.—SAVANNAH

1½ cups all-purpose flour

¼ teaspoon baking soda

¼ teaspoon baking powder

¼ teaspoon kosher salt

8 tablespoons (1 stick) unsalted butter, at room temperature

1 cup granulated sugar

1 large egg

1½ teaspoons pure vanilla extract

⅓ cup plus 2 teaspoons finely chopped raw pecans

1 cup semisweet chocolate chips

½ of a 14-ounce can sweetened condensed milk

36 raw pecan halves

Confectioners' sugar for dusting

Set racks in the upper and lower thirds of the oven and preheat the oven to 350°F.

In a medium mixing bowl, combine the flour, baking soda, baking powder, and salt. Whisk to blend. Set aside.

In a large mixing bowl, using an electric hand mixer, cream the butter and granulated sugar until fluffy. Add the egg and vanilla and mix until combined. Gradually add the dry ingredients and mix until thoroughly blended.

Form the dough into 1-inch balls and place on ungreased baking sheets 2 inches apart. Push the center of each ball with your thumb about halfway down, making a well in the center of each cookie. Fill each hole with ½ teaspoon of the chopped pecans. Set aside.

In a small saucepan, combine the chocolate chips and condensed milk. Heat over low heat, stirring occasionally, until the chocolate melts. Using a teaspoon, put about 1 level spoonful of the fudge glaze on each filled hole, covering the pecans. Place 1 pecan half on each fudge center and push down lightly.

Place in the oven and bake until firm, 12 to 14 minutes. To ensure even baking, rotate the sheets top to bottom and front to back halfway through.

Remove from the oven and let the cookies rest on the baking sheets for 5 minutes, then transfer them to a wire cooling rack to finish cooling. Once cooled, dust the cookies with confectioners' sugar. Store in an airtight container.

hallie's mixed berry pie

makes one 9-inch pie

■ **FROM THE MARKET**

Fresh raspberries (1 pint)

Fresh blueberries (2 pints)

Lemon (1)

Unsalted butter
(½ pound, or 2 sticks, plus
1½ tablespoons)

Milk, whole or low-fat
(2 tablespoons)

Coarse or decorating
sugar, or granulated sugar
(1 tablespoon)

■ **FROM THE PANTRY**

All-purpose flour (2½ cups
plus extra for flouring the
work surface and dusting)

Granulated sugar
(½ cup plus 1 teaspoon)

Kosher salt

Cornstarch (3 tablespoons)

Ground cinnamon (pinch)

Pure vanilla extract
(¼ teaspoon)

My first pie was born out of a misunderstanding. My boyfriend, Sam, and I decided to go berry picking. Sam had never gone berry picking before and when we reconvened at the end of the day, he had amassed over 25 pounds of berries. He hadn't realized you are charged by the weight! We went home, prepared to eat only smoothies for a month. About a week later we were invited to a community potluck and I turned to the mounds of berries in the freezer, and with this my first pie was created. —HALLIE

2½ cups all-purpose flour plus extra for flouring the work surface and dusting

½ cup plus 1 teaspoon granulated sugar (you may need a little more sugar depending on the sweetness of the berries)

1 teaspoon kosher salt

½ pound (2 sticks) plus 1½ tablespoons unsalted butter, very well chilled

4 cups fresh blueberries

2 cups fresh raspberries

3 tablespoons cornstarch

Pinch of ground cinnamon

¼ teaspoon pure vanilla extract

1 tablespoon fresh lemon juice

1 teaspoon finely grated lemon zest

2 tablespoons whole or low-fat milk

1 tablespoon coarse or decorating sugar (granulated may be substituted)

Fill a small mixing bowl with water and ice and set aside.

In a large mixing bowl, combine the flour, 1 teaspoon of the granulated sugar, and the salt.

Working quickly so it stays cold, dice ½ pound of the butter into ¼- to ½-inch cubes. Add these to the flour and, using your hands, blend into a coarse meal. (If you pinch some of the crumbly dough, it should stick together.)

Begin to add ice water to the dough 1 tablespoon at a time. After each spoonful, lightly knead the dough. Continue to add the water until the dough holds together when shaped. Do not exceed 8 tablespoons; too much water or handling will make a tough dough.

Divide the dough into two pieces, one slightly larger than the other. Flatten them into disks and wrap in plastic. Refrigerate for at least 30 minutes and up to 2 hours. Place a rolling pin in the freezer.

Set a rack in the middle of the oven and preheat the oven to 375°F. Place a rimmed baking sheet in the oven.

Combine the blueberries and raspberries in a large mixing bowl. In a small mixing bowl, combine ½ cup of granulated sugar, the cornstarch, cinnamon, vanilla, lemon juice, and lemon zest. Pour this onto the berries and mix gently to blend. (Taste and use a little more sugar, depending on the sweetness of the berries.) Set aside.

Lightly flour your work surface. Remove the larger piece of dough from the refrigerator and transfer to the work surface. Dust the top of the dough with flour. Remove the rolling pin from the freezer and begin to roll out the dough, slowly pushing from the center out, turning the dough as you roll so that it is uniform. Roll into a disk about 12 inches in diameter and ⅛ inch thick.

Carefully place the disk onto a 9-inch pie plate. Press the dough down onto the bottom and sides of the pan. Trim any excess dough hanging off the edge to ½ inch.

(recipe continues)

Pour the berries and any accumulated juices into the pie crust. Cut the remaining 1½ tablespoons of butter into thin slivers and dot the top of the filling. Sprinkle a thin coating of flour on top.

Remove the second piece of dough from the refrigerator and roll it into a disk 13 to 14 inches in diameter and ⅛ inch thick. Drape this disk over the berry filling. Working around the rim, pinch the upper and lower crusts together with your fingers or crimp with a fork.

Brush a thin coating of milk over the top and edges of the pie and sprinkle the coarse sugar on top. Cut 4 to 6 slits in the center of the dough.

Place the pie onto the preheated baking sheet and bake for 20 minutes. Reduce the oven temperature to 350°F and bake until the crust is deep golden brown and the juices are bubbling, 30 to 40 minutes; if the edges are getting too brown, cover them with foil. Cool on a wire cooling rack and serve at room temperature.

mack and cam's mini pecan tarts

makes 2 dozen tarts

■ **FROM THE MARKET**

Cream cheese (3 ounces)

Unsalted butter
(9 tablespoons, or
1 stick plus 1 tablespoon)

Large egg (1)

■ **FROM THE PANTRY***

All-purpose flour (1 cup)

Dark brown sugar (¾ cup)

Pure vanilla extract
(1 teaspoon)

Kosher salt

Raw pecans (1 cup)

*You will need a mini muffin
pan or pans that will hold a
total of 24 tarts.

My dad and I love pecan pie, so I brainstormed with my grandmother for recipe ideas, and we came up with one for mini pecan tarts. These bite-size treats are easy to bake and fun to eat. With each bite you get it all—creamy filling, crunchy nuts, and flaky crust. Cameron and I enjoy preparing them for the whole family, and once they hit the table, they are immediately devoured. —MACKLIN

FOR THE CRUST

3 ounces cream cheese, at room
temperature

8 tablespoons (1 stick) unsalted butter,
at room temperature

1 cup sifted all-purpose flour

FOR THE FILLING

1 large egg

¾ cup packed dark brown sugar

1 tablespoon unsalted butter,
at room temperature

1 teaspoon pure vanilla extract

Pinch of kosher salt

⅔ cup chopped raw pecans

FOR THE CRUST

Combine the cream cheese and 8 tablespoons of butter in a large mixing bowl and mix with a wooden spoon until thoroughly blended. Add the flour and continue mixing until the dough comes together. Form it into a ball, flatten the top, wrap it in plastic, and place it in the refrigerator for 1 hour.

Set a rack in the middle of the oven and preheat the oven to 325°F. Set aside an ungreased mini muffin pan or pans that will hold a total of 24 tarts.

FOR THE FILLING

Using an electric hand mixer or a stand mixer, combine the egg, brown sugar, 1 tablespoon of butter, vanilla, and salt. Beat until smooth, 2 to 3 minutes. Set aside.

Remove the dough from the refrigerator and shape it into 24 one-inch balls. Place a ball in each muffin cup, and with your fingers press out the dough to completely line the bottom and sides of the cup.

Evenly distribute ⅓ cup of the pecans in the pastry-lined cups. Add about 1 teaspoon of filling to each cup and top with the remaining nuts.

Place the pan(s) in the middle of the oven and bake until the filling is set and the crust is browned, 25 to 30 minutes. To ensure even baking, rotate the pan(s) top to bottom and front to back halfway through. Let the tarts cool in the pan on a wire cooling rack. Arrange the tarts on a platter and serve.

micaela's nirvana bars

makes 3 dozen 1½-inch bars

My mom always made these bars when she was a teenager, so I decided to give them a try and make a batch for my friends. I made my own edits to the recipe and brought them into class the next day. Following the consumption of the first few, word of the bars quickly spread and soon I was in a swarm of hungry teenagers attracted to the smell of chocolate, nuts, coconut, and all the rest of the chewy, crunchy deliciousness. Within five minutes the container was empty, and I was already taking orders for more. Now, these Nirvana bars have become a favorite middle-of-the-night, sneak-into-the-kitchen treat for friends who sleep over. —MICAELA

■ **FROM THE MARKET**

Unsalted butter
(6 tablespoons, or ¾ stick)

Graham crackers
(9 full cracker sheets)

White chocolate chips
(½ cup)

Bittersweet or dark chocolate chips (½ cup)

■ **FROM THE PANTRY***

Kosher salt

Raw walnuts or pecans
(1¼ cups)

Semisweet chocolate chips
(½ cup)

Sweetened shredded or flaked coconut (1 cup)

Sweetened condensed milk
(½ of a 14-ounce can)

*You will need
parchment paper.

6 tablespoons (¾ stick) unsalted butter, melted

9 full graham cracker sheets, crushed into coarse crumbs

¼ teaspoon kosher salt

1 cup chopped raw walnuts or pecans

½ cup semisweet chocolate chips

½ cup white chocolate chips

½ cup bittersweet or dark chocolate chips

1 cup sweetened shredded or flaked coconut

½ of a 14-ounce can sweetened condensed milk

Set a rack in the middle of the oven and preheat the oven to 350°F. Line the bottom of a 9-inch square baking pan with parchment paper.

In a large mixing bowl, combine the butter, graham cracker crumbs, and salt; stir to mix well. Press the crumbs into the bottom of the baking pan. Layer on the chopped nuts, then the semisweet chocolate chips, white chocolate chips, and bittersweet chocolate chips. Sprinkle the coconut evenly on top. Lastly, drizzle on the condensed milk, covering everything with a thin layer.

Bake until golden brown, about 25 minutes. Let cool completely in the pan, then cut into 1½-inch bars. Store in an airtight container.

isaac's mexican wedding cookies

makes about 3½ dozen cookies

■ **FROM THE MARKET**

Unsalted butter
(½ pound, or 2 sticks)

■ **FROM THE PANTRY***

Confectioners' sugar
(1½ cups)

Pure vanilla extract
(2 teaspoons)

All-purpose flour (2 cups
plus more for shaping)

Kosher salt

Raw pecans (1¼ cups)

Ground cinnamon
(½ teaspoon)

Ground cardamom
(¼ teaspoon)

Ground nutmeg
(¼ teaspoon)

*You will need
parchment paper.

These Mexican wedding cookies were one of the first things I learned to make, and the first recipe that I committed to memory (with my own variations, of course). The recipe came from a wonderful chef who visited my middle school weekly for eagerly anticipated lessons in Latino cuisine. These cookies were the unanimous favorite. –ISAAC

½ pound (2 sticks) unsalted butter,
    at room temperature

1½ cups confectioners' sugar

2 teaspoons pure vanilla extract

2 cups all-purpose flour plus more
    for shaping

¼ teaspoon kosher salt

1 cup finely chopped raw pecans

½ teaspoon ground cinnamon

¼ teaspoon ground cardamom

¼ teaspoon ground nutmeg

Place the butter and ½ cup of the confectioners' sugar in a deep mixing bowl. Using an electric hand mixer or a stand mixer, beat until light and fluffy. Add the vanilla, and with the mixer on low speed, very gradually add the flour and salt. Next, stir in the pecans using a wooden spoon.

Form the dough into a ball, flatten slightly, wrap in plastic, and chill in the refrigerator for about 20 minutes.

Set racks in the upper and lower thirds of the oven and preheat the oven to 350°F. Line two rimmed baking sheets with parchment paper.

With floured hands, roll rounded teaspoonfuls of the dough into 1-inch balls. Arrange them on the baking sheets in rows, about 1 inch apart.

Bake until the cookies turn a pale golden brown, about 20 minutes. To ensure even baking, rotate the sheets top to bottom and front to back halfway through.

Meanwhile, in a small mixing bowl, combine the remaining 1 cup of confectioners' sugar with the cinnamon, cardamom, and nutmeg. Set aside.

Let the cookies cool slightly for 3 to 4 minutes. While they are still slightly warm, remove a few at a time from the baking sheets and roll them in the spiced sugar, making sure they are evenly coated. Transfer the cookies to a wire cooling rack to finish cooling. Once cool, roll them again in the sugar mixture. Store in an airtight container.

nana fox's oatmeal cookies

makes 3½ dozen cookies

■ **FROM THE MARKET**

Unsalted butter
(½ pound, or 2 sticks)

Large egg (1)

■ **FROM THE PANTRY***

Dark brown sugar (1 cup)

Granulated sugar (1 cup)

All-purpose flour (1 cup)

Baking soda (1 teaspoon)

Baking powder (1 teaspoon)

Kosher salt

Pure vanilla extract
(1 teaspoon)

Sweetened shredded or
flaked coconut (¾ cup)

Old-fashioned rolled oats
(2¼ cups)

*You will need
parchment paper.

This old Irish recipe for oatmeal cookies was given to Michael's mother by a friend of hers years ago. We get to enjoy these cookies whenever Nana Fox comes to visit. Coconut is the secret ingredient that makes these cookies so incredible.

½ pound (2 sticks) unsalted butter,
  at room temperature

1 cup firmly packed dark brown sugar

1 cup granulated sugar

1 large egg

1 cup all-purpose flour

1 teaspoon baking soda

1 teaspoon baking powder

¼ teaspoon kosher salt

1 teaspoon pure vanilla extract

¾ cup sweetened shredded or
  flaked coconut

2¼ cups old-fashioned rolled oats

Set racks in the upper and lower thirds of the oven and preheat the oven to 375°F. Line two baking sheets with parchment paper.

Combine the butter, brown sugar, granulated sugar, egg, flour, baking soda, baking powder, salt, vanilla, coconut, and rolled oats in a large mixing bowl and mix until well blended. Using half the dough, form into 1-inch balls and place them on one of the parchment paper–lined baking sheets 3 inches apart. Press flat with a fork. Repeat with the remaining dough.

Bake for 12 minutes or until the edges are golden brown. To ensure even baking, rotate the sheets top to bottom and front to back halfway through.

Let cool for 2 minutes on the baking sheet, then transfer the cookies to a wire cooling rack to finish cooling. Store in an airtight container.

raspberry pudding cake

6 servings

"Pudding" brings to mind British desserts, but this super scrumptious pudding cake is all-American. Raspberries are one of our favorite berries and adding a bit of jam amplifies the tart-sweet flavor.

8 tablespoons (1 stick) unsalted butter, melted and cooled slightly, plus extra for greasing the pan

¾ cup granulated sugar

1 tablespoon fresh lemon juice

1 teaspoon cornstarch

2 cups fresh raspberries

½ cup raspberry jam

1 cup all-purpose flour

1¾ teaspoons baking powder

¼ teaspoon kosher salt

1 large egg

½ cup whole milk

1 teaspoon pure vanilla extract

Set a rack in the middle of the oven and preheat the oven to 375°F. Butter a 9-inch square baking pan.

In a small saucepan over low heat, stir together ¼ cup of the sugar, ¼ cup of water, the lemon juice, and cornstarch and bring to a simmer. Add the raspberries and the raspberry jam and cook, stirring, for an additional 3 minutes. Set aside.

In a medium mixing bowl, whisk together the flour, baking powder, salt, and the remaining ½ cup of sugar.

In a large mixing bowl, whisk together the egg, milk, melted butter, and vanilla. Add the dry ingredients and stir with a wooden spoon until just combined.

Spread the batter into the baking pan and top with the raspberry sauce.

Bake until a cake tester inserted in the center of the cake just comes out clean, 20 to 25 minutes. Cool in the pan on a cooling rack for 5 minutes and serve.

■ **FROM THE MARKET**

Lemon (1)

Fresh raspberries (1 pint)

Raspberry jam (½ cup)

Large egg (1)

Whole milk (½ cup)

Unsalted butter
(8 tablespoons, or 1 stick, plus extra for greasing the pan)

■ **FROM THE PANTRY**

Granulated sugar (¾ cup)

Cornstarch (1 teaspoon)

All-purpose flour (1 cup)

Baking powder
(1¾ teaspoons)

Kosher salt

Pure vanilla extract
(1 teaspoon)

streusel-topped apple cake

10 servings

■ **FROM THE MARKET**

Granny Smith apples
(3 pounds, about 7 large)

Unsalted butter (10 ounces,
or 2½ sticks, plus extra for
greasing the pan)

Whole milk (½ cup)

Large eggs (2)

■ **FROM THE PANTRY**

Ground cinnamon
(3 teaspoons)

Granulated sugar
(2 cups plus 1 tablespoon)

All-purpose flour
(4 cups plus 2 tablespoons)

Baking powder
(½ teaspoon)

Baking soda (2 teaspoons)

Kosher salt

Dark brown sugar (¾ cup)

An abundance of apples accounts for this cake taking top honors on the family's most wanted list. We blend apples into the batter, resulting in a cake that's deliciously moist. And we add apples to our streusel, creating a fruity note to our crunchy topping.

FOR THE CAKE

½ pound (2 sticks) unsalted butter, at room temperature, plus extra for greasing pan

3¾ cups peeled and diced Granny Smith apples, cut into ¼-inch cubes (3 large)

2 teaspoons ground cinnamon

2 cups plus 1 tablespoon granulated sugar

2 large eggs

4 cups sifted all-purpose flour

½ teaspoon baking powder

2 teaspoons baking soda

½ teaspoon kosher salt

½ cup whole milk

FOR THE TOPPING

4 cups peeled and sliced Granny Smith apples, cut into ¼-inch-thick slices (4 large)

4 tablespoons (½ stick) unsalted butter, cut into small pieces

¾ cup firmly packed dark brown sugar

1 teaspoon ground cinnamon

2 tablespoons all-purpose flour

Set a rack in the middle of the oven and preheat the oven to 350°F. Butter a 9 by 13-inch baking pan.

FOR THE CAKE

In a large mixing bowl, toss the chopped apples with 2 teaspoons of cinnamon and 1 tablespoon of the granulated sugar. Set aside.

Using a stand mixer or an electric hand mixer, combine the remaining 2 cups of granulated sugar and 2 sticks of butter and cream until fluffy. Beat in the eggs.

Add 4 cups of flour, the baking powder, baking soda, salt, and milk and mix until combined. Stir in the apples and spoon the batter into the pan.

FOR THE TOPPING

Arrange the sliced apples in slightly overlapping rows to completely cover the batter. In a small mixing bowl, add 4 tablespoons of butter, the brown sugar, 1 teaspoon of cinnamon, and 2 tablespoons of flour. Using a fork or your fingers, combine the mixture until the crumbs are pea-size. Sprinkle the topping over the apples.

Bake until the topping is brown and a cake tester inserted in the center comes out with a few crumbs clinging to it, 50 to 60 minutes. To ensure even baking, rotate the pan halfway through. Cool slightly in the pan on a wire cooling rack and serve warm.

crispy crunchy apple crumble

10 servings

By popular demand a crumble appears at all of our big family dinners. The fruits can change with the seasons—rhubarb and strawberries may appear in spring, peaches and blueberries in summer, pears and cranberries in fall or winter. The apple spans all seasons and it's the one that's requested most of all.

FOR THE FILLING

4 pounds apples (8 or 9, assorted varieties), peeled, cored, and cut into ½-inch slices

¼ cup granulated sugar

1 tablespoon fresh lemon juice

2 teaspoons ground cinnamon

¼ teaspoon ground nutmeg

½ teaspoon finely grated fresh ginger

2 tablespoons quick-cooking tapioca or all-purpose flour

⅛ teaspoon kosher salt

FOR THE CRUMBLE TOPPING

1¼ cups all-purpose flour

1¼ cups old-fashioned rolled oats

1¼ cups firmly packed dark brown sugar

½ teaspoon ground cinnamon

⅛ teaspoon kosher salt

12 tablespoons (1½ sticks) unsalted cold butter, cut into small cubes

■ **FROM THE MARKET**

Apples, assorted varieties (8 or 9 apples, 4 pounds)

Lemon (1)

Fresh ginger (1 small knob)

Quick-cooking tapioca (2 tablespoons; optional)

Unsalted butter (12 tablespoons, or 1½ sticks)

■ **FROM THE PANTRY**

Granulated sugar (¼ cup)

Ground cinnamon (2½ teaspoons)

Ground nutmeg (¼ teaspoon)

Kosher salt

All-purpose flour (1¼ cups plus 2 tablespoons if not using tapioca)

Old-fashioned rolled oats (1¼ cups)

Dark brown sugar (1¼ cups)

Set a rack in the middle of the oven and preheat the oven to 375°F.

FOR THE FILLING

Place the apples in a large mixing bowl. Add the granulated sugar, lemon juice, 2 teaspoons cinnamon, nutmeg, ginger, tapioca, and ⅛ teaspoon of salt and gently toss to combine. Spoon the filling into an ungreased 9-inch round, 2-inch-deep pie dish or an 11-inch oval, 2-inch-deep pie dish.

(recipe continues)

FOR THE CRUMBLE TOPPING

In a medium mixing bowl, whisk together the 1¼ cups flour, rolled oats, brown sugar, ½ teaspoon cinnamon, and ⅛ teaspoon of salt. Add the butter and, working with your fingertips, a fork, or a pastry blender, combine the mixture until the crumbs are pea-size.

Spoon the topping evenly, but thickly, over the fruit filling.

Place the baking pan on a baking sheet or sheet of foil (this will catch any spills) on the middle rack of the oven. Bake until the fruit is bubbling and the top is nicely browned, about 1 hour. To ensure even baking, rotate the baking dish halfway through. (If the top begins to get too brown, cover it with a sheet of foil.)

Serve warm.

key lime pie
with walnut oatmeal crust

6 to 8 servings

In our family Key lime pies are so loved, they are demanded for special occasions. Happily, they're the quickest pies to make. Ours has a nutty crust, not the classic graham cracker one, and a heavenly smooth filling.

FOR THE CRUST

1½ cups old-fashioned rolled oats

¾ cup finely chopped raw walnuts

4 tablespoons packed dark brown sugar

6 tablespoons (¾ stick) unsalted butter, melted

FOR THE FILLING

4 large egg yolks

One 14-ounce can sweetened condensed milk

7 tablespoons fresh Key lime juice (from 8 to 10 Key limes) or good-quality bottled

■ **FROM THE MARKET**

Fresh Key limes (8 to 10), or good-quality bottled Key lime juice (7 tablespoons)

Unsalted butter (6 tablespoons, or ¾ stick)

Large eggs (4)

■ **FROM THE PANTRY**

Old-fashioned rolled oats (1½ cups)

Raw walnuts (1 cup)

Dark brown sugar (4 tablespoons)

Sweetened condensed milk (one 14-ounce can)

Set a rack in the middle of the oven and preheat the oven to 350°F.

FOR THE CRUST

Spread the oats in an ungreased 9-inch pie pan and bake until lightly browned, 15 to 20 minutes. Leave the oven on. Transfer the oats to a medium mixing bowl and add the walnuts, sugar, and melted butter. Mix with a fork until combined.

Using your fingers or the back of a soup spoon, press the crust evenly onto the bottom and the sides of the same pie pan. Refrigerate for at least 15 minutes.

FOR THE FILLING

Whisk the egg yolks in a mixing bowl. Add the condensed milk and lime juice and continue whisking until combined and the filling thickens slightly.

Pour the filling into the crust and bake until set, about 15 minutes. (It should be wobbly in the center.) Chill for at least 1 hour before serving.

caramelized peaches à la mode with raspberry sauce

4 servings

■ **FROM THE MARKET**

Fresh ginger (1 knob)

Fresh raspberries (½ pint)

Peaches (4)

Unsalted butter
(3 tablespoons)

Vanilla or coffee ice cream
(1 pint)

Cinnamon stick (1)

■ **FROM THE PANTRY***

Granulated sugar (½ cup)

Bay leaf (1)

Dark brown sugar
(3 tablespoons)

Balsamic vinegar
(1 tablespoon)

*You will need
parchment paper.

Broiling peaches caramelizes them and intensifies their flavor; adding scoops of ice cream and a drizzle or two of raspberry sauce turns these peaches into an impressive dessert.

½ cup granulated sugar

1 cinnamon stick

1 bay leaf

1 tablespoon finely grated fresh ginger

1 cup fresh raspberries

3 tablespoons unsalted butter

3 tablespoons dark brown sugar

4 peaches, halved and pitted

1 tablespoon balsamic vinegar

1 pint vanilla or coffee ice cream

Set racks in the middle and the upper third of the oven and preheat the oven to 400°F. Line a rimmed baking sheet with parchment paper.

In a small saucepan, combine the granulated sugar, cinnamon stick, bay leaf, ginger, raspberries, and ¼ cup of water. Simmer, stirring occasionally, for 8 minutes, until slightly thickened. Discard the cinnamon stick and the bay leaf, and set aside.

In another small saucepan, melt the butter. Add the brown sugar and stir.

Arrange the peaches cut side up on the baking sheet. With a pastry brush, spread on the butter mixture. Drizzle each half with vinegar. Roast until the peaches are tender, 8 to 10 minutes. Remove the baking sheet from the oven.

Set the oven to broil. Return the baking sheet to the top rack of the oven, and broil until the sugar begins to bubble and caramelize, about 5 minutes.

To serve, arrange two peach halves each in four individual bowls. Top each serving with a scoop of ice cream and drizzle with the raspberry sauce.

nectarine blueberry cobbler with praline crumble

8 to 10 servings

During the summer, we love to make desserts with fresh fruits picked at their absolute sweetest. This cobbler is one of our favorites. You can substitute peaches and blackberries or raspberries. Choose whatever looks most enticing at your local farmstand or farmers' market.

¼ cup plus 2 tablespoons firmly packed light brown sugar

8 tablespoons (1 stick) unsalted butter, at room temperature

¼ teaspoon ground nutmeg

¼ teaspoon kosher salt

1½ cups all-purpose flour

½ cup roughly chopped raw pecans

5 cups sliced unpeeled nectarines, cut into ½-inch-thick slices

¾ cup granulated sugar

1 teaspoon fresh lemon juice

1 cup fresh blueberries

1½ teaspoons baking powder

¾ cup buttermilk

Set a rack in the middle of the oven and preheat the oven to 350°F.

To make the praline crumble topping, in a medium mixing bowl, combine the brown sugar, 4 tablespoons of the butter, the nutmeg, and ⅛ teaspoon of the salt; mix well. Add ¾ cup of the flour and the pecans. Stir until blended and crumbly.

In a large skillet over medium heat, combine the nectarines, ¼ cup of the granulated sugar, and the lemon juice. Cook the mixture at a simmer for 4 minutes. Add the blueberries, stir until incorporated, and remove from the heat.

In a small saucepan over medium heat, heat the remaining 4 tablespoons of butter until it begins to brown and emits a nutty aroma, about 4 minutes. Pour the browned butter into an 8-inch square baking dish and set aside.

To make the batter, combine the remaining ¾ cup of flour, the remaining ½ cup of granulated sugar, the baking powder, and the remaining ⅛ teaspoon of salt in a medium mixing bowl. Slowly stir in the buttermilk and mix just enough to moisten the dry ingredients.

Pour the batter into the baking dish over the butter in an even layer, taking care not to mix the two together. Pour the fruit and all the accumulated juices evenly over the batter. Cover with the praline crumble topping. Bake until golden and bubbling, 45 to 50 minutes. Serve warm.

acknowledgments

FOR THE FOUR OF US THIS COOKBOOK PROVED TO BE A REAL "COMMON POT." With love and gratitude we want to thank all the exceptional and talented people who helped turn our brainchild into a beautiful and accessible cookbook.

First and foremost, we want to thank our husbands and children, who had no clue what they were getting into when they thought our writing a cookbook was a good idea.

An immense thank-you to Michael Pollan, who generously offered to write a foreword before we even finished our proposal, and whose loving guidance has been extraordinary.

Our dear friend Lucy Kaylin was our first reader and her suggestions, editing, and belief in our project kept us going even when we had doubts.

Michael Fox's generosity of time and inspired input were invaluable gifts to the writing of our book.

Mitchell Stern's dedicated energy, valued counsel, and unfailing support kept us going all through the process.

Our gracious, collaborative editor, Shannon Welch, embraced this book and lavished it with loving attention. Her superb editing guided us from beginning to end. Thank you to our publisher, Nan Graham, whose enthusiasm and positive energy were infectious. Heartfelt thanks to our amazing team at Scribner: Roz Lippel, John Glynn, Kara Watson, Caitlin Dohrenwend, Tal Goretsky, Brian Belfiglio, Lauren Lavelle, Gwyneth Stansfield, Mia Crowley-Hald, Katie Rizzo, Stacey Kulig, Suzanne Fass, and Gabriele Wilson. We also want to give a special thanks to Jan Derevjanik, who helped create a gorgeous book.

Amanda Urban of ICM immediately fell in love with our proposal and took a chance on four would-be authors and has been cheering us on ever since. Without her support this book would not have come to fruition. Andrea Barzvi, our initial agent, championed us from the beginning, and her passion for our concept was a driving force. Kari Stuart seamlessly took over as our agent and unfailingly answered all of our questions, big and small. Her upbeat spirit was always a breath of fresh air.

We had a vision for how our recipes would look in print, and the work of our brilliant creative team surpassed our expectations. John Kernick's stunning photographs brought all of our dishes to life on the page. Digital tech Rizwan Alvi's warmth, kindness, and funny asides made every day on the set a pleasure. Our food stylist, Susie Theodorou, had the uncanny ability to make order out of chaos. Her talent, skills, and artistic eye are brilliant. Our prop stylist, Amy Wilson, with her care and attention to detail, created a beautiful setting for each dish. Their assistants, Monica Pierini and Nina Lalli, proved indispensable to the shoot. Thanks also to our own Amuna Ali, the indefatigable kitchen wonder. When writing a cookbook, all the recipes should be tested by a professional, and we give thanks to Denise Landis for this huge undertaking.

An additional thank-you to the talented Quentin Bacon, Mariana Velasquez, and Bette Blau, along with Madeline Miller and Kristen Walther, for the elegant photo of our Citrus-Roasted Chicken with Grand Marnier.

Thank you to our fantastic publicists Leslie Sloane and Jami Kandel for their tenacious dedication to our project. Also a big thank-you to Nanci Ryder. Judith Belzer's keen artistic eye and feedback proved invaluable. Also thanks to Cindy Gold, our unofficial/official family photographer, for preserving so many special moments. This book would not have been possible without the support and hard work of Jamey Cohen, Mary Grieco, Harris Salat, Joseph Sperduto, and Michael Tolani, and much gratitude to Tony Breznica, Bernice Gaspard, Iwalani Goldstein, Mabel James, Glenn Koetzner, Nina Tringali, and Nelly Vasquez.

For their valiant efforts to make us look beautiful, thank you to Ronald Westcott, Ryan Trygstad, and the team from Mary Brunetti: Nicolette Flynn, Joylyn Porter-Long, and Maria Tavella.

For their generosity, a very special thank-you to Sur La Table for their handsome and high-quality cookware, and to ABC Carpet and Home for their gorgeous tableware.

Finally, big thanks to our devoted Facebook friends for their staunch support and encouragement.

TRACY: Much of the credit for my participation in this book goes to my family. Their deep appreciation for our family meals inspired me to want to share the experience with others. Michael, you are the kindest person I know, the best friend a girl could ask for, and the love of my life. Thank you for having enough optimism for the both of us.

And much love goes to my little guinea pigs. Sam, my "super taster," how is it you always know the exact missing ingredient in any dish? Aquinnah, your gusto and gratitude for a good meal rivals only my own. Schuyler, your enthusiasm and compassion have kept me from second-guessing myself in the kitchen. And Esmé, the ultimate team player, you dare to try so many new foods when I know you really only want meatballs.

Many thanks to Jennifer Grey, Judith Belzer, Cindy Gold, Carolyn Schenker, Joyce Cohen, Jill Olonoff, Jean Monaco, Ali Wentworh, and Pamela Mitchell, and all of my other girlfriends, each of you in your own way has contributed to this project. Thank you for your loving

Nina, Amy, Susie, Rizwan, Amuna, John, and Monica

support and all the times you have saved a seat for me at your own family tables. I have tremendous gratitude to Iwa, for your friendship, hard work, and awesome organizational skills, and to Amuna "Grasshopper" Ali, for being my taster, tester, and sous chef.

Thanks to you, Dad, I grew up believing I could accomplish absolutely anything; your belief in us kids was that powerful. Working with one's mom and sisters and brother could easily be a recipe for disaster, but the truth is very few adults get to spend so much quality time with their parents and siblings. Who knew when we had this crazy idea to write a book what we were getting ourselves into? These last two years creating, cooking, eating, laughing, and sharing panic attacks have been some of the absolute highlights of my life. I will treasure these memories always, thank you.

DANA: I am eternally grateful to my husband and three children—and treasure our family meals together. Mitchell, thank you for your unwavering support, wisdom, and never-ending affection—and for always making me laugh. You are my best friend. I love you always.

Macklin, my "first" picky eater, for inspiring me to create meals you would eat—many of which appear in this book—and for the joy and enthusiasm you display over a delicious dinner. Savannah, my tireless at-home "recipe tester," your invaluable opinions and clever suggestions provided important contributions to many of these recipes. I especially loved working together side by side in your bedroom—you tackling your homework while I fine-tuned recipes. Cameron, for your incredible patience and boundless love throughout the process of writing this book and for allowing me to work on it, in your words, "all the time."

My dad, Stephen, for instilling in me the idea that you can accomplish whatever you set your mind to and for modeling your remarkable work ethic.

And my mom, Corky: I feel so lucky to have grown up with the delicious family meals you made for us. Your passion for food and cooking are truly inspiring. And my siblings—you are the best sisters and brother a sister could have.

I want to thank some special friends. Clare Garfield, thank you for your wonderful friendship and support. My Studio School buddies: I cherish our breakfasts together and look forward to a lot more of them now that this book is completed. Thank you to Judith Belzer, Lisa Penberthy, and Robin Bidner, and all of my other dear friends for their patience and understanding when I was constantly caught in the kitchen up to my elbows in kale.

LORI: I have a group of truly wonderful women in my life who are my village, and I cannot thank them enough for their support, encouragement, and love. Thank you to Caren Austen, my other sister—our children grew up sharing dinners together just as we did; to Judith Belzer, my other, other sister, so insightful and always ready to lend an ear; to Melissa Benzuly, my best sounding board and beach plum jelly–granola-making kitchen companion; and to Lucy Kaylin—how lucky I am to have such a dear friend and comrade living right upstairs. A special mention must go out to my book club cronies and the B Jesh ladies— sharing meals and our lives is what we do, and it's how we sustain each other. To the rest of my treasured friends—thank you for your patience when I couldn't always come out to play, let alone return your emails. Thank you to Allan—together we found the recipe for three incredible kids.

I am deeply grateful to my family: to my parents, Corky and Stephen, who have always believed in me and nourished my dreams. They have taught me that the work is the reward and that family is to be cherished. Thank you to Michael, Tracy, and Dana, who always, no matter what, have my back and who believe that it's part of our sibling job to make each other laugh.

Most of all I am so grateful to Mica, Jack, and Hallie, my three compassionate and amazing children. You are my eager taste testers, thoughtful reviewers, and now, accomplished and exuberant cooks yourselves. The greatest privilege I have is to share a family table with the three of you; not only are you the loves of my life, but you are also the most interesting and entertaining dinner companions that I could ever ask for. Your enthusiasm for and generosity toward this project has touched me so deeply. You bring me infinite joy.

CORKY: With love and a very special thanks to my husband, Stephen, my biggest supporter. His enthusiasm for our book was limitless and steadfast. He gamely tolerated my crazy work schedule and deadlines that often cut into our time together. And he happily consumed everything I put before him— my successes along with those dishes still in need of work.

To my daughters Lori, Tracy, and Dana for coming up with the idea for this cookbook. Their exceptional talents constantly astonish me. They made cooking together, writing together—even commiserating together—an amazing experience. This project was one of pure joy.

To my daughter-in-law, Judith, a dearest friend whose wise advice and precious insights I cherish. And to my son, Michael, who was always there for us, generous with his time, knowledge, and wisdom.

To my grandkids, so lavish with their praise that they constantly inspire me. Observing their evolution from picky eaters to gourmands has been a delight, and their love for desserts has transformed me from a main course–kind of cook to a pastry aficionado.

To my sister, Joyce, my very first cooking partner. At an early age we both learned the joy of cooking from our mother, Mary, a true inspiration in the kitchen.

To my dad, Max, who introduced me to what really fresh fruits and vegetables taste like, and whose love of gardening inspired my own.

To Sally Mettler, Deborah Harkins, Susan Soriano, Ali Berlow, and my dear friends who have put up with my endless emails canceling our lunches and museum visits because of looming deadlines. They have constantly cheered me on and—happily—still count me as their friend.

index

12/8/14